AF893839

CHINESE FLOWER PAINTING
MADE EASY

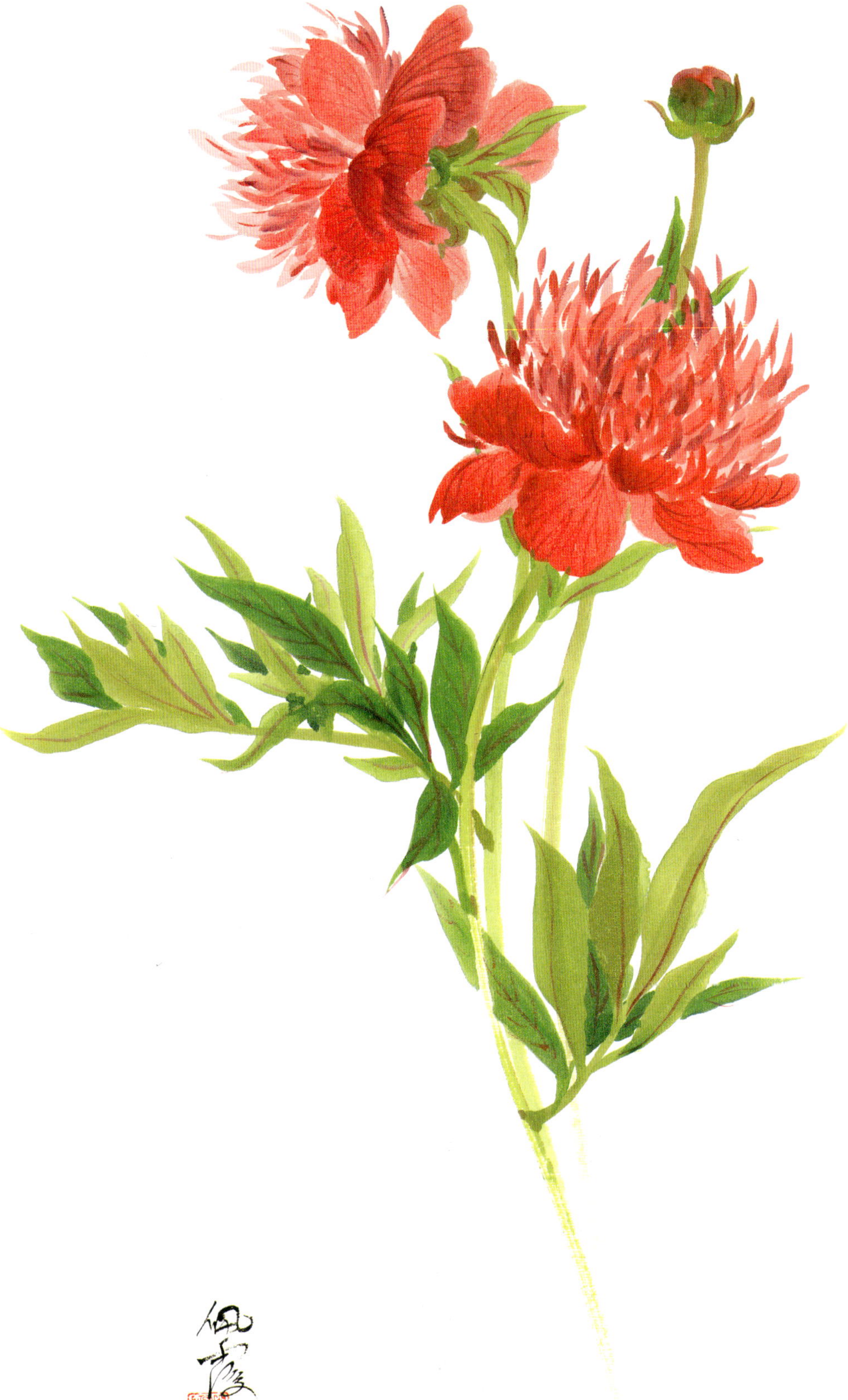

CHINESE FLOWER PAINTING MADE EASY

REBECCA YUE

COLLINS & BROWN

First published in Great Britain in 2004 by
Collins & Brown
The Chrysalis Building
Bramley Road
London W10 6SP

An imprint of Chrysalis Books Group

Distributed in the United States and Canada by Sterling Publishing Co., 387 Park Avenue South, New York, NY 10016, USA

Copyright © Collins & Brown 2004
Text copyright © Rebecca Yue 2004
Photographs copyright © Chrysalis Books Group 2004

All rights reserved. No part of this publication may be reproduced, stored in a retrieval system, or transmitted in any form or by any means, electronic, mechanical, photocopying, recording or otherwise, without the prior written permission of the copyright owner.

1 3 5 7 9 8 6 4 2

British Library Cataloguing-in-Publication Data:
A catalogue record for this book is available from the British Library.

ISBN 1 84340 142 8

Commissioning editor: Marie Clayton
Project editor: Miranda Sessions
Copy editor: Fiona Biggs
Designer: Brian Flynn
Photographer: Nicki Dowey
Hand illustrations: Juliet Percival

Reproduction by Anorax Imaging Ltd, England
Printed and bound by Kyodo Printing Co Pte Ltd, Singapore

CONTENTS

Introduction 8

CHAPTER 1 — **Materials and equipment** 12–25
Chinese brushes 14
Paper 20
Ink, colours and other accessories 24

CHAPTER 2 — **Basic techniques** 26–41
Using a Chinese brush 28
Wrist movement 32
Elbow movement 34
Press and lift technique 36
Two-tone effects 38
Multi-colour effects 39

Project 1 — Painting a Chinese orchid 40

CHAPTER 3 — **Brushstrokes** 42–117

Brushstroke 1
Dot 44
Lilac flower heads 46
Buddleia and lavender 47
Astilbe and gypsophila 48
Trees and climbers 49

Brushstroke 2
Long dot 50
Bleeding heart flower stalks 52
Hydrangea flower heads 53
Daffodil flowers 54
Lilac leaves 55
Morning glory leaves 56
Water lily leaves 57

Project 2 — Painting lilac 58

Brushstroke 3
Short brushstroke 60
Chrysanthemum flowers 62
Honeysuckle flower head 63
Lily flowers 64
Water lily flowers 65
Lotus flowers 66
Azalea flower heads with leaves 67
Painting leaves with short brushstrokes 68
Wisteria leaves 72

Bamboo leaves 73
Camellia leaves 74
Rose leaves 75
Lily leaves 76
Honeysuckle leaves 77
Clematis leaves 78
Hydrangea leaves 79
Hibiscus leaves 80
Pansy leaves 81
Poppy leaves 82
Bleeding heart leaves 83

Brushstroke 4
Long brushstroke 84
Long slender leaves 86
Tulip leaves 87
Iris leaves 88
Peony leaves 89

Project 3 Painting daffodils 90

Brushstroke 5
Side brushstroke 92
Bamboo trunks 94
Trunks and branches of younger trees 95
Old tree trunks 95
Stalks 96
Climbers 97

Project 4 Painting bamboo 98

Brushstroke 6
Fan brushstroke 100
Plum blossom 102
Geraniums flower heads 103
Wisteria flower head 104
Hibiscus flowers 105
Geraniums leaves 106
Chrysanthemum leaves 107

Project 5 Painting plum blossom 108

Brushstroke 7
Reverse fan brushstroke 110
Shirley poppy flowers 112
Roses 113
Morning glory flowers 114
Chrysanthemum leaves 115

Project 6 Painting chrysanthemums 116

Chapter 4 **Combining Brushstrokes** 118–129
Clematis flowers 120
Camellia flowers 121
Iris flowers 122
Tulip flowers 124
Peony flowers 125
Pansy flowers 126
Lotus leaves 127
Poppy flowers 128

Chapter 5 **Gallery** 130–151
Geraniums 132
Clematis 133
Honeysuckle 134
Iris 135
Lily 136
Wisteria 137
Hibiscus 138
Shirley poppy 139
Camellia 140
Hydrangea 141
Tulip 142
Rose 143
Bleeding heart 144
Pansy 145
Poppy 146
Peony 147
Azalea 148
Water lily 149
Lotus 150
Morning glory 151

Appendices
Mounting a Xuan paper artwork 152
Adding a colour wash 154
A water line 155
Greens 155

Suppliers 156
Index 158
Acknowledgments 160

INTRODUCTION

There are two styles of Chinese brush painting: the outline style and the non-outline style. The outline style starts with drawing the outlines of the objects. The spaces are then filled with colour, layer after layer creating tones until the desired effect is achieved. The resulting artwork is very detailed. The non-outline style is a very expressive way of painting and is the one described in this book. A shape created by the brush on paper is called a 'brushstroke'. Proper manoeuvring of the brush will create a brushstroke that not only expresses the shape but also carries different colours in a variety of tones. For example, a lilac leaf created by the brushstroke 'long dot' will have a green heart shape tinted with a brown edge. By arranging the dots in different positions, the leaf can be open or folded or in any posture. A reverse fan brushstroke can create a dancing Shirley poppy petal with a dark red edge fading into light pink towards the centre. By using this amazing painting style all these effects are produced by a single touch of the brush on paper.

Traditionally, learning Chinese flower painting always begins with learning the basic techniques used to paint the four Chinese flowers: plum blossom, orchid, chrysanthemum and bamboo. In the ancient concept, the teaching of the four Chinese flowers involves not only painting but also the philosophy of life. A reputable master not only teaches the pupils techniques of painting, but also guides them in their thinking, life style and future outlook. Each of the four flowers is a symbol of virtue. The pupils are encouraged to model their lives on these virtues. On the technical side, there are many reasons to choose the four flowers for learning. The four flowers represent the four seasons. In learning to paint the four flowers, you also learn about the moods of the four seasons, what colours to use and the accompaniments that go with the flowers. The four flowers also bring all the basic techniques together. The orchid is a perfect example of using the three fundamental basic techniques: wrist and elbow movements, press and lift technique and the two-tone or multi-colour loading of the brush. Painting bamboo involves the use of the side of the brush. The painting of the plum blossom introduces the fan brushstroke, an essential brushstroke for painting many flowers. It also extends the use of the side brushstroke to paint the tree trunks and branches. Painting the chrysanthemum concentrates on graceful posture and the composition, especially the complicated technique of painting leaves in groups. There

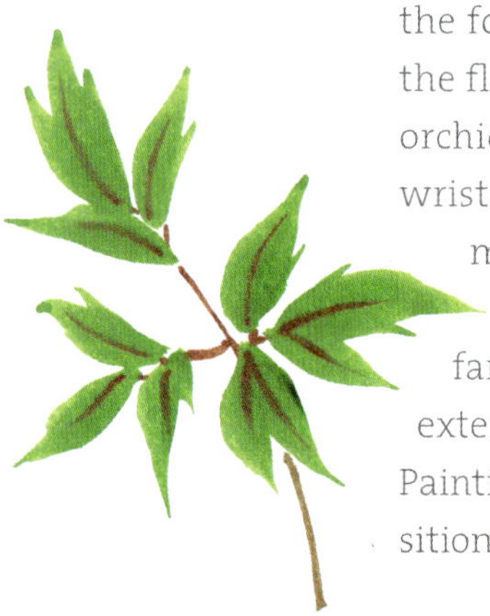

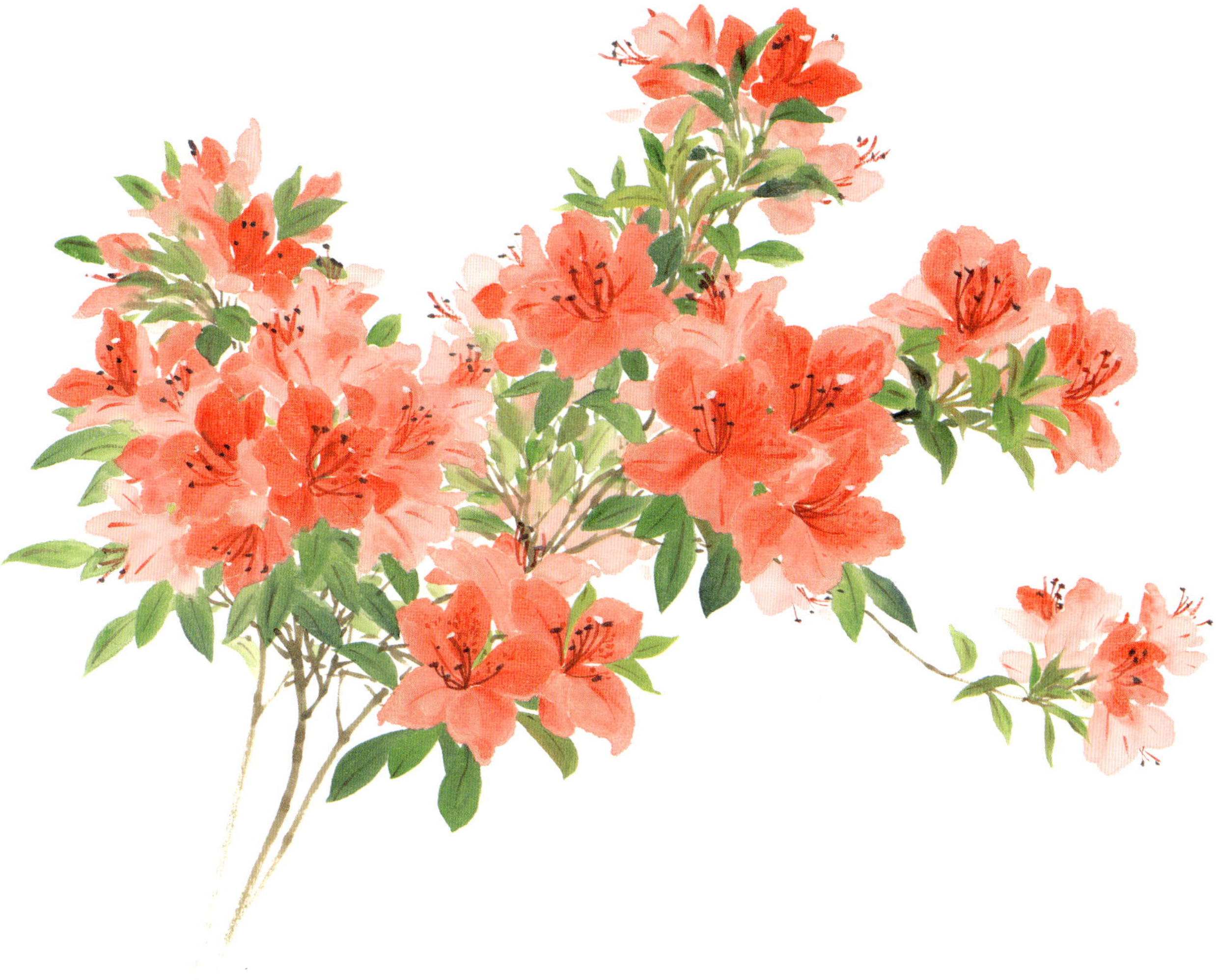

is a Chinese saying: 'If you can master the painting of chrysanthemum leaves, you will not have trouble painting the leaves of any flowers.'

Now you can probably understand that when finished learning the four Chinese flowers, any pupil will have acquired a wide range of basic techniques for flower painting. These basics serve well for painting flowers in the traditional way. Modern Chinese flower painting has developed greatly since ancient times. We are painting many flowers that were never used by the ancient masters, and artists throughout history have developed lots of new techniques. Modern Chinese flower painting is very exciting.

Pupils coming to my painting classes begin by painting the four Chinese flowers because I want them to experience the traditional way of learning the

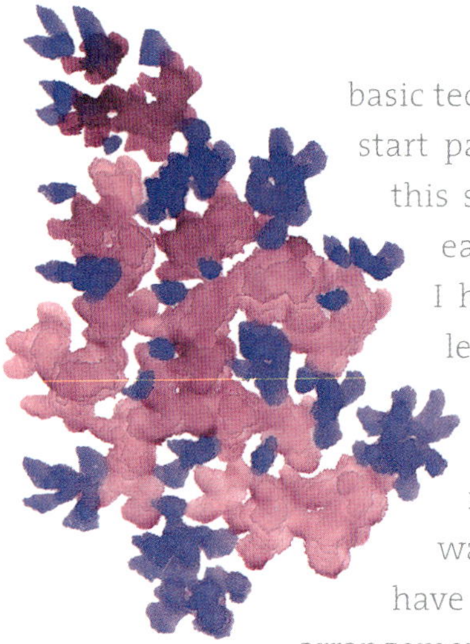

basic techniques. When they are familiar with these techniques, they will start painting other flowers, applying what they have learned. During this stage I teach each individual additional techniques according to each person's progress. I cannot teach in the same way in a book, so I have modified my way of teaching to provide a comprehensive learning programme in flower painting. Instead of beginning with the four Chinese flowers, I have integrated all the basics for painting the four Chinese flowers with the other techniques for modern flower painting, presenting them in a very systematic way. Do not feel that you have missed out on anything because you have not begun with the traditional method. I assure you that this arrangement is very thorough and you will gain a complete picture of what is needed for painting flowers. The four traditional Chinese flowers – orchid, bamboo, plum blossom and chrysanthemum – will also be covered.

The learning process begins with the basic techniques: wrist movement and elbow movement, press and lift technique, two-tone and multi-colour loading of the brush. The wrist and elbow movements show you how to control the movement of your hand and your arm so that you will learn to be active and expressive when you paint. The press and lift technique explores the potential of the brush and how you can use this potential to make shapes. You can paint almost any shape of flower when you combine press and lift technique with wrist and elbow movements. The two-tone and multi-colour loading of the brush adds a wide range of colour effects to your brushwork. The chapter on basic techniques is an important one. It is not only vital to flower painting but is fundamental for using the Chinese brush.

Equipped with these basic techniques, you will learn to construct brushstrokes. I have included all the necessary brushstrokes for flower painting, starting with the simplest 'dot', then building up to the more complicated brushstrokes one by one. Each brushstroke is described in detail. Any flower or leaf or stem that uses that brushstroke will be presented separately, with full instructions for each. When you have learnt sufficient techniques to construct a flower, I will demonstrate in a project how to assemble these techniques together to complete a flower painting.

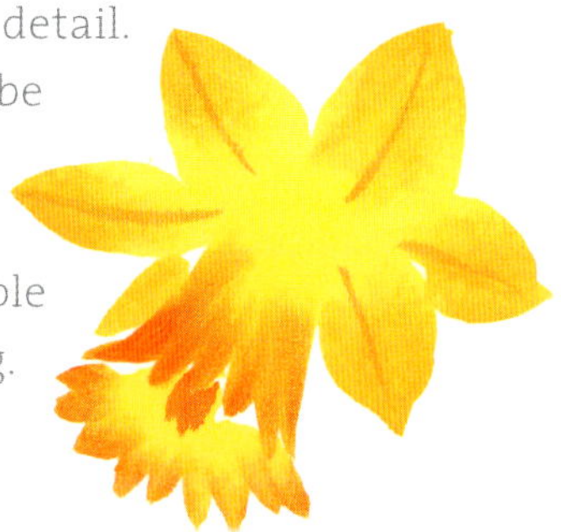

For example having learnt 'dots' and 'long dots', you can learn how to paint lilac.

Some flowers and leaves cannot be expressed with a single type of brushstroke. They need combinations of different brushstrokes to construct them. So, after the chapter on brushstrokes, there is a chapter about using a combination of brushstrokes to create more complicated flowers and leaves.

The teaching process concludes with a gallery of my flower paintings. It is then time to put related flowers, leaves and stems together. I can include only a limited variety of flowers in the gallery, so the flowers selected are representative of different types. You can easily apply the techniques used to paint these flowers to others not included in this book.

When you have produced paintings of flowers and want to present them in a professional way, you can learn how to mount them on thicker paper with my unique method of mounting. The process of mounting is described in step-by-step instructions at the end of this book.

Most of the flowers painted in this book can be found in ordinary gardens. I grow most of them in my own. When the flowers bloom in succession in the summer, my pupils and I always have fun painting them from life.

This book is not intended for an intensive course that gives instant results. You have to taste it slowly and take time to digest it, constantly retracing your steps to see what you have missed. Like many other styles of painting, you need time to build up your techniques and confidence. So for the time being, please be patient in your learning process. Every step is an awakening of a little of that creative potential in you. It is a very rewarding journey. Enjoy it.

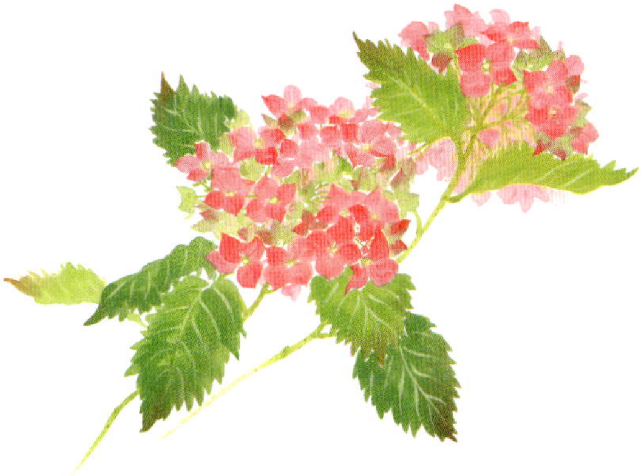

CHAPTER I

MATERIALS AND EQUIPMENT

Paper, brush, ink stick and ink stone are known in Chinese painting as the scholar's four treasures. Traditionally, ink is made by grinding an ink stick on an ink stone. With the quality of liquid ink improving all the time nowadays, it is definitely worth using it, especially if you are using a lot for practice.

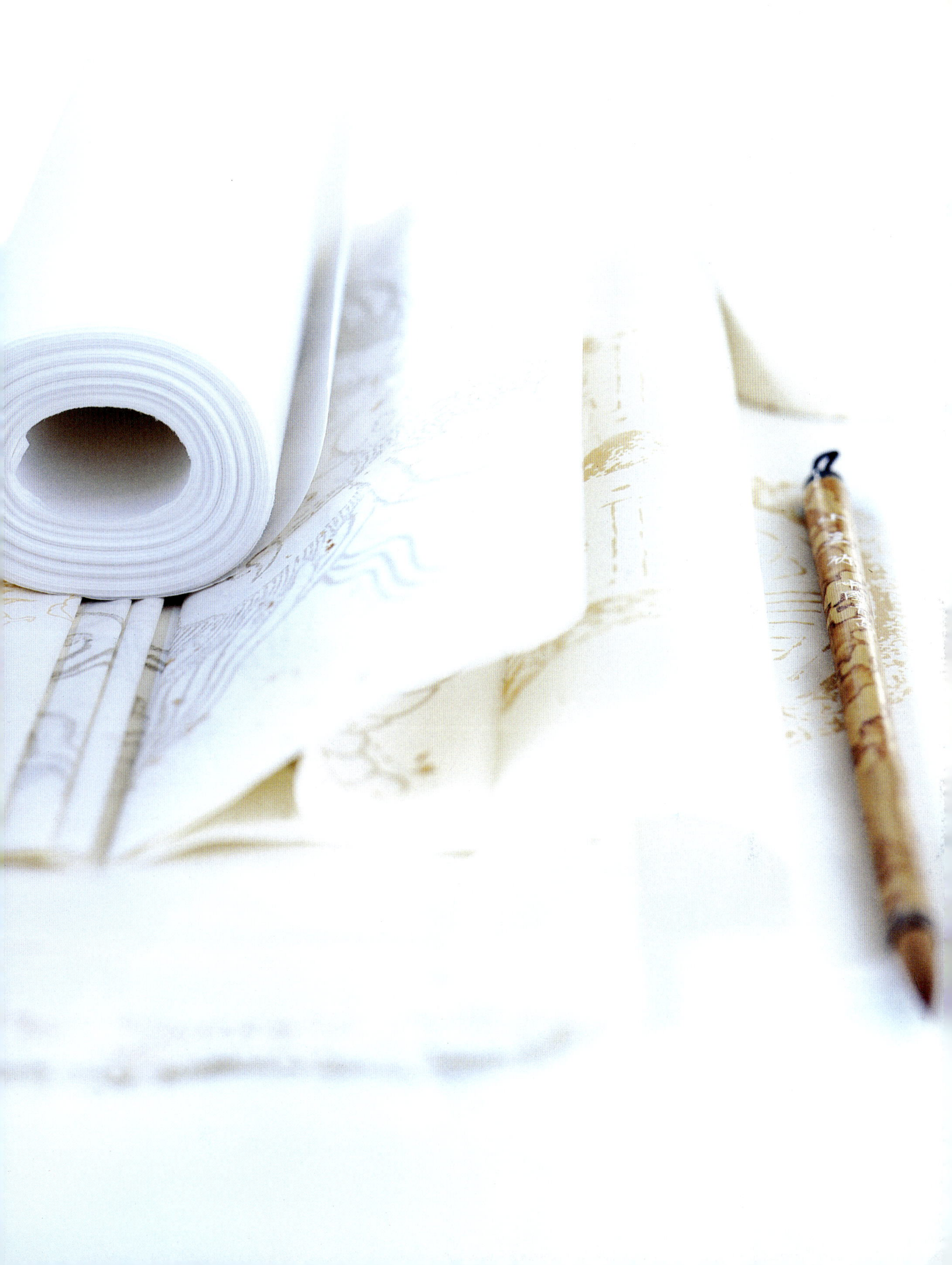

CHINESE BRUSHES

TYPES OF BRUSHES

A Chinese brush is made up of a handle and a brush tip. The handle is traditionally made of bamboo. The brush tip is made of animal hair.

Animal hair for making a brush is usually classified by the colour it is dyed. There are white-hair brushes, brown-hair brushes and black-hair brushes.

White hair comes from goats, chickens or lambs. Brushes made of this hair are very soft and are usually referred to as 'soft-hair' brushes. They can carry a lot of moisture, making them suitable for doing big and expressive brushstrokes. Brushes for calligraphy are also usually made of soft hair because they can carry more ink to sustain the writing. However, beginners in Chinese painting may find it difficult to control the excessive moisture carried by these brushes. Soft-hair brushes also have a negative characteristic. When a wet brush tip is pressed hard in painting, the tip very often will not go back automatically to an upright position with a point.

A Hake brush 底紋筆 is a wide brush. The hair can be black or white. The white ones are made of goat hair. They are used for colour washes (see Appendices). There are five widths of this type of brush. They are 1 in (2.5 cm), 1½ in (4 cm), 2 in (5 cm), 2½ in (6.5 cm) and 3 in (7.5 cm). Hake brushes wider than 3 inches are usually made for mounting in the traditional way. If you want to do the colour washes described in the appendices, get a Hake brush of at least 2 inches width. Do not buy those with metal necks because they will eventually rust after getting wet a few times.

Brown hair comes from foxes, wolves, rabbits, camels and many other animals. Brushes made of this hair are firmer and are usually referred to as 'tough-hair' brushes. These brushes carry less moisture and are more flexible than the soft-hair ones. When the tips are pressed, they fan out easily but always return to the upright position when they are lifted. Such qualities make them suitable for general non-outline painting, especially flower painting. It is advisable for newcomers to Chinese painting to start with this type of brush.

There are brushes that are made of a mixture of soft hair and tough hair. Those made for painting usually have the tough hair on the outside of the brush tips and soft hair at the centres.

Black-hair brushes are made of even firmer hair. The hair is that of horses, hogs, squirrels, racoons, and other animals with tougher hair. These brushes carry even less moisture than the brown-hair ones. Experienced artists make use of this to create expressive rough and dry brushwork in landscape painting and animal painting. In flower painting, these brushes are perfect tools for painting tree trunks and branches, especially those requiring rough and dry effects such as wisteria and plum blossom. Although similar results can be achieved with a wolf-hair brush used on the dry side, it is always nice to have one of these brushes for expressive flower painting. Brushes in this category are more expensive because the hair used has to be of very high quality. The hairs cannot be too old or too hard or the brush will not hold moisture. They cannot be too soft either or they will not create the special dry and rough effects. Many black brushes sold to tourists in Asia are dyed black just for appearance and are not the type of brush I am talking about here. So if you buy brushes while touring Asia, do ask what kind of hair they are made of.

A very popular black-hair brush is the Mountain and Horse brush 山馬筆 It is made of horse hair and is a very good brush for general use. The Mountain and Horse brush comes in six sizes. They are big size, medium size, small size, extra small size 1, extra small size 2 and extra small size 3. A small size Mountain and Horse brush will be adequate for flower painting. There are cheaper versions of Mountain and Horse brushes. The brush tips of one type are made entirely of brown hair and those of another type are made of a mixture of black and brown hair. I prefer those made entirely of horse hair.

The hairs of a brush tip are assembled according to a formula that stipulates the proportion of hairs to be used and the way that the tip should be trimmed. Many popular traditional brushes are made according to formulas passed down from ancient times, but there are many modern ones too. Manufacturers safeguard modern formulas like secrets. Those made according to traditional formulas may vary because different manufacturers would have adjusted the formulas when they made such brushes in modern times. That is why a named brush would have many versions, depending on where it is made. As the quality of a brush varies, so does the price. You will have this problem when you try to buy the brushes I introduce to you. Usually the price indicates the quality of a brush. My advice is to start with those in the middle price range. When you are more used to painting with Chinese brushes, treat yourself to expensive ones.

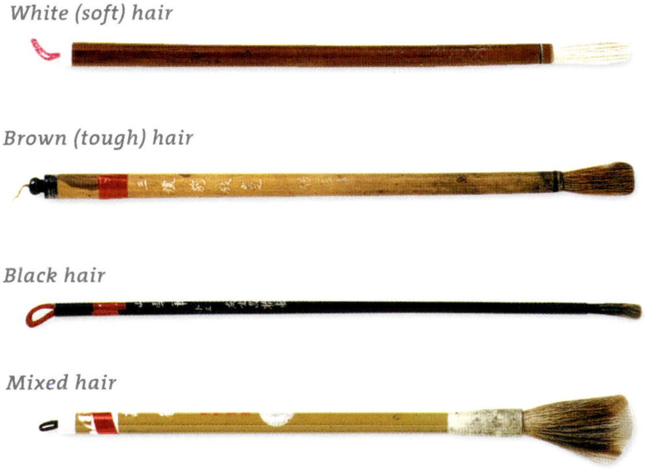

Different types of Chinese brushes

I always advise beginners to start with four brushes of different sizes for flower painting. Below are the four brushes of my choice. They are labelled **B1, B2, B3,** and **B4** for ease of reference throughout this book. The photograph on page 17 shows the actual sizes of the four brushes. The photograph shows the brushes before they are 'opened', that is, while they are still bound together with gum. These gummed brushes are what you will see in art shops. You will learn to remove the gum before using the brushes for painting. If you cannot find all the brushes I choose for painting flowers you should go for brushes of similar sizes. All the brushes selected for painting in this book are the brown-hair type.

These are the brushes of my choice:

B1 **A small size Orchid and Bamboo brush** 小蘭竹

B2 **A size 3 Leopard and Wolf brush** 三号豹狼毫

B3 **A Red Bean brush** 紅豆

B4 **A No.1 small Wolf-hair brush** 一号狼毫國畫筆

The **Orchid and Bamboo brush** is one of the most popular brushes for flower painting. There are three sizes available – large, medium and small. B1 is the small size. This brush is made according to one of the oldest formulas. Many manufacturers make it, so size and quality vary a lot. While most versions of this brush are reliable, I advise you to get one in the middle price range. When you are more experienced in painting, invest in a more expensive one. This brush is generally available where Chinese brushes are for sale so it should not be difficult to obtain one. Those available in this country are of average quality. B1 is the largest of the four brushes I have chosen.

Hairs for making the **Leopard and Wolf brush** are always of excellent quality, making these brushes the finest ones for painting flowers. My pupils call B2 the 'magic' brush. It comes in three sizes, 1, 2 and 3. B2 is size 3 and is the smallest of the Leopard and Wolf brushes. Again, it is made according to a very traditional formula. However, the brush tips of all Leopard and Wolf brushes are never long, making it a medium brush for painting. This brush is generally available throughout Asia but I have not come across any elsewhere so you probably will not find one. The best alternative is to look for a wolf-hair brush of the same size. Tell the shop assistant that you are looking for a brush of similar size for flower painting. Do not accept a brush for landscape painting. There are wolf-hair brushes for landscape painting that are of similar sizes, but brushes for landscape painting are tougher.

The **Red Bean brush** is also made to a traditional formula. When it was first made it was probably dyed with red bean colouring but nowadays manufacturers use red dyes just to keep up the tradition that this brush originally was made in red. There are quite a few red Chinese brushes but this Red Bean brush is special. The point of the brush tip of the Red Bean brush is trimmed so that it is very slender, making it one of the best brushes for small and slender brushwork. It is an excellent brush for painting small petals and leaves.

If you cannot get hold of this brush, buy the small brush called 宜書宜畫 (meaning 'suitable for writing and painting'). It is a similar size wolf-hair brush but it is not trimmed to the same shape as the Red Bean brush. This brush is generally available in art shops.

The final **Wolf-hair brush**, B4, is a tiny brush. It belongs to a group of tiny, thin brushes made with either goat hair or wolf hair. The formula for the wolf-hair type has four sizes – 0, 1, 2 and 3. The difference in size between them is actually very slight. This brush is used for final touches in flower painting. The craftsmanship involved is amazing. Each tiny brush tip is actually held by two extra bamboo rings before being tucked into the bamboo handle. The extra bamboo rings keep the tiny bundle of hair secured. Some are made without the extra bamboo rings. Look for those with these extra bamboo rings. This brush is usually available where Chinese brushes are sold.

As I mentioned earlier, you can add a 3-inch Hake brush and a small size Mountain and Horse brush to your list.

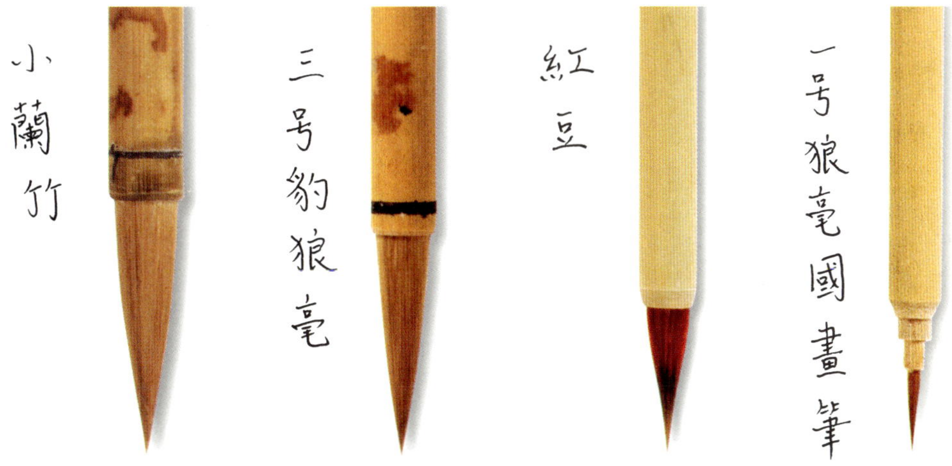

Actual sizes of the four brushes selected by the author

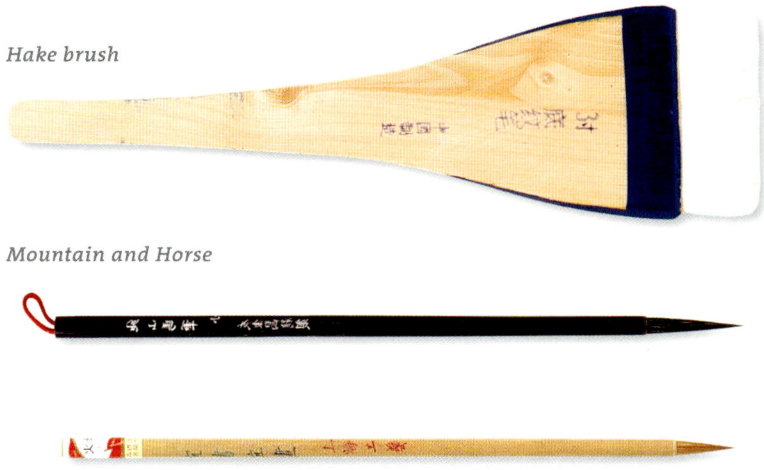

A 3-in (7.5 cm) wide hake brush and a small Mountain and Horse brush. The small brush is 宜書宜畫

'OPENING' A CHINESE BRUSH

The tip of a new Chinese brush is held together by gum. This is for the purpose of presentation only. The tip is usually protected with a bamboo or plastic cover when it is new. Before using a Chinese brush for painting, the brush needs to be 'opened'. 'Opening' a brush means removing the gum and loosening the hair. Begin this process by soaking the brush tip in cold water. Avoid using warm water. People use warm water to hasten the process of removing gum, but using warm water does not save time. Treat your brushes gently and with respect. Give them enough time to be properly 'opened'. Two things happen when you use warm or hot water for the opening process. Hot water shrinks the hair, making it tougher and causing it to lose its shape. The brush tip is attached to the handle with a little bit of glue. Warm water will loosen this and will cause the tip to fall prematurely. Prolonged soaking of the brush in water will also do this. That is why you should never soak brushes in water when they are not in use.

Soak your new brush in a jar with sufficient cold, clean water to cover the brush tip. For the majority of brushes, 20 minutes will usually be sufficient to loosen the gum and the brush tips. Some brushes, such as the Leopard and Wolf brushes, need about half an hour for soaking. After soaking the new brush in water for 20 minutes, press the brush tip gently with your fingers. If the hairs are soft and separate, the brush is properly 'opened'. If the tip is still hard and will not separate, do not force it by bending. Return it to the water and soak for longer. When the brush is fully opened, rinse it thoroughly in clean water to remove all the gum. Dry it between tissues or a soft towel. The brush is now ready to serve you.

Gummed

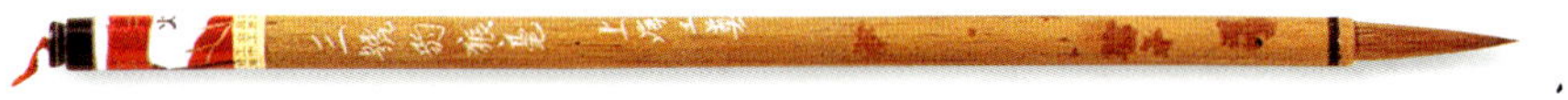

Fully open

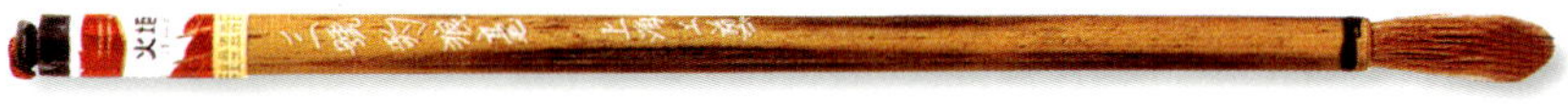

A new brush before being 'opened' and a fully 'opened' brush

CARING FOR CHINESE BRUSHES

There are a few things you can do to keep your brushes in good condition and enable them to last longer.

Do not put your 'opened' brush back into the cover. When a brush is opened, the brush tip will be too big for the cover. Squeezing it into the cover will damage the brush tip.

Do not store wet or damp brushes in airtight containers like plastic bags. Chinese brushes are made of natural materials and they can rot in damp conditions. Always dry them completely before storing them away. When the brushes are not in use, you can store them in opened jars with the brushes pointing up. If you need to carry the brushes with you on painting trips or to and from classes, the best way is to wrap them in specially made brush mats. A brush mat is made up of thin bamboo sticks bound together. Brush mats have gaps that allow brushes to breathe and dry. However, if you are not careful, brushes will fall out from the open ends and get lost. To keep the brushes securely in place on the mat, cut a length of dress elastic equal to the width of the mat. Thread it through the gaps of the mat and secure the two ends of the elastic with stitches. The loops formed by the elastic are perfect places for holding brushes.

After each painting session, always clean your brushes and rid them of ink and colours. Wipe off excess moisture before storing them. Do not clean any of your brushes with soap or washing liquid which, once attached to the hair, is difficult to get rid of. Sometimes this forms a barrier in the brush and you may have a problem in picking up colours with it.

The brush tip of a quality brown-hair or black-hair brush always returns to a point when wet. When this fails to happen, the brush has passed its serving time and you should consider replacing it with a new one. However, do not discard the old one. Old brushes can be used for mixing colours and the big ones are perfect for rough and dry brushworks.

PAPER

Absorbent Xuan paper 宣紙 is used for non-outline painting. The Chinese, the Japanese and the Koreans make this type of paper. It is available in loose sheets or in long continuous rolls in different thicknesses.

We call the thinnest 'one sheet' 單宣 the next thickness 'two sheet' 雙夾宣 then 'three sheet' 三夾宣 and the thickest 'four sheet' 四夾宣

'One sheet' are very thin. Newcomers to non-outline Chinese painting may find it difficult to control the amount of moisture during painting on 'one sheet' paper. I usually use 'one sheet' Xuan paper for practice and demonstrations. It is relatively cheap so it is very economical to use for practice. 'Two sheet' are more suitable for non-outline painting but does cost more. 'Three sheet' and 'four sheet' Xuan papers are not available outside of Asia. Even in Asia, only shops specializing in quality Chinese painting materials stock 'three sheet' and 'four sheet'.

Xuan papers are made of a mixture of tree barks, bamboo, cotton and other materials. Each manufacturer has its own formula for making Xuan paper. The name of the formula is usually printed at one corner of the paper or across the side of a pack of 50 sheets. The traditional size of a sheet of Xuan paper is approximately 26 in x 51 in (66 cm x 132 cm) though some varieties may be bigger. Very often, the paper is cut into half lengthwise and sold as rolls of 12 or 15 half sheets. 中國宣紙 (Chinese Xuan paper) and 中國書畫宣紙 (Chinese Xuan paper for calligraphy and painting) are the names of such rolls and are sold in most shops that stock Chinese painting materials. Usually they are of the 'one sheet' type. Occasionally you can find rolls of the 'two sheet' type. These rolls have the labels printed on the wrapping.

'Moon Palace' 月宮殿 is the name given to a Xuan paper of 'two sheet' thickness. It is a continuous roll, usually 50 ft (15 m) long. There are three widths available, 15 in (38 cm), 18 in (45.5 cm) and 24 in (61 cm). 'Moon Palace' was originally made by the Japanese, but nowadays China, Korea and Taiwan also make this paper. It is a reasonable paper for beginners to use when learning Chinese non-outline painting. Many art shops stock it. I usually recommend my pupils to start with 'Moon Palace'. The paper has a smooth side and a rough side. Use the smooth side for painting.

Coloured paper, speckled gold paper

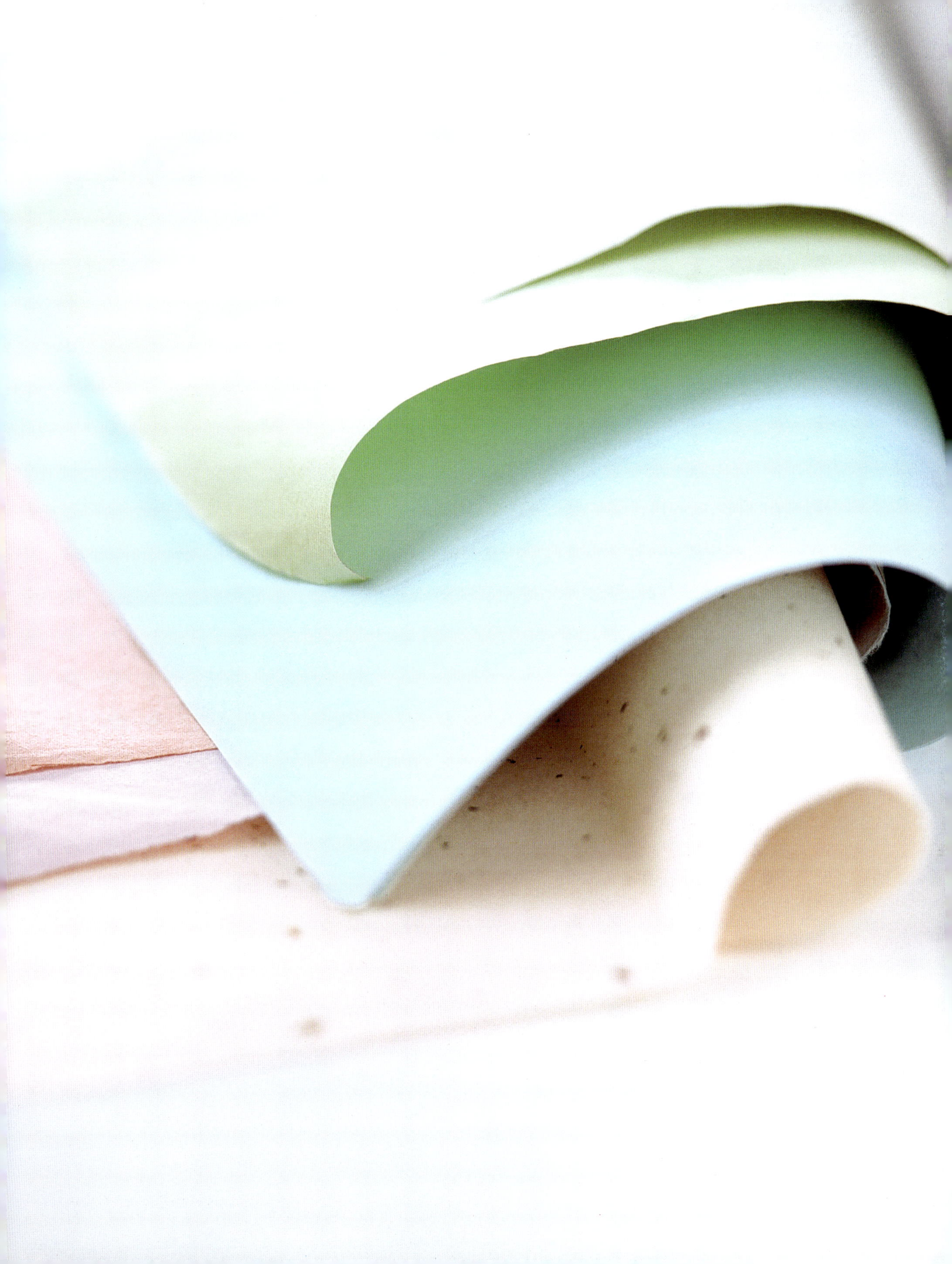

There are many specialized Xuan papers. Some are dyed with colours. Speckled gold papers have bits of gold paper mixed in the pulp when the papers are made. There are also Xuan papers with patterns of good wishes or luck printed on them.

Mulberry paper 麻紙 is a good quality paper for non-outline painting. The mulberry paper made for Chinese painting is not the same as those made for craftwork. Those made for Chinese painting have a tighter texture. The Chinese make two types of mulberry paper. One type is coarse with beautiful patterns of mulberry fibre and the other one has a smooth texture. These are excellent papers for painting.

Cotton paper 棉紙 is becoming more and more popular. It is not entirely made of cotton, with other ingredients like tree bark and bamboo being used. It is a softer paper and is very pleasant to use.

Xuan paper can be sized with alum and gum. Alum-sized Xuan paper is used for outline painting. Alum-sized silk is also made for outline painting.

You can cut a piece of absorbent Xuan paper with a wet brush. Draw a line with a wet brush where you want to cut, then pull the paper apart. The two sides of the paper will separate.

A roll of 'Moon Palace' and folded sheets of Xuan paper and Mulberry paper

INK

You can make ink by grinding an ink stick on an ink stone or you can use ready made liquid ink. In recent years, liquid ink of very good quality has become available so it is certainly acceptable to use it for painting. The ink shown below in the photograph is a type produced for general use, manufactured by 一得閣 one of the oldest ink makers in China.

Writing ink is not suitable for Chinese painting or calligraphy because it runs badly on absorbent paper. Chinese ink has gum in it. When it is dry, it is permanently fixed on the paper. So do avoid splashing if you are wearing good clothing while painting.

It is better to serve ink in a utensil separate from the one used for mixing colours. You can use the traditional ink stone or a small ceramic dish or even a small plastic container. Make sure that you clean the ink server every time you finish painting. Any leftover ink will harden up and will be very difficult to remove.

New ink freshly poured out of the bottle may be a bit thin but it will thicken up quickly. I usually allow fresh ink to stand for five minutes before using. However, ink thickens up very quickly if it is left in the open air. When ink becomes too thick, add a bit of fresh ink to thin it. Never add water to thin the ink since this will make the ink paler.

If you want to make ink from an ink stick, you will need an ink stone. Place a few drops of clean water on the ink stone. Hold the ink stick vertically on the water and grind it against the surface of the stone in circular movements. You will see dark colour beginning to appear. Add a few more drops of water and grind again. Repeat the process of adding a few drops of water followed by grinding until you have made sufficient dark ink. Always clean the ink stone after use. Any dry leftover ink on the stone will be very difficult to remove. Clean the stone using soft tissues with cold water and dry it properly before storing it away. Hard and abrasive material will damage the delicate surface of the stone.

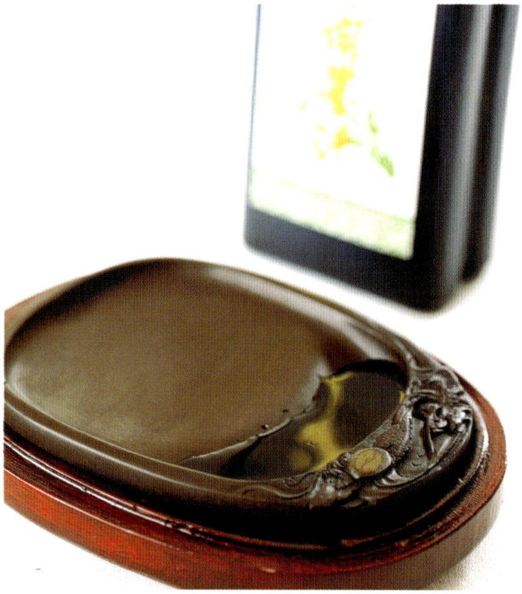

A bottle of ink and an ink stone

COLOURS

Some people will insist on using Chinese or Japanese colours for Chinese painting. I do not see any reason why watercolours cannot be used. Most of my pupils use watercolours with excellent results. They offer more choices of colour and they are easily available anywhere. Chinese and Japanese colours have gum in them. This makes life easier when it comes to mounting Chinese painting artworks because you have to wet your paintings in the process of mounting and watercolours tend to run when you wet your paintings. My modern method of mounting eliminates this problem and all my pupils find my method a complete success. I use watercolours in all the illustrations in this book. You will find instructions for this mounting method in the appendices.

If you are a beginner to watercolours, the following is a list of the colours I used in this book. You can add any of your favourite colours to this list.

Sap green   indigo   burnt sienna   gamboge   alizarin crimson   cobalt blue   lemon yellow

mauve   cadmium red   permanent rose   process white   cadmium orange

OTHER ACCESSORIES

A big jar or yoghurt pot for water

A mixing dish or a big, light-coloured dinner plate for mixing colours

Lots of newspaper to protect the surface you are painting on

A newsprint for laying your Xuan paper on. This is for absorbing the excess moisture during painting. When the newsprint gets too wet and muddy, you can change to a new one. Traditionally artists use a large piece of flannel to lay the painting paper on. These flannels are available in the art shops where you can buy your Chinese painting materials. I find them too soft and they can be a hindrance to any expressive movement. Newsprint serves the same purpose. Most art shops and craft shops stock newsprint. If they do not, they can easily order it for you.

Some weights such as small stones or horse brasses to keep your painting paper from moving when you are painting

A cheap painting brush or an old Chinese brush for mixing colours

CHAPTER 2

BASIC TECHNIQUES

Anyone can pick up a brush and paint. However, if you want to use your brush effectively, the techniques described in this chapter will help you.

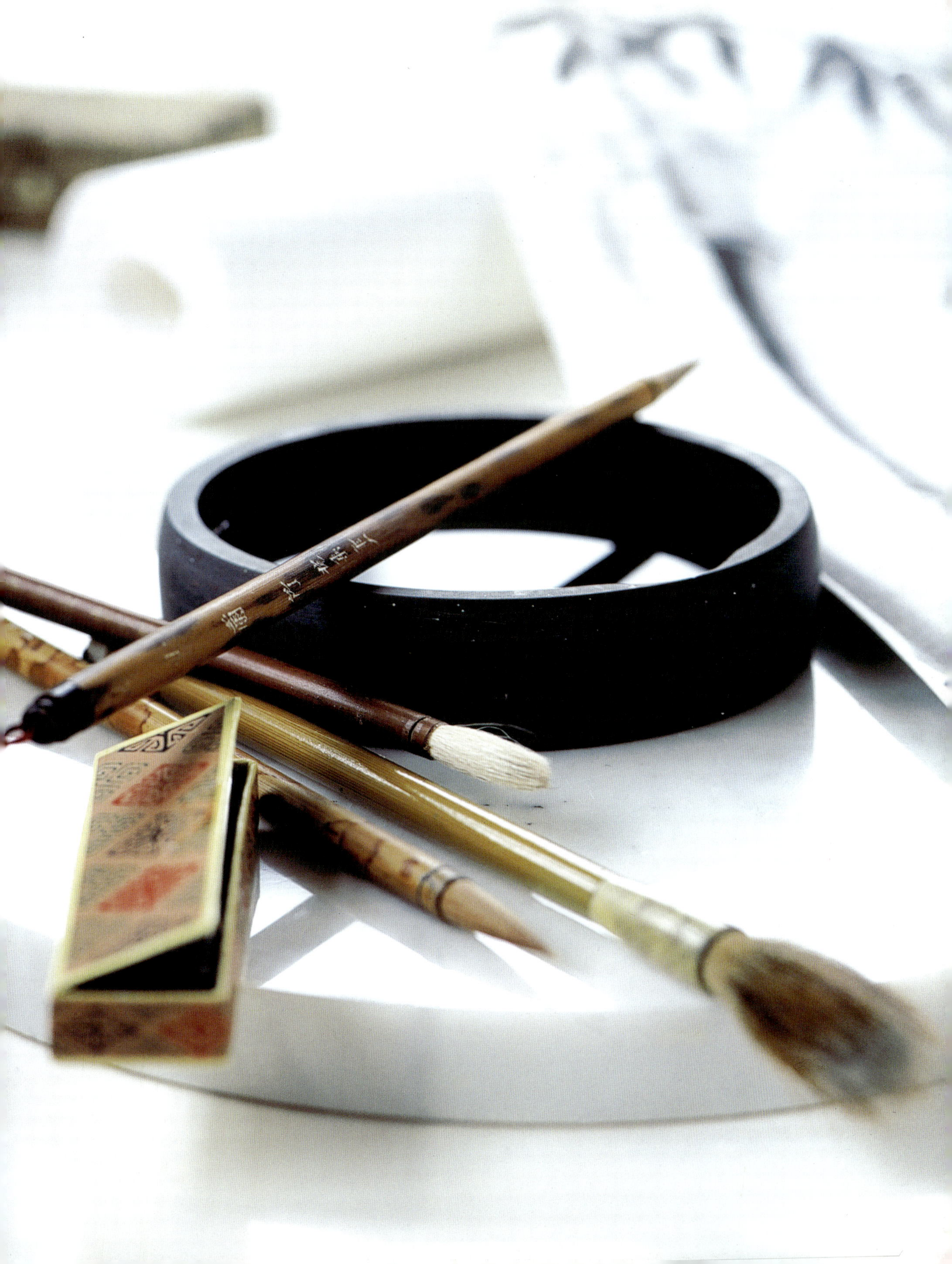

USING A CHINESE BRUSH

Anyone can pick up a Chinese brush and paint. However, if you understand how a brush works and how your hand and arm work, it will help you to use the brush more effectively.

HOW TO HOLD A CHINESE BRUSH

The length of the handle of a brush is carefully measured in proportion to the size of the brush tip and in accordance with the way the brush is designed to be used. For example, a brush with black hair has a longer handle in comparison to a brush of the same size but made with a different type of hair because black-hair brushes are usually used for more expressive brushworks when the artist needs to swing the arm. Too short a handle will restrict such swinging movements.

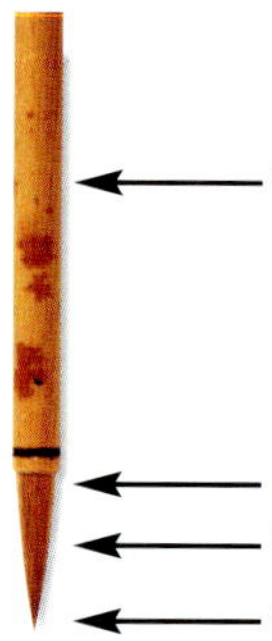

Hold the brush in the middle of the handle. Too low a position will restrict the movement of the brush. Too high a position will mean that the painting movement will be too shaky. Experienced artists sometimes vary the position for special effects. For new users of the Chinese brush, it is better to keep to the middle position until they are more familiar with how a brush behaves.

The simplest way to hold a brush is between your thumb and your four fingers. Another way is to hold it with two fingers on one side of the brush and the other two on the same side of the thumb. You can use either way as long as you are comfortable with it. The most important rule is to be able to hold the brush upright and firmly. Always begin painting by holding the brush in an upright position (see the illustration). Rotate your wrist to manoeuvre the angle of the brush to the paper and the direction the handle points. Both the angle of the brush to the paper and the direction the handle points are important to the painting movement. Firmness is absolutely important and necessary for expressive painting.

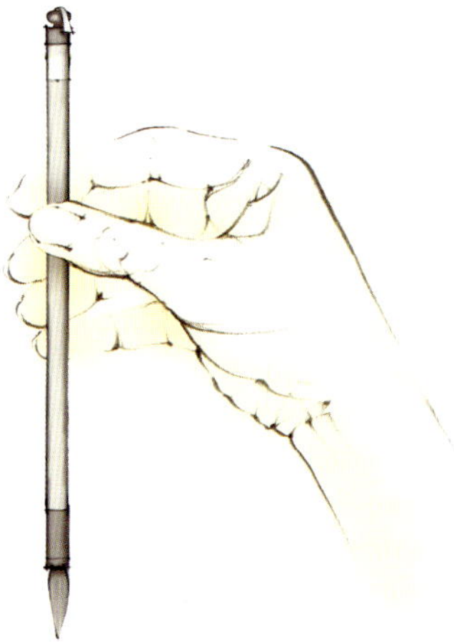

One way of holding the brush is with four fingers on one side of the brush and the thumb on the other side.

Hold the brush at the middle of the handle.

Hold the brush in an upright position.

You probably realize that when you hold the brush at the middle of the handle, your wrist will not be able to touch the paper. Your hand will always be away from the painting surface. Chinese brush painting is a very expressive way of painting, and brushes are designed to be used with free move-

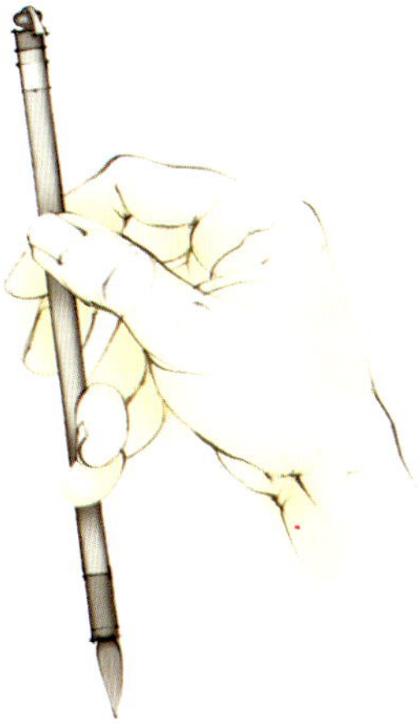

Another way is to hold the brush with two fingers on one side and two fingers on the side of the thumb.

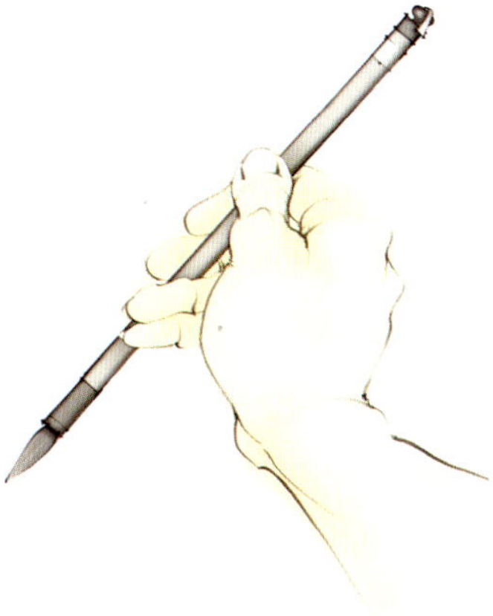

You can vary the angle of the brush to the paper by rotating the wrist.

ments. It is better for your hand and arm to have no restriction during painting. However, if you are a newcomer to using the Chinese brush and you feel that you need some support to anchor your hand and arm, you can rest your elbow on the painting surface, but once you gain more confidence, do try to lift your arm away from the surface so that you can move without restraint.

ANGLE OF THE BRUSH TO THE PAPER

Hold the brush vertically in an upright position. When you rotate your wrist, the brush will be at an angle to the paper. The lower the angle, the more of the brush tip will be in contact with the paper, so a brushwork made by using a low angle is bigger. Brushstrokes affected by the angle of the brush to the paper are the long dots, side brushstrokes, fan brushstrokes and reverse fan brushstrokes. You can vary the sizes of these brushstrokes by varying the angle of your brush to the paper.

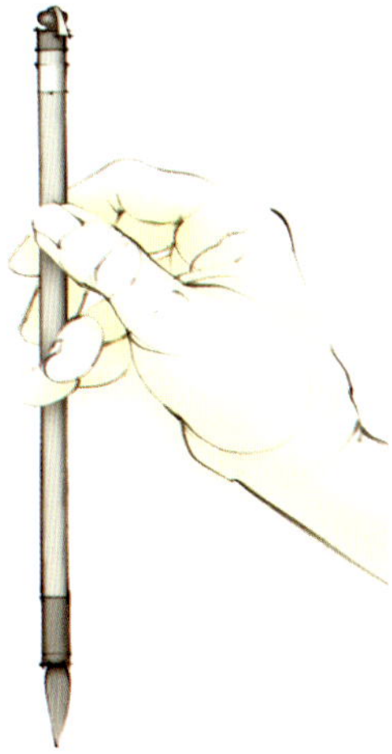

When the brush is held at a high angle, the resulting brushwork is smaller.

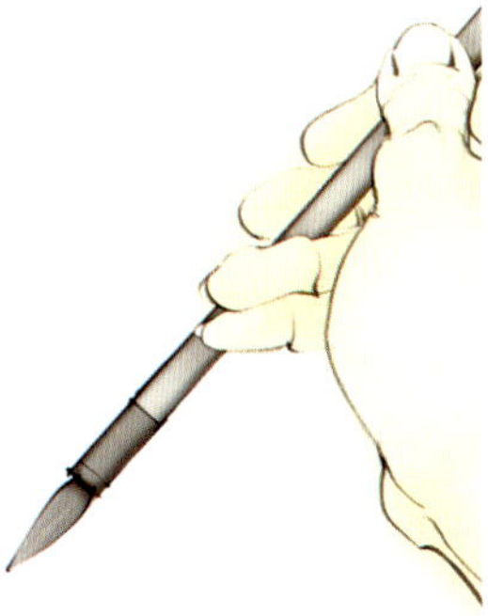

When the brush is held at a low angle, the resulting brushwork is bigger.

DIRECTION OF THE BRUSH HANDLE

The rotation of the wrist not only controls the angle of the brush to the painting surface, it also controls the direction in which the handle of the brush is pointing, and so dictates where the nib of the brush tip lands on the paper. For example, if the handle is pointing to the right, the nib will land on the furthest point left of the brushstroke. It is important because it determines how you load the colours onto the brush. In the example above the colour on the nib will be at the furthest point left of the brushstroke. So if the handle is pointing to the left, the colour at the nib will be on the point furthest to the right. When the handle of the brush is pointing away from you, the colour at the nib will be nearest to you and vice versa.

The direction in which the handle of the brush is pointing also controls the painting movements of certain brushstrokes. In painting short brushstroke, you always move the brush towards where the handle is pointing. In painting long brushstroke, you also move towards where the handle is pointing and when the brushstroke changes direction you also change the direction of the handle. To paint side brushstroke, you always move your brush at right angles to where the handle is pointing. You will learn about this topic in detail later when I discuss using the different brushstrokes.

The following illustrations show you the different directions in which the handle of the brush can point. Fully load your brush with alizarin crimson and dip the nib of the brush into ink. Touch the paper with the brush at every position and observe the effects of the colours on the brushwork.

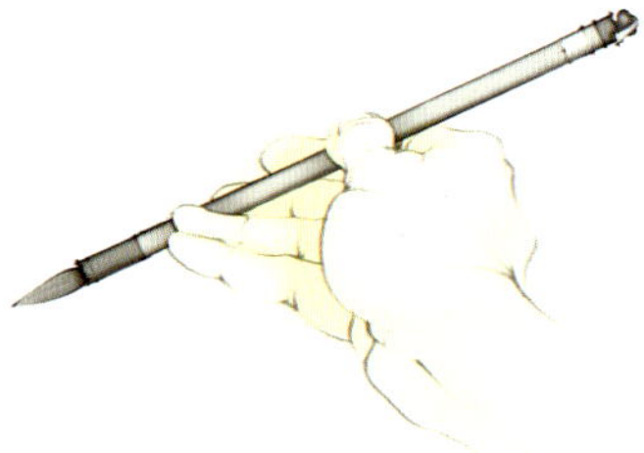

The handle of the brush points to the right at an angle to the surface.

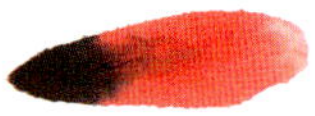

The resulting brushwork

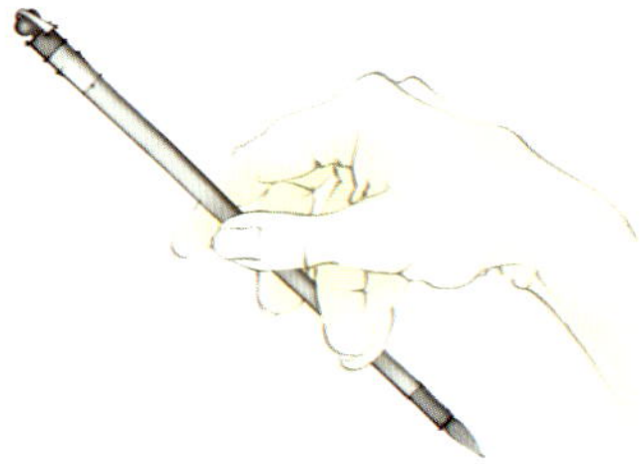

The handle of the brush points to the left at an angle to the surface.

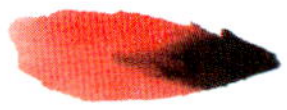

The resulting brushwork

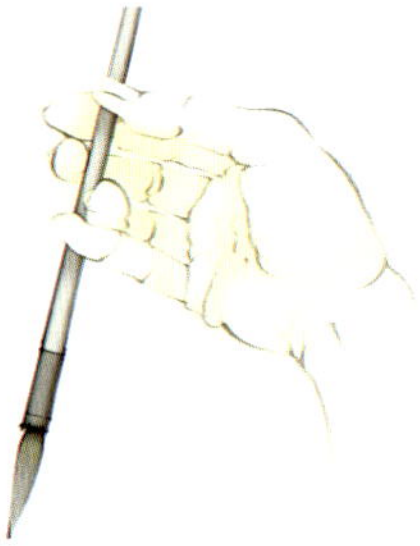

The handle of the brush points away from you at an angle to the surface.

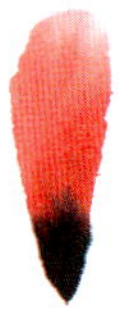

The resulting brushwork

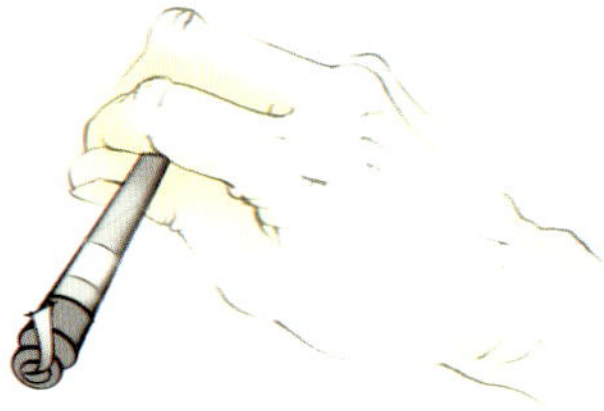

The handle of the brush points towards you at an angle to the surface.

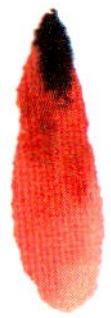

The resulting brushwork

LOADING A BRUSH WITH INK OR COLOURS

Colours work their way up a wet brush. Where a brush is loaded with two tones of a colour, or two colours, or three colours, the colours at the lower part of a brush work their way up after a while. The resulting brush-work may not have the effect you planned. To avoid this happening, always half load or dip the nib of the brush into a second and a third colour just before painting. Clean the brush after a few repeat multi-loadings and load the brush again with fresh colours.

There are many ways of loading a brush with ink or colours. The following are the ones I use in this book.

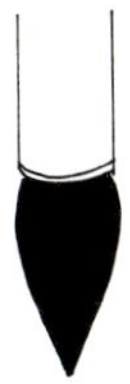

Fully loading a brush
Dip the brush into ink or colour. Roll the brush until the whole brush tip is full of ink or colour.

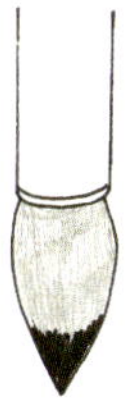

Loading a brush with two tones of colour
Fully load a brush with a diluted colour and dip the nib of the brush into a darker tone of the same colour.

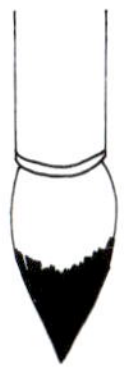

Half-loading a brush
Dip the lower half of the brush tip into ink or colour and lift it out immediately.

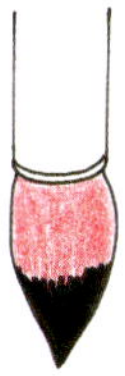

Loading a brush with two colours
Fully load a brush with one colour. Then half-load or dip the nib of the brush into a second colour.

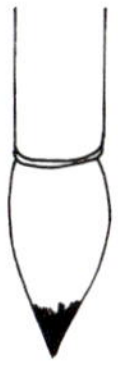

Loading the nib of a brush
Dip only the nib of a brush tip into ink or colour. You can control how much of the ink or colour appears in the final brushwork by how much you dip the nib of the brush into the ink or colour. The more you load the nib with a colour, the more the colour will appear in the brushwork.

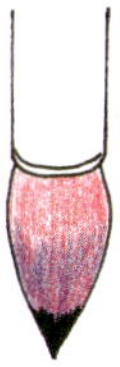

Loading a brush with three colours
Fully load a brush with one colour, then half-load the brush with a second colour and, finally, dip the nib of the brush into a third colour.

See also
brush sizes p14
using the brush p28

WRIST MOVEMENT

Movements made by rotating the wrist are small. Such movement are used for drawing small objects. They are perfect for painting blossoms, flowers with small petals, and small leaves. You can move your hand up and down, to the right and to the left by rotating the wrist. Fully load **B3** with ink for all the brushwork.

Short vertical lines
Hold the brush in a vertical position. Draw the short vertical lines by rotating the wrist upwards or downwards. Follow the directions indicated by the arrows.

Short horizontal lines
Hold the brush in a vertical position. Draw the short horizontal lines by rotating the wrist to the right or to the left. Follow the directions indicated by the arrows.

Small curves
Hold the brush in a vertical position. Draw the small curves by rotating the wrist. Follow the directions indicated by the arrows.

Small rounds
Hold the brush in a vertical position. Draw the small rounds by rotating the wrist. Follow the directions indicated by the arrows.

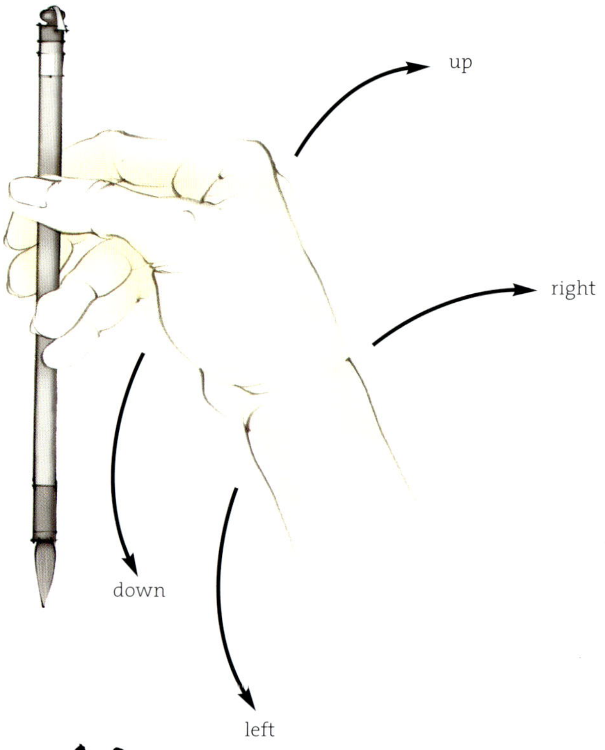

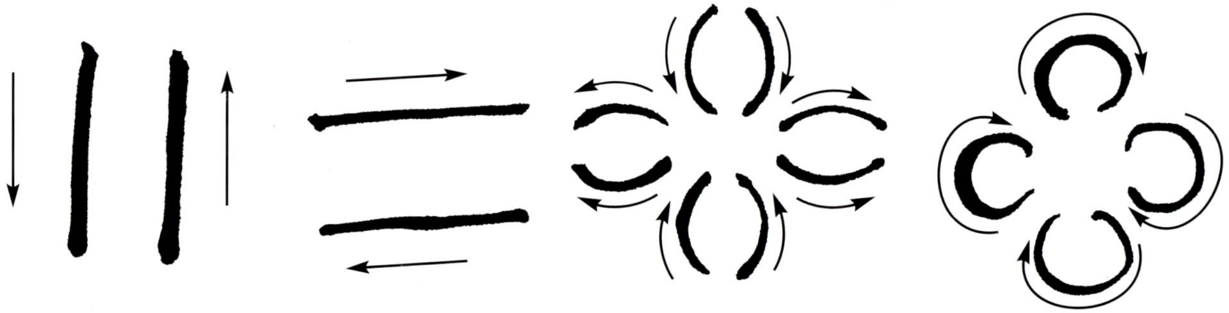

Short vertical lines *Short horizontal lines* *Small curves* *Small rounds*

FURTHER PRACTICE

We can use the wrist movement to draw small objects like small leaves and small flower petals. Below are some examples for you to practise. I am sure you can find many other interesting objects around you for practising the wrist movements. Load **B3** with ink to practise all the drawings.

A small leaf

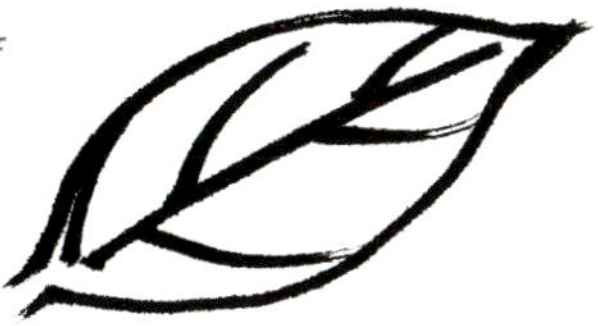

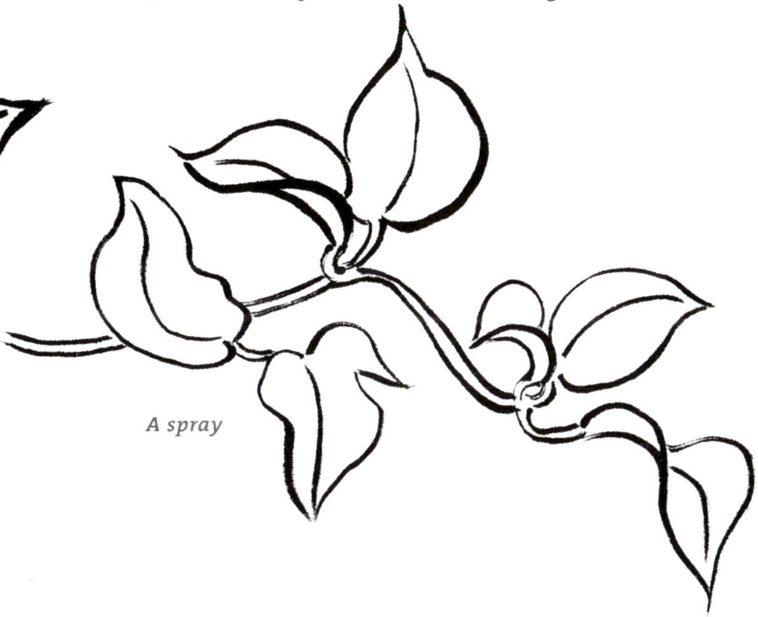

A spray

A small flower

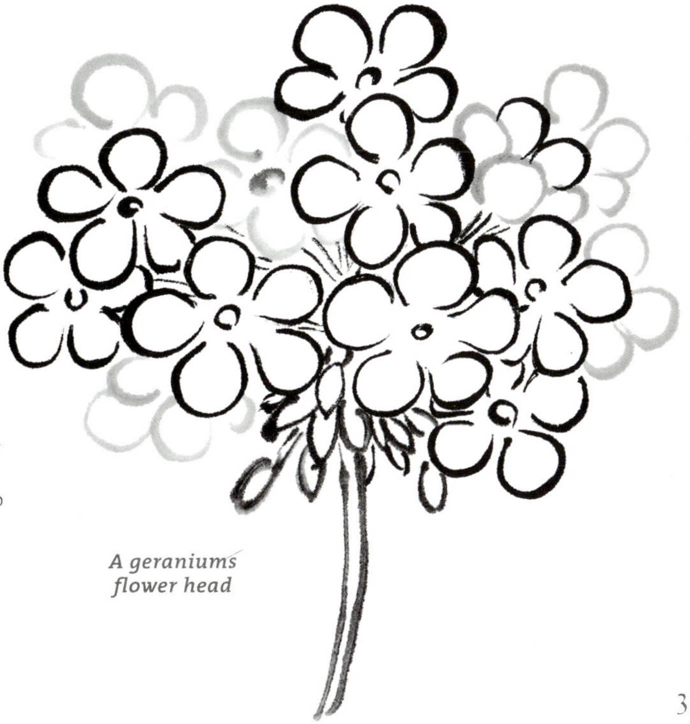

A geraniums flower head

A small leaf
Draw the outline of the leaf. Then add the veins.

A small flower
Draw five small rounds for the petals. Use short lines and dots to draw the centres.

A spray
Draw the leaves. Then add stalks to connect the leaves.

A geraniums flower head
Start the flower head with the flowers at the front of the flower head. Clean your brush and reload it with diluted ink. Draw the background flowers. Finally, dip **B3** into dark ink. Add the small stalks connecting the flowers. Paint a few buds and the main stalk of the flower head.

See also

brush sizes p14
using the brush p28

ELBOW MOVEMENT

Long vertical lines
Hold the brush in a vertical position. Draw long vertical lines by moving your elbow forwards and backwards. Follow the directions indicated by the arrows.

Long horizontal lines
Hold the brush in a vertical position. Draw long horizontal lines by rotating your elbow to the right or to the left. Follow the directions indicated by the arrows.

When you draw large objects like the long leaves of irises, spreading branches or twisting climbers, you can no longer use the wrist movements. The small movements produced by rotating the wrist cannot create such brushwork. You need continuous sweeping curves to express these objects. Rotating your elbow will enable you to reach a bigger area. You can move your elbow back and forth or you can rotate it to the left or to the right.

Fully load **B3** with ink for practice. Lift your hand and arm away from the painting surface. You do not want to have any restriction when you paint with elbow movement.

Move your arm forwards and backwards, to the right and to the left by rotating your elbow.

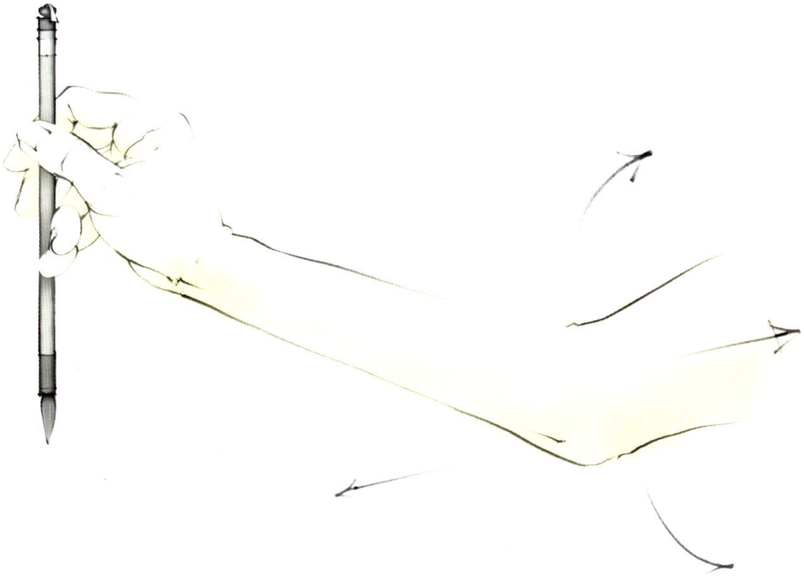

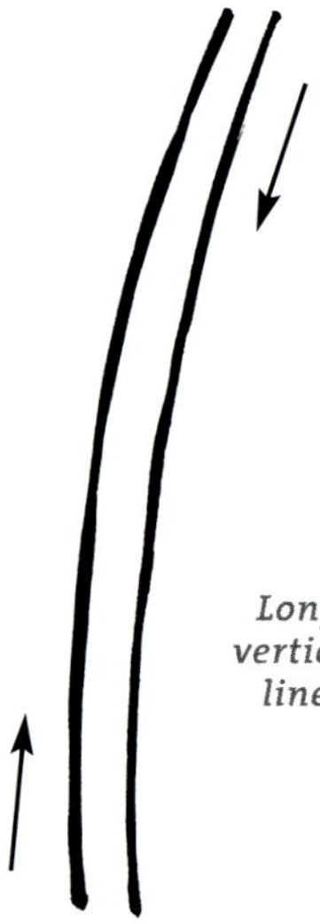

Long vertical lines

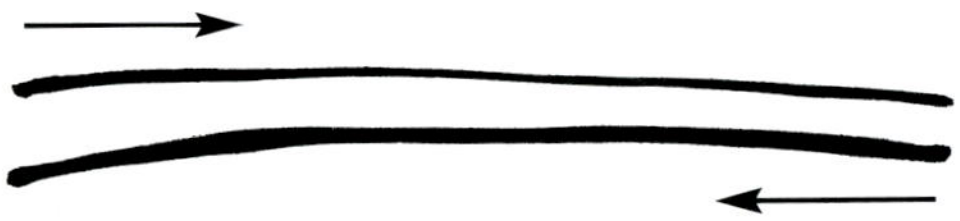

Long horizontal lines

See also
wrist movement P32
elbow movement P34

FURTHER PRACTICE

Drawing real objects is different from drawing long lines. Real objects curve, bend and twist. You have to constantly rotate your elbow to adjust to the changing directions. The more you practise, the more flexible your movement will be and the more lively your brushwork.

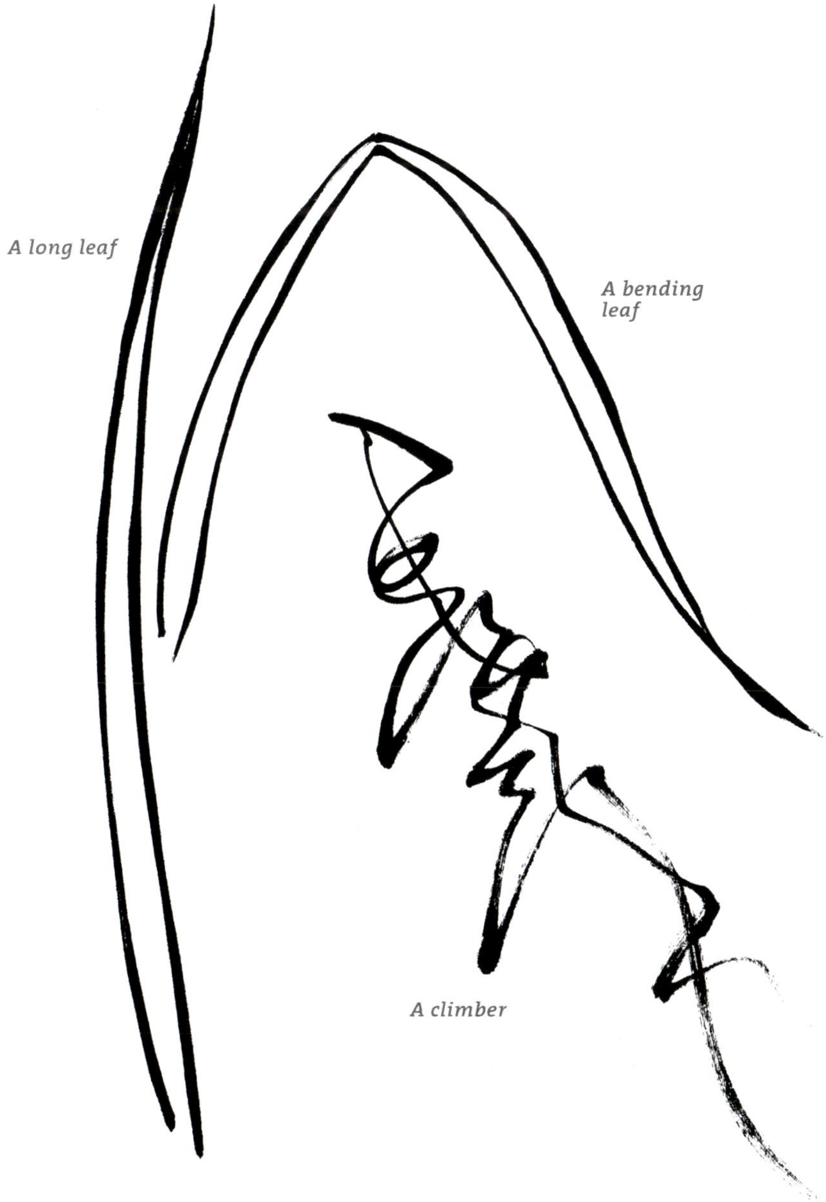

A long leaf
Use two sweeping lines to form a long leaf. Don't hesitate when you draw the lines. Don't stop half way.

A bending leaf
Drawing a bending leaf does not mean that you stop or lift the brush away from the paper at the bend. Keep going and change direction at the bend and, if possible, do not let your brush leave the paper until you finish.

A climber
Painting a climber is a challenge. A climber has many turns and curves. You have to use both elbow and wrist movement. Move with elbow movement along the curve of the climber and at the same time rotate your wrist to draw all the bends and small curves.

See also
using the brush p28
wrist movement p32
elbow movement p34

PRESS AND LIFT TECHNIQUE

When you press the brush, it will spread and give width to your brushwork. When you lift the brush, it will come back to a point and your brushwork will finish with a point. By pressing and lifting the brush, you can vary the widths at different parts of a single brushwork. The size of the brushwork depends on the size of the brush. A bigger brush creates bigger brushwork. It also depends on how hard you press the brush. The harder you press the brush, the bigger the brushwork will be. Combine the press and lift technique with the wrist movement. The result is a short brushwork looking like a bamboo leaf. Combining the press and lift technique with the elbow movement results in a long brushwork looking like a long daffodil leaf.

Press and lift with wrist movement

Step 1 Fully load **B2** with dark ink. Hold the brush at a slight angle to the paper. Point the handle of the brush to the right. Press at the beginning.

Step 2 Rotate your wrist towards the right to lengthen the brushwork.

Step 3 Lift the brush as you move towards the end of the shape.

Fig. 1 A brushwork made by **B2**.

Fig. 2 Press and lift with wrist movement using **B1**: The brushwork is bigger compared to the one made by **B2**.

Fig. 3 Press and lift with wrist movement using **B3**: The brushwork is smaller compared to the one made by **B2**.

Fig. 4 When you press **B2** hard, the shape is larger.

Fig. 5 When you press **B2** lightly, the shape is thinner.

Fig. 6 Practise painting the shape pointing in different directions. Each time when you change the direction in which the shape is pointing, remember to change the direction in which the handle of the brush will be pointing before you paint.

Step 1

Step 2

Step 3

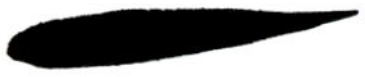

Fig. 1

Fig. 2

Fig. 3

Fig. 4

Fig. 5

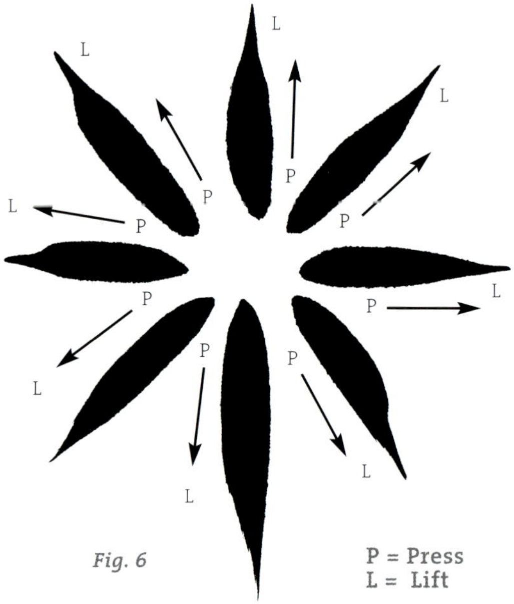

Fig. 6

P = Press
L = Lift

COMBINING PRESS AND LIFT TECHNIQUE WITH ELBOW MOVEMENT

Fig. 1 This is a shape made by combining simple press and lift technique with the elbow movement. The four steps are marked along the brushwork.

Step 1 Fully load **B2** with ink. Hold the brush at an angle to the surface with the handle pointing to where the brush is moving. Press to start.

Step 2 Move by swinging the elbow towards where the shape is pointing.

Step 3 Halfway through the brushwork start lifting the brush. Do not rush the lifting. Lifting the brush gradually will achieve a more natural curve.

Step 4 Continue to move by rotating the elbow and lifting until the brush leaves the surface.

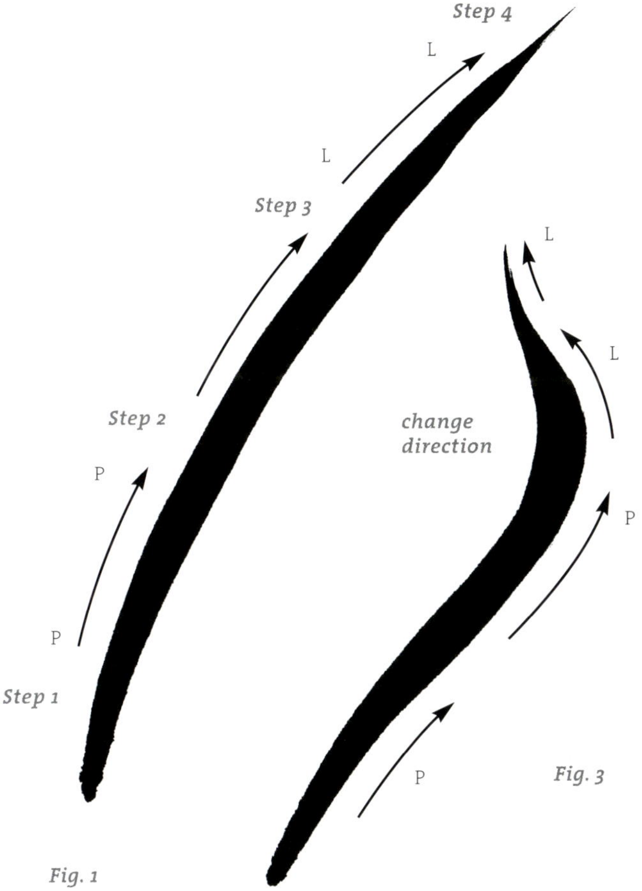

Fig. 1

Fig. 2

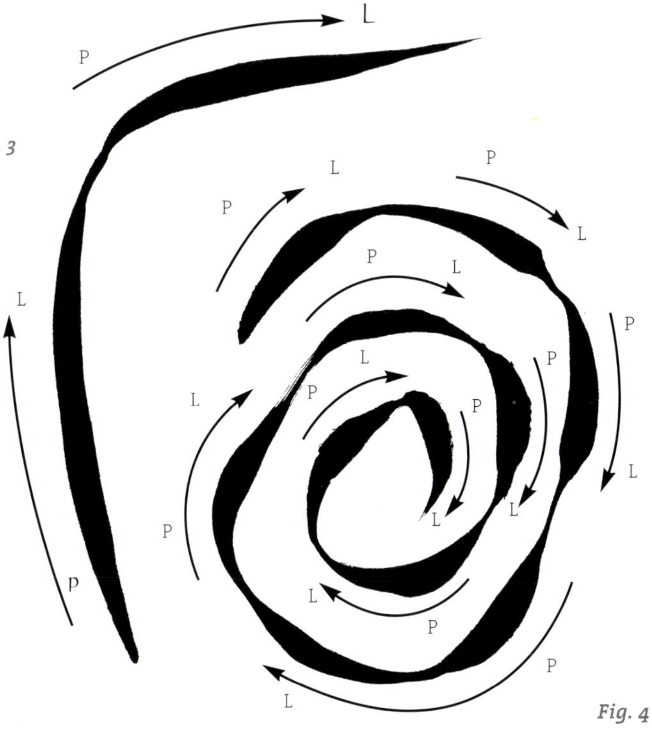

Fig. 3

Fig. 4

Fig. 2 This shape changes direction at the upper half. Change direction by rotating the wrist.

Fig. 3 This shape is made up of two press and lift brushworks. Paint the second press and lift after the first one without the brush leaving the paper. The second press and lift also changes direction.

Fig. 4 Practise this swirl using the press and lift technique according to the instructions given in the illustration. Use elbow movement to move along the swirl but rotate the wrist to change the direction of each press and lift.

See also

brush sizes p14
wrist movement p32
elbow movement p34

TWO-TONE EFFECTS

Loading a brush with two tones of ink or two tones of a colour

Fig. 1 Fully load **B2** with diluted ink and load the nib of the brush with a tiny bit of dark ink. Press and lift with wrist movement. This shape has only a tiny dark shading.

Fig. 2 Fully load **B2** with diluted ink and dip the nib of the brush deeper into dark ink. Press and lift with wrist movement. This shape has more dark shading.

Fig. 3 Fully load **B2** with diluted alizarin crimson and then the nib of the brush with a tiny bit of a darker tone of alizarin crimson. Press and lift with wrist movement.

Fig. 4 Fully load **B2** with diluted alizarin crimson then half-load the brush with a darker tone of alizarin crimson. Press and lift with wrist movement.

Fig. 5 Load **B2** with two tones of ink. Press and lift with elbow movement following the direction as indicated.

Fig. 6 Load **B2** with two tones of alizarin crimson and paint a press and lift brushwork with elbow movement. This brushwork has two presses and lifts and changes direction after the first.

Fig. 7 Load **B2** with two tones of sap green and press and lift with elbow movement.

If you fully load a brush with diluted ink and dip the nib of the brush in dark ink, a brushwork using this brush will carry the two tones of inks or, rather, a gradual toning of ink from dark to light. You will have a similar result if you load the brush with a diluted colour and dip the nib of the brush into a darker tone of the same colour. Different amounts of dark colour or ink loaded onto the nib of the brush will determine how much dark shading there will be on the final brushwork. By combining this effect with the press and lift technique, and with the wrist and elbow movements, you will be able to create a wide range of brushworks.

Fig. 1 *Fig. 2*

Fig. 3 *Fig. 4*

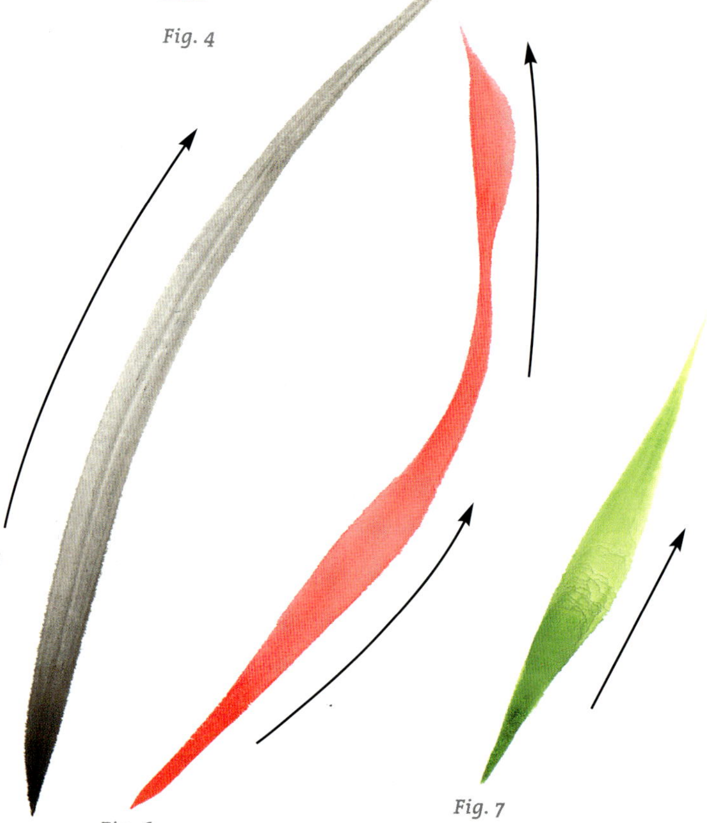

Fig. 5 *Fig. 6* *Fig. 7*

See also

brush sizes p14
using the brush p28
wrist movement p32
elbow movement p34
press and lift p36

MULTI-COLOUR EFFECTS

When you load a brush with one colour and dip the nib into another colour, the resulting brushwork will have two colours. With a big brush, you can load three colours in succession. Fully load the brush with the first colour, then half-load the brush with the second colour and, finally, dip the nib of the brush into the third colour. The final brushwork will carry all three colours in succession. Colours mix if left on the brush for some time. To avoid this happening, dip the nib into the second and third colour just before you are going to paint the brushwork. Clean the brush after a few brushworks and reload with fresh colours.

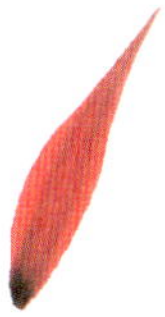

Fig. 1

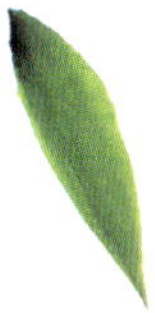

Fig. 2

Fig. 3

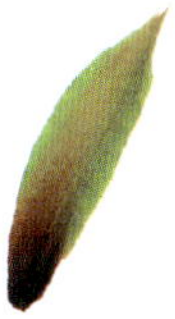

Fig. 4

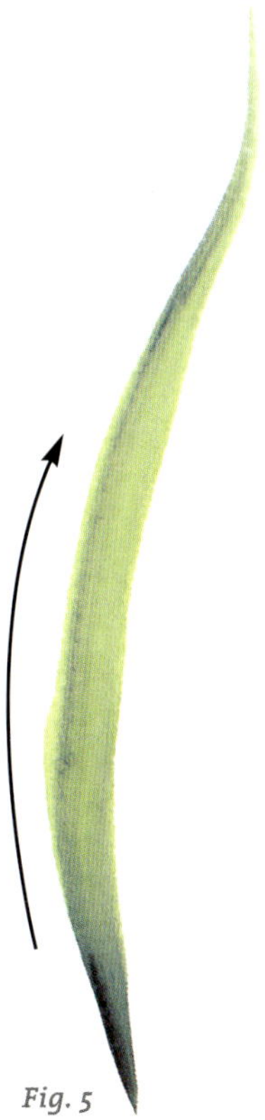

Fig. 5

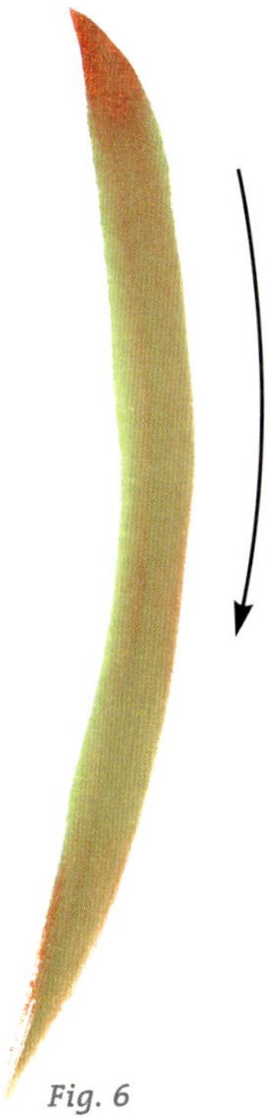

Fig. 6

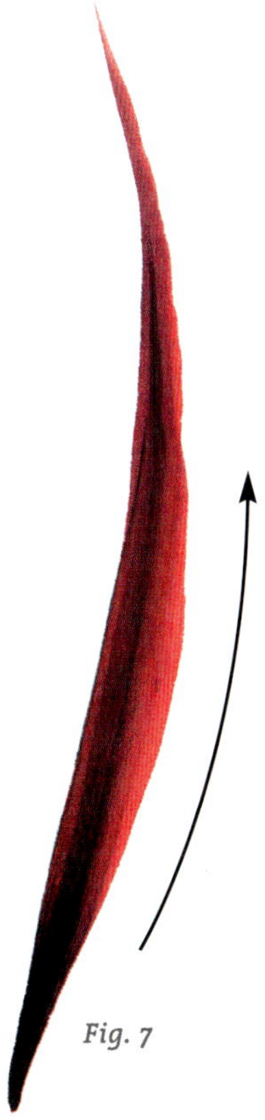

Fig. 7

Loading a brush with two colours

Fig. 1 Fully load **B2** with alizarin crimson and dip the nib of the brush into ink. Press and lift with wrist movement.

Fig. 2 Fully load **B2** with sap green and dip the nib of the brush into indigo. Press and lift with wrist movement.

Fig. 3 Fully load **B1** with permanent rose and dip the nib of the brush in mauve. Paint a press and lift brushwork with wrist movement.

Fig. 4 Fully load **B1** with sap green, then half-load the brush with burnt sienna and, finally, dip the nib of the brush into ink. Paint a press and lift brushwork with wrist movement.

Fig. 5 Fully load **B1** with sap green and then dip the nib of the brush into indigo. Paint a press and lift brushwork with elbow movement in the direction indicated by the arrow.

Fig. 6 Fully load **B1** with sap green and then dip the nib of the brush into burnt sienna. Paint a press and lift brushwork with elbow movement in the direction indicated by the arrow.

Fig. 7 Fully load **B1** with alizarin crimson, then half-load the brush with mauve and finally dip the nib of the brush in ink. Paint a press and lift brushwork with elbow movement in the direction indicated by the arrow.

PROJECT I
PAINTING A CHINESE ORCHID

Colour Palette

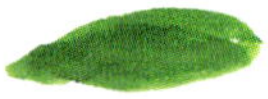

Sap green

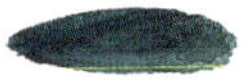

Indigo

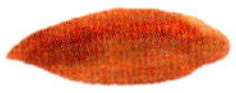

Burnt sienna

Ink

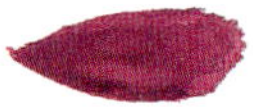

Mauve

Before you learn how to construct brushstrokes, you could try painting a Chinese orchid in a traditional pattern with all the basic techniques you have learned so far.

The composition of an orchid painting is always simple, yet every leaf and every flower has to be an execution of the basic techniques in perfect order. Ancient masters have a traditional pattern for learning to paint an orchid. This pattern, though simple, has achieved all the elements of a varied but balanced composition. In four brushstrokes, you will paint a long leaf, a short leaf, crossing leaves and a bending leaf, using different combinations of colours. The masters have cleverly used an orchid to bring together all the basic techniques in a very beautiful way.

Brushes to use: B1, B2, B3, B4

Step 1 You can use **B1** or **B2** to paint the leaves. **B1** will make bigger brushworks so the painting will be bigger. Load **B1** or **B2** with sap green and then the nib of the brush with indigo. Paint a long leaf using press and lift technique with elbow movement (marked step 1). All other leaves are also painted with press and lift techniques using the elbow movements.

Step 2 Rinse the nib of the brush to get rid of the indigo. Load the brush again with sap green and then the nib with burnt sienna. Paint the second leaf. The second leaf is shorter than the first one which it crosses.

Step 3 Make a dark green by mixing two parts of sap green with one part of indigo. Load the brush with this dark green and dip the nib of the brush into ink. Paint a short leaf crossing the second leaf as shown in the illustration.

Step 4 Clean the brush again. Load the brush with sap green and dip the nib of the brush into ink. Paint the last leaf. Press and lift until you come to a point at the top where the bend is, then change direction and press and lift as you come down. Try not to lift the brush out of the paper at the turning, but if you do, it is not very important.

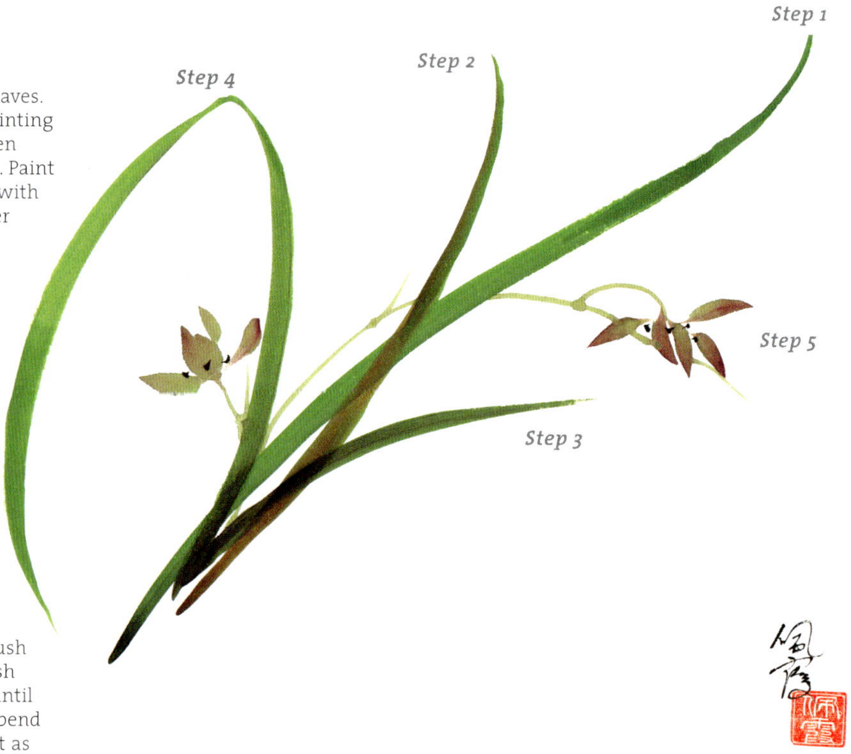

Step 5
Add the flowers. Refer to the instructions for painting orchid flowers on page 41.

PAINTING ORCHID FLOWERS

Paint the petals using press and lift technique with wrist movement. Practise painting a few petals before assembling them to form flowers. Some varieties of orchid have many flowers on a single stalk. In other varieties, each flower has a separate stalk. If you are using **B1** to paint the leaves, then use **B2** to paint the flowers. If you are using **B2** to paint the leaves, then use **B3** to paint the flowers.

Step 1 Fully load **B2** or **B3** with sap green and dip the nib of the brush into mauve. Use press and lift technique with wrist movement to paint each petal. Start from the outside of the petal and move towards the centre of a flower. This gives each petal a wider outside and a more slender end towards the centre of the flower.

Step 2 There are five petals on each flower. Dip **B4** into sap green and add a short stalk to each flower.

Step 3 Dip **B4** into dark ink. Paint a few dots to represent the centre of each flower.

Step 4 Some orchids have separate stalks for each flower while some have many flowers on a single stalk.

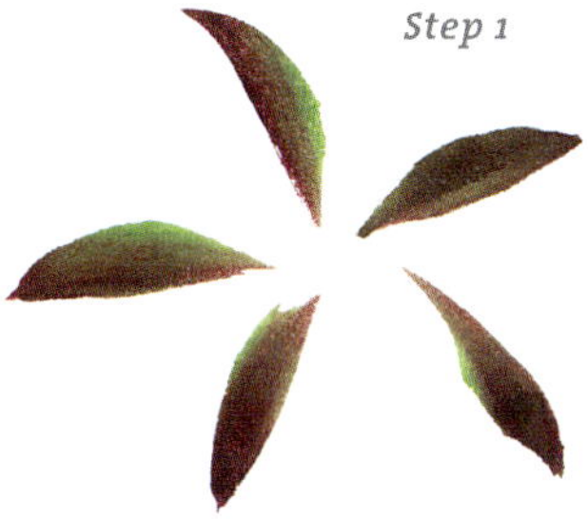

Step 1

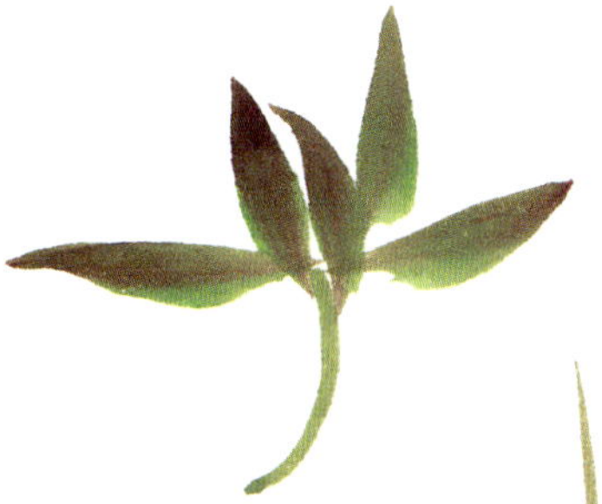

Step 2

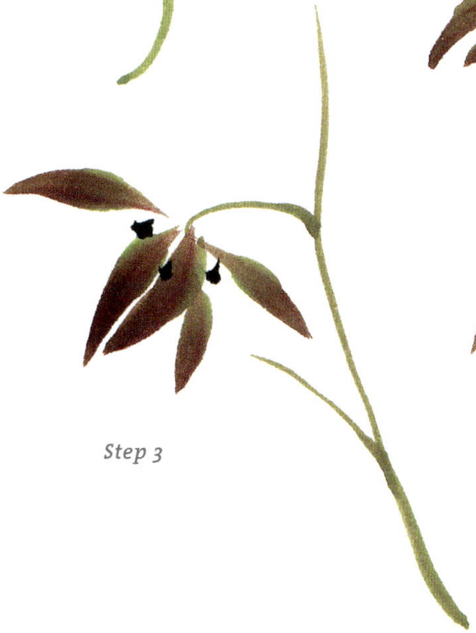

Step 3

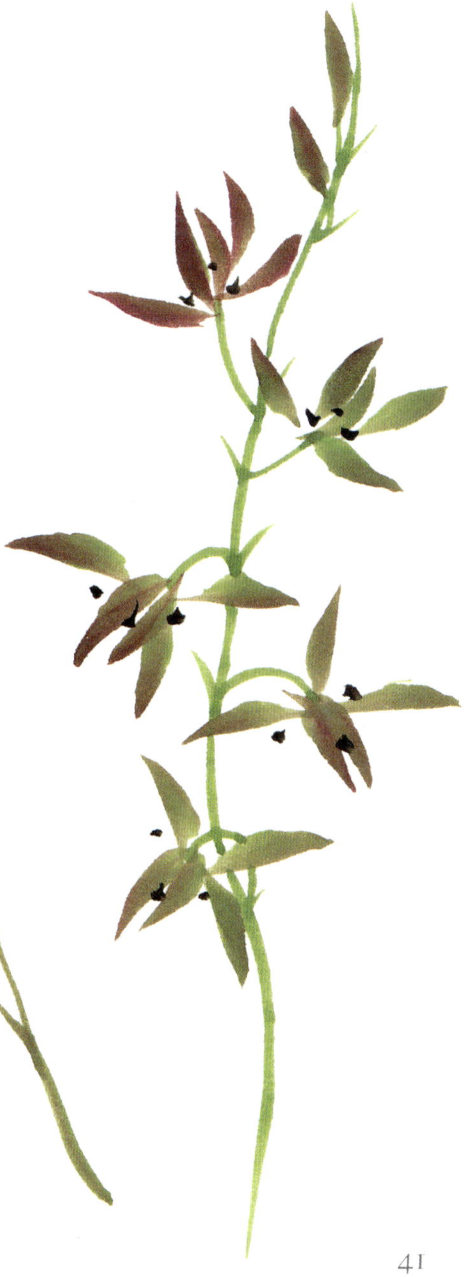

Step 4

CHAPTER 3

BRUSHSTROKES

Brushstrokes for painting flowers are dot, long dot, short brushstroke, long brushstroke, side brushstroke, fan brushstroke and reverse fan brushstroke. I will guide you through them one by one and show you many applications for each. Projects are provided at intervals.

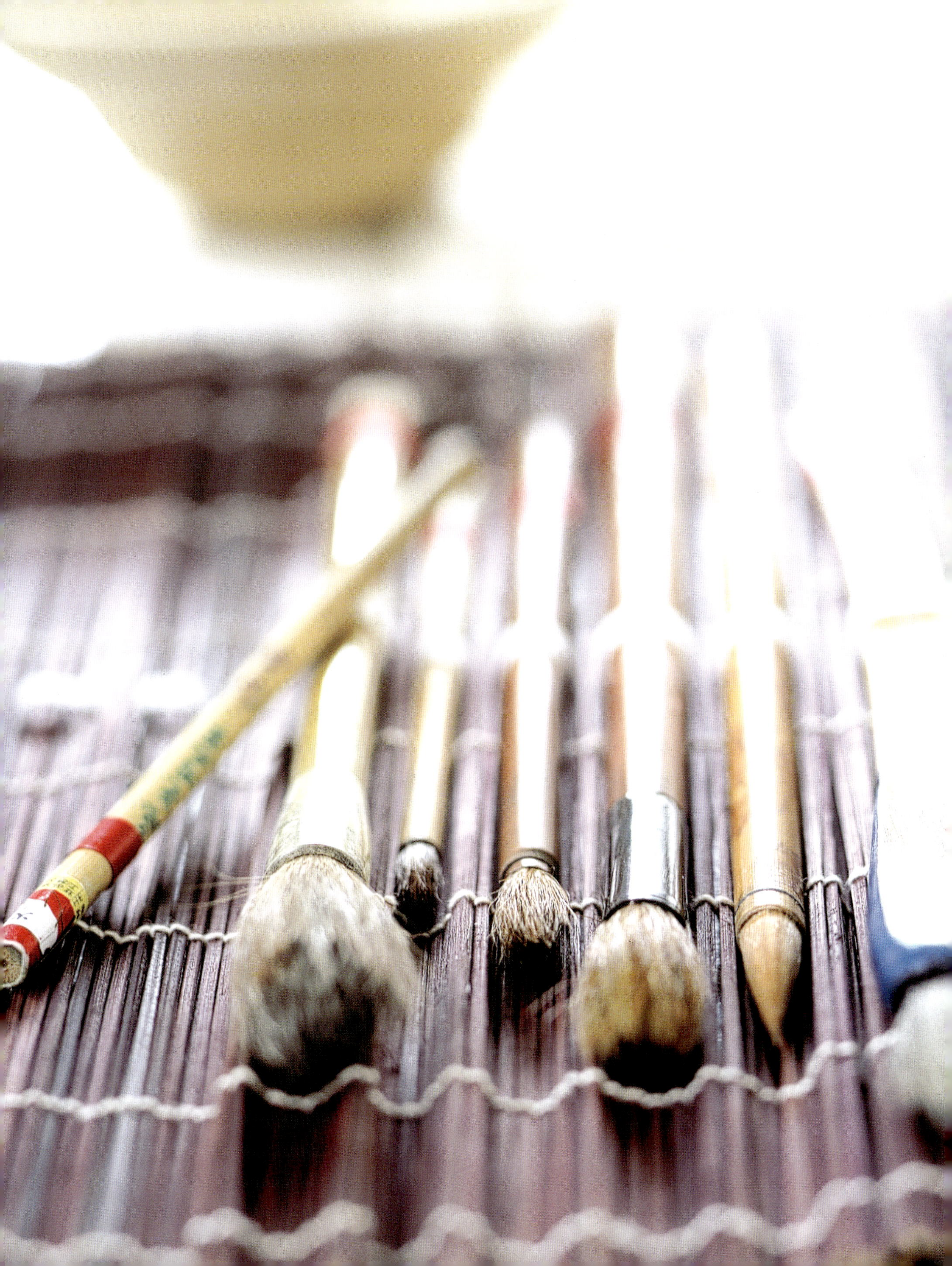

See also
brush sizes p14
using the brush p28

BRUSHSTROKE I DOT

When you touch the paper with a brush loaded with ink or colour, a dot is formed. A dot is the simplest brushstroke. Any brush can paint dots, but a bigger brush creates bigger dots than a smaller brush. The size of a dot also depends on how fully you load a brush. A dot created by a wet brush is bigger than one made by a dry brush. Pressing a brush hard on paper during painting will also create bigger dots.

Dots are used to add ruggedness to tree trunks, branches and climbers. Dots are also used to paint flowers with very small petals such as lilac, buddleia, astilbe, lavender, heather, broom and gypsophila.

Fig. 1

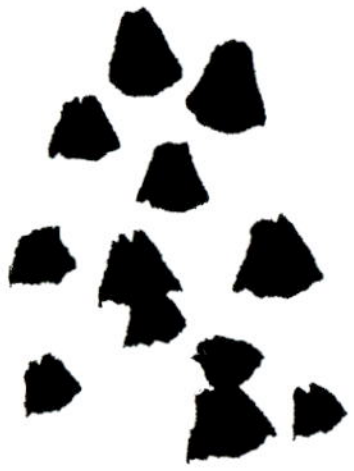

Fig. 2

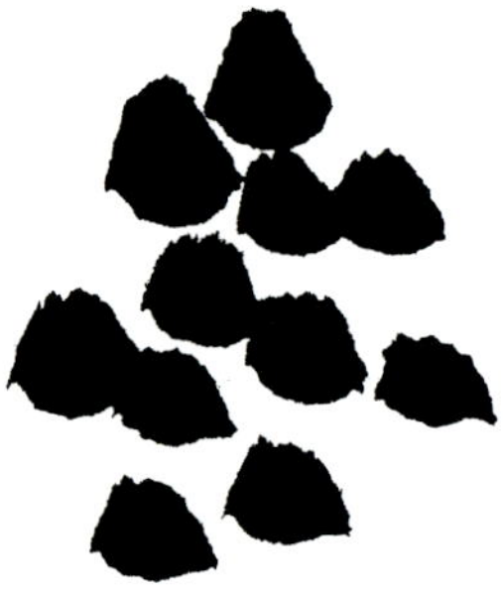

Fig. 3

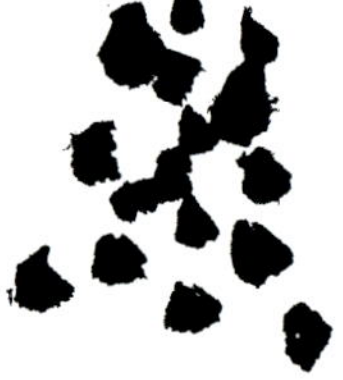

Fig. 4

Fig. 1 Load a brush with ink. Wipe off excess ink at the edge of the mixing dish. Hold the brush in a vertical position. Touch the paper. A dot is formed.

Fig. 2 Dots created by **B2**.

Fig. 3 **B1** creates bigger dots than those made by **B2**.

Fig. 4 **B3** creates smaller dots than those made by **B2**.

PRACTISING THE DOTS

Besides using different brushes, the way you load the brush and how hard you press the brush on paper will also affect the sizes of dots you make. Dots made by a wet brush are bigger than those made by a dry brush because the paper absorbs more moisture and makes the dots bigger. When you press your brush hard on paper, the tip of the brush spreads out and dots are bigger.

You can paint with a brush loaded with two tones of ink, or two tones of a colour. Dots of the darker tone appear before the lighter ones. You can vary the positions of dots with different tones to create special effects. When you load a brush with two colours or three colours, dots of the colour at the nib of the brush appear first, followed by the others. Again you can vary positions of dots of different colours to create interesting effects.

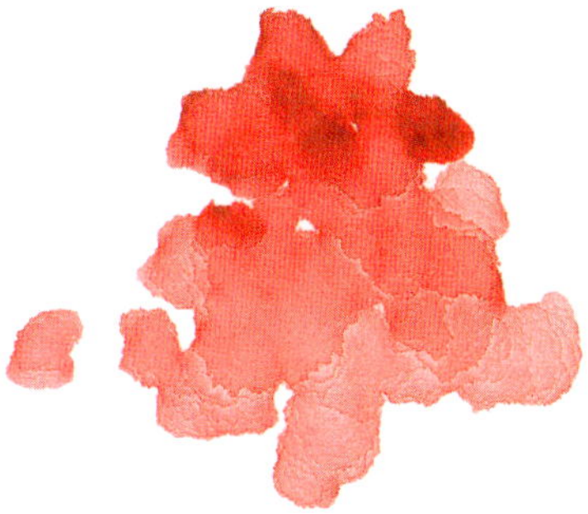

Fig. 1

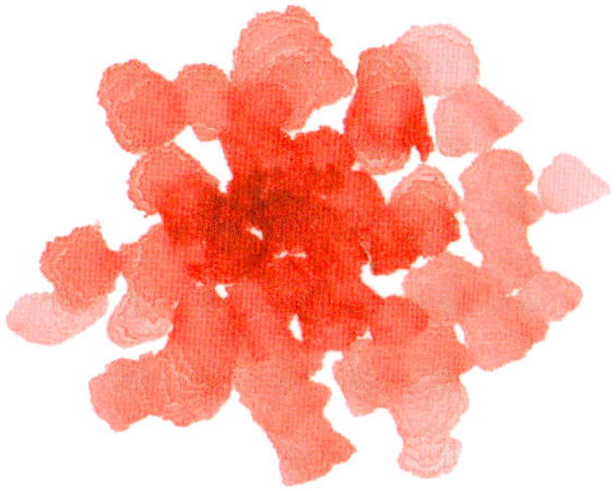

Fig. 2

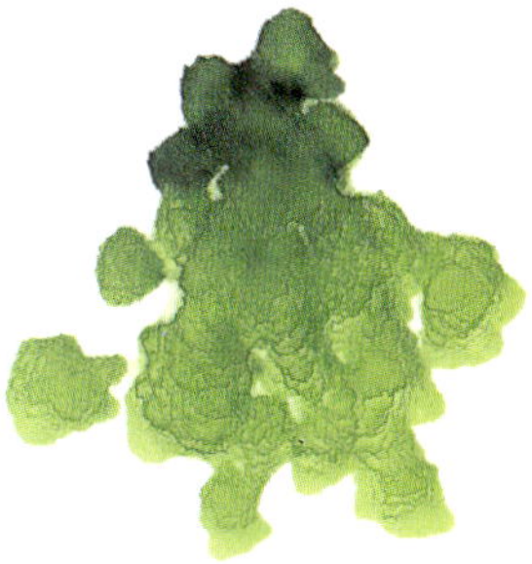

Fig. 3

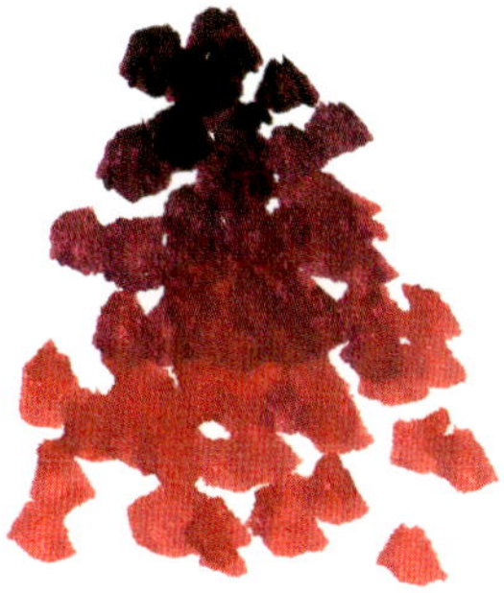

Fig. 4

Fig. 1 Load **B2** with diluted alizarin crimson and dip the nib of the brush into a darker tone of alizarin crimson. Paint a group of dots. Dots of darker colour appear before those of lighter colour.

Fig. 2 You can vary the positions of dots of darker tone and dots of lighter tone to create interesting effects. Load **B2** with diluted alizarin crimson and dip the nib of the brush into a darker tone of alizarin crimson. Paint dots at the centre before moving outwards. This group of dots has a darker centre.

Fig. 3 Load **B2** with sap green and dip the nib of the brush into indigo. Paint a group of dots. Dots of indigo appear before the dots of sap green.

Fig. 4 Load **B2** with alizarin crimson, then load the lower half of the brush with mauve and finally dip the nib of the brush in ink. Paint a group of dots. Black dots appear first, followed by mauve ones and, finally, red ones.

See also

leaves p55
finished painting p59

LILAC FLOWER HEADS

Colour Palette

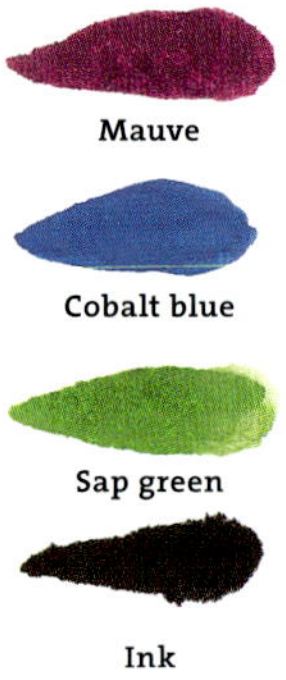

Technical information: A lilac flower head is made up of many tiny flowers. Each flower has four petals. Paint each petal with a dot.

To paint a flower head, always start with the flowers at the front. Position the front flowers and use them to sketch out the size and shape of the flower head. Then use a darker colour to add more flowers to fill the spaces in between. The darker flowers will make the flowers in the front stand out. This technique creates a three-dimensional effect.

Step 1

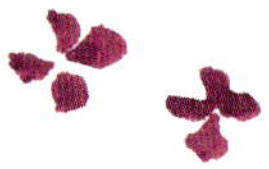

Step 2

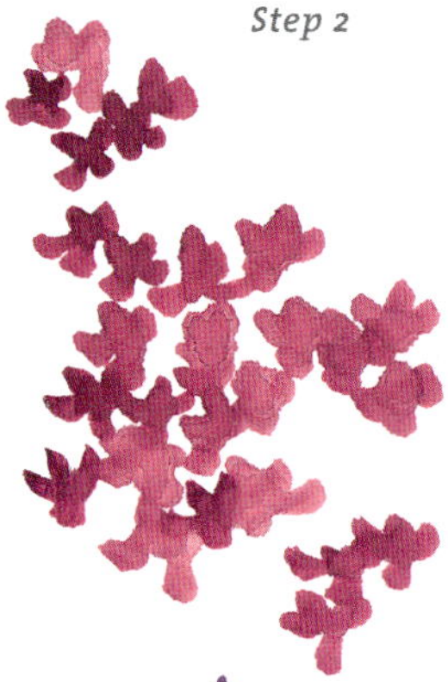

Step 3

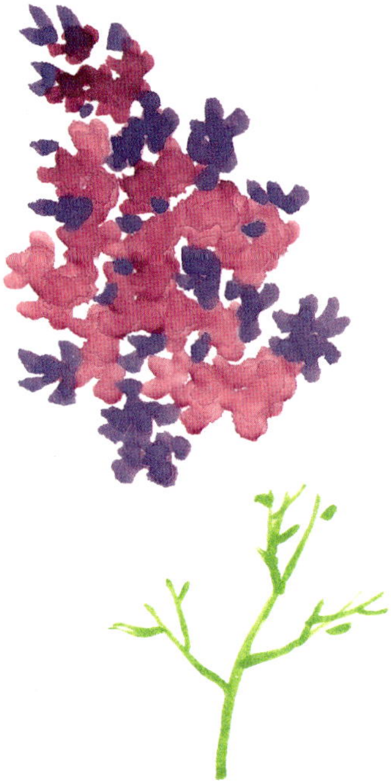

Step 4

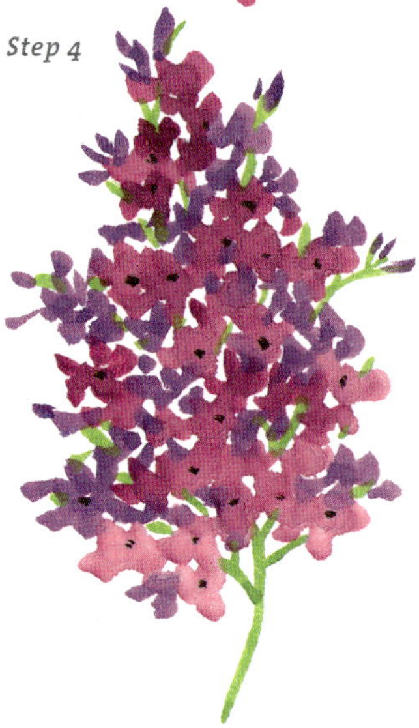

Brushes to use: B2, B3, B4

Step 1 Fully load **B2** with mauve. Paint a dot to represent a petal. Each flower has four petals.

Step 2 Start painting the flower head with flowers in mauve. Position these flowers in the front of the flower head. Use these flowers to sketch out the shape and the size of the flower head.

Step 3 Make a purple colour by mixing two parts of mauve with one part of cobalt blue. Use this purple to add more flowers. Maintain a cone shape to the flower head. Paint some buds using a small purple dot for each bud.

Step 4 A central stalk runs through the flower head from top to bottom. Each flower is connected to the central stalk by a shorter stalk. Fully load **B3** with sap green. Paint sections of the centre stalk to the flower head where it is visible. Add shorter stalks in between flowers. Dip **B4** into ink and paint a tiny dot at the centre of each flower at the front.

BUDDLEIA AND LAVENDER

Technical information: You can use the same techniques for painting lilac flower heads to create a buddleia flower head, but a buddleia flower head is longer than a lilac flower head.

Lavender also has small flower heads. A lavender flower head looks like a small tube. There are five petals to each lavender flower. A few small flowers usually appear at leaf joints.

Colour Palette

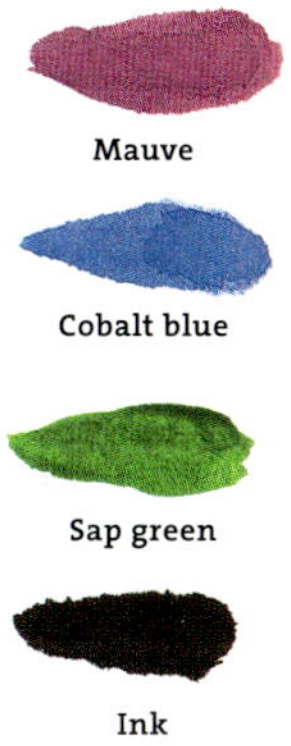

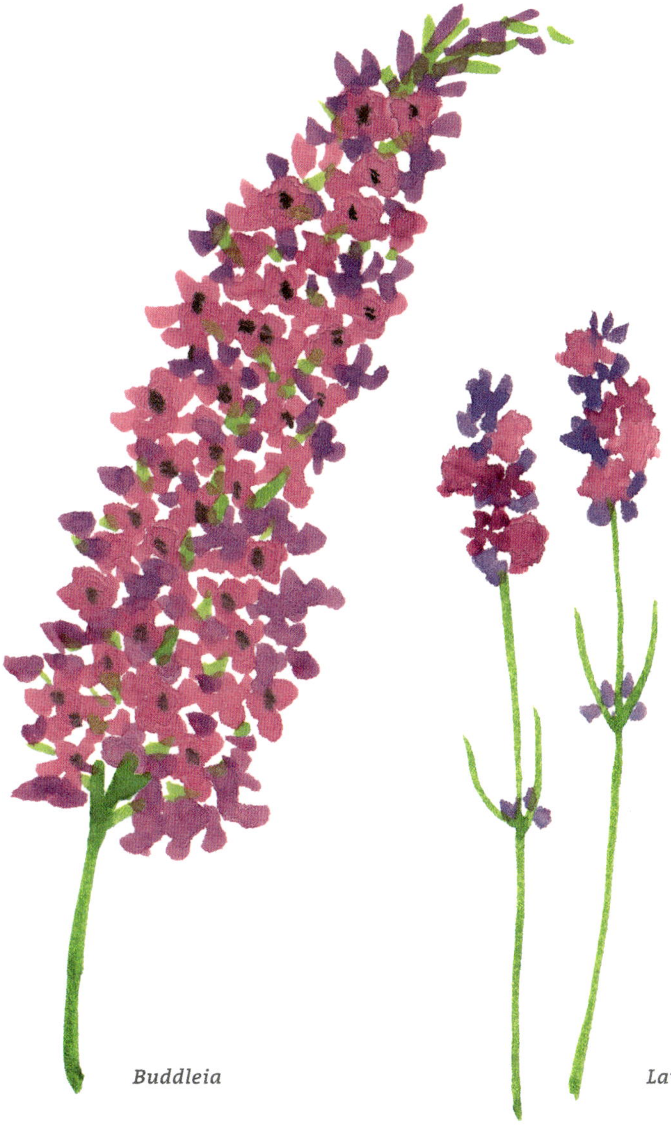

Buddleia *Lavender*

Brushes to use: B2, B3, B4

Buddleia

Fully load **B2** with mauve to paint the flowers at the front of the flower head. Each flower has four petals. Paint a dot for each petal. Make a purple by mixing one part of cobalt blue with two parts of mauve. Use this purple to paint more flowers to make up the cone shape of the flower head. A buddleia flower head is longer than a lilac flower head. Fully load **B3** with sap green and paint sections of the main centre stalk where it is visible. Add shorter stalks to connect the flowers to the main stalk. Dip **B4** into ink and paint a dot at the centre of each flower in the front.

Lavender

Fully load **B3** with sap green. Paint lines for the stalks. Add two short lines for leaves at the lower ends. Fully load **B2** with mauve and paint a few flowers at the front of the flower head. Each flower has five petals. Paint a dot for each petal. Mix two parts of mauve and one part of cobalt blue to make a purple colour. Fully load **B2** with this purple and add further flowers to finish painting the flower heads. The shape of the flower head is like a small tube. There are usually a few flowers at the leaf joints.

See also

washes p154

ASTILBE AND GYPSOPHILA

Colour Palette

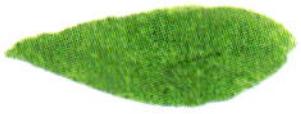

Sap green

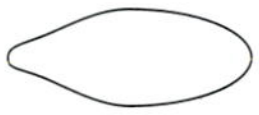

Process white

Technical information: Astilbe and gypsophila flowers are very small. They can be represented by dots. I use coloured paper for painting because I like to show off the white flowers. You can make coloured paper yourself by applying colour washes to Xuan paper. Refer to the Appendices for instructions for applying washes to Xuan paper.

Other plants with small flowers such as broom and heather can also be represented by dots.

Brushes to use: B2, B3

Astilbe

Astilbe flowers are packed closely together on a framework of long and short stalks. Fully load **B2** with process white and paint dots for flowers. Paint the dots close together. Fully load **B3** with sap green and add the long and short stalks.

Gypsophila

Gypsophila flowers are scattered within a framework of long and short branches. Fully load **B3** with sap green and paint long and short lines to create a framework of stalks. Dip **B2** into process white and add dots to the stalks as flowers.

Astilbe

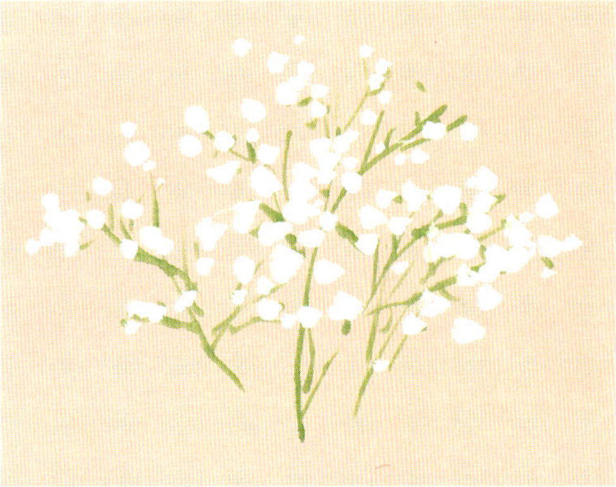

Gypsophila

See also

tree trunks and branches p95

TREES AND CLIMBERS

Dots are used to add ruggedness to tree trunks and branches, especially old tree trunks and climbers. Trees such as plum blossom and climbers such as wisteria are perfect subjects for this technique. Use the same size of brush as that with which you paint the tree trunk or the climber. Fully load it with ink and dot the tree trunk or the climber, usually at joints and places with broken branches. Do not add too many dots or the dots will look like leaves. Painting tree trunks and climbers will be dealt with in the section on 'Side Brushstroke'.

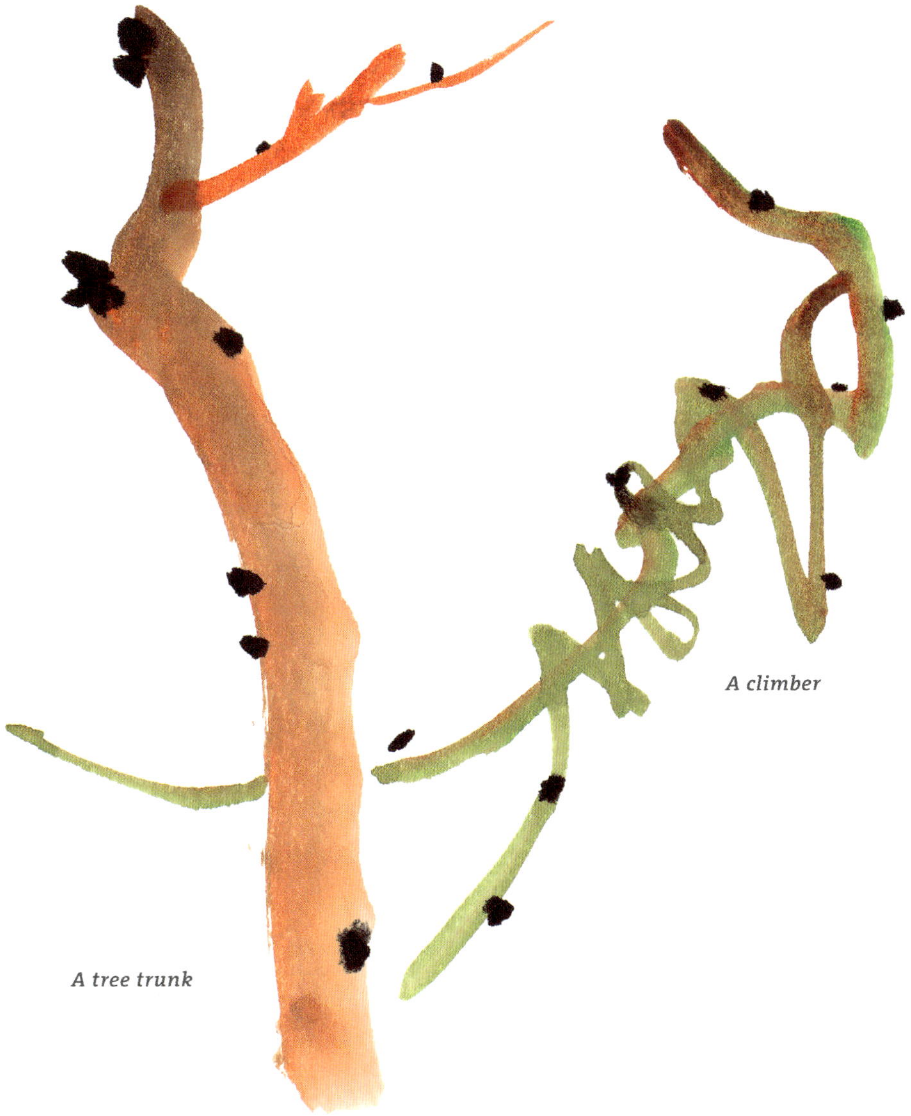

A tree trunk

A climber

See also

brush sizes **p14**
holding the brush **p28**

BRUSHSTROKE 2
LONG DOT

Fig. 1 Load the brush with ink. Hold the brush at an angle of 45 degrees to the paper. Press on the paper. A long dot is formed.

Fig. 2 Hold the brush at a higher angle, that is, more than 45 degrees. The long dot will be shorter.

Fig. 3 Hold the brush at a lower angle, that is, less than 45 degrees. The long dot will be longer.

Fig. 4 Load **B2** with ink. Paint two long dots side by side to form a bigger dot.

Fig. 5 Load **B2** with ink. Paint a long dot. Slide the brush in the direction indicated by the arrow during painting. The result is an extra long dot.

A dot is made with the brush held vertically. Rotate your wrist so that the brush is held at an angle to the paper. A dot made with this position of the brush will be longer. We call it a 'long dot'. A long dot has a narrow end where the tip of the brush touches the paper and a wider end where the wider part of the brush tip touches the paper. The length of a long dot varies according to the angle of the brush to the surface. The lower the angle, the longer the dot will be. Sliding the brush during painting will also result in a longer dot. Many factors affect the size of a long dot. Bigger and wetter brushes create bigger dots. If you press the brush hard on touching the paper, you will make bigger dots. You can also paint double long dots side by side to make bigger shapes.

You can use double long dots to create heart-shaped brushworks. They are perfect for painting bleeding heart flowers, lilac leaves and morning glory leaves. The wider petals of hydrangea and daffodils are also painted with double long dots. The daffodil trumpets and water lily leaves can be constructed using extra long dots by sliding the brush during painting.

Fig. 1

Fig. 2

Fig. 3

Fig. 4

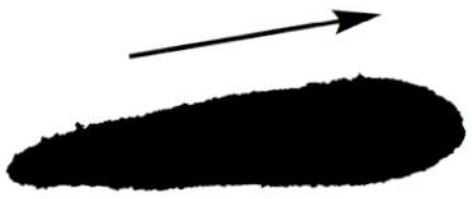

Fig. 5

PRACTISING THE LONG DOT

A bigger brush creates a bigger long dot and a smaller brush creates a smaller long dot. A wet brush makes a bigger dot because the paper absorbs more moisture from the brush. When you press the brush hard on paper, the brush tip spreads and the resulting dot is bigger.

You can also increase the size of a long dot by painting two long dots side by side. This is a technique that is usually used for painting wide petals with pointed tips. When you slide the brush during painting a long dot, you will end up with an extra long dot.

Fig. 1 Practise painting long dots, each pointing in a different direction. For each long dot, remember to adjust the handle of the brush to point in the direction indicated by the arrows. This exercise is to train you to paint long dots pointing to different positions.

Fig. 2 Practise painting some extra long dots with different postures. Remember to adjust the handle of the brush to point to the direction indicated by the arrow.

Fig. 3 Load the brush with diluted ink and dip the nib into dark ink. The resulting long dot has two tones of ink.

Fig. 4 Load the brush with diluted alizarin crimson and dip the nib into darker alizarin crimson. The resulting long dot has two tones of the colour.

Fig. 5 Load the brush with alizarin crimson and dip the nib of the brush into ink. The resulting long dot has two colours.

Fig. 6 Load the brush with sap green. Then load the lower half of the brush with burnt sienna and, finally, dip the nib of the brush into ink. The resulting long dot has three colours.

Fig. 7 Load the brush with sap green. Then load the lower half of the brush with burnt sienna and, finally, dip the nib of the brush into ink. Paint a long dot and slide the brush at the same time in the direction indicated by the arrow. The result is an extra long dot with three colours.

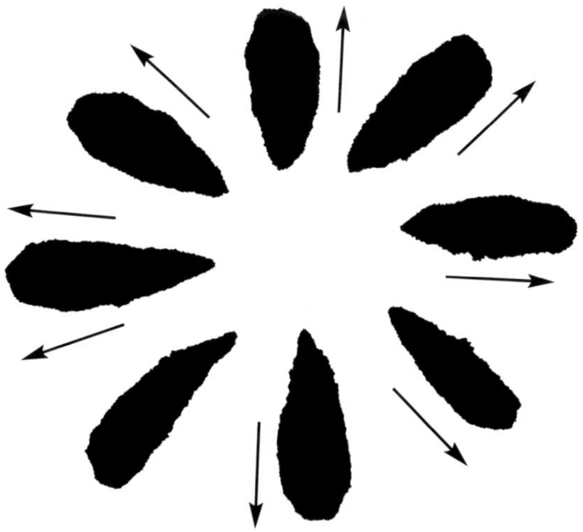

Fig. 1

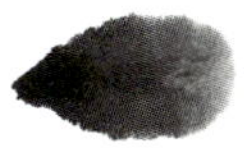

Fig. 3

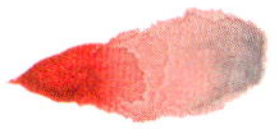

Fig. 4

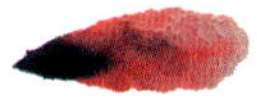

Fig. 5

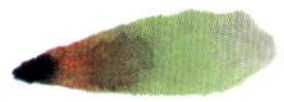

Fig. 6

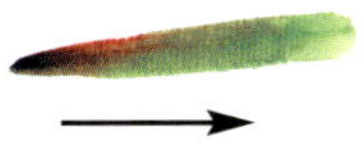

Fig. 7

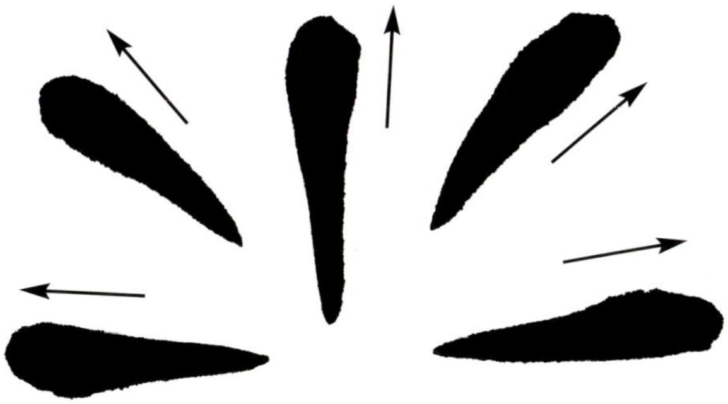

Fig. 2

See also

leaves	p83
finished painting	p144
water line	p155

BLEEDING HEART FLOWER STALKS

Colour Palette

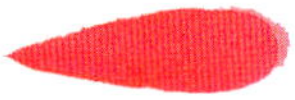

Permanent rose

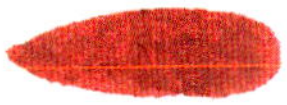

Alizarin crimson

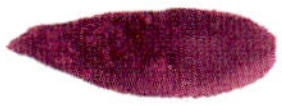

Mauve

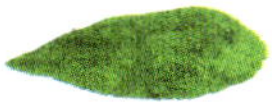

Sap green

Technical information: Bleeding heart flowers are heart-shaped. A single flower has three layers of heart-shaped petals. We can only see the red outer layer wrapping around the white second layer. Long dots are perfect for painting the red outer petals.

A bleeding heart plant has many long flower stalks. Usually at least ten flowers will hang from a stalk. Use a water line to mark the position of the stalk. Flowers can then be painted along the water line.

Step 1

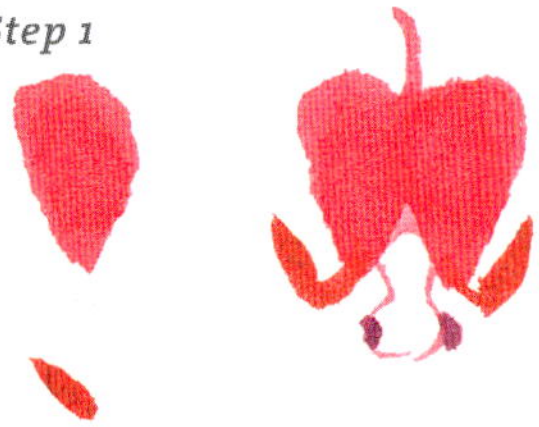

Step 2

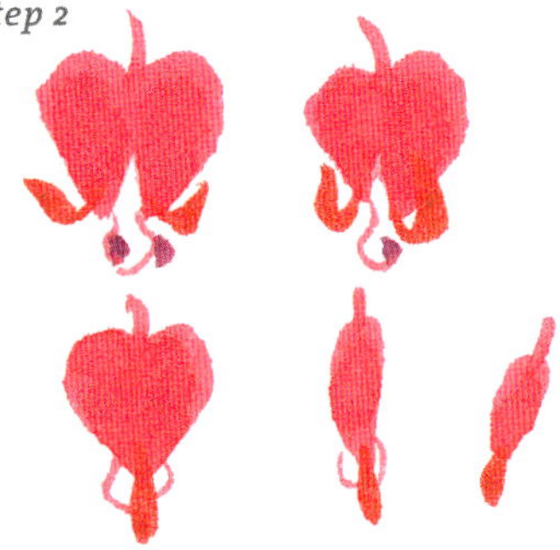

Step 3

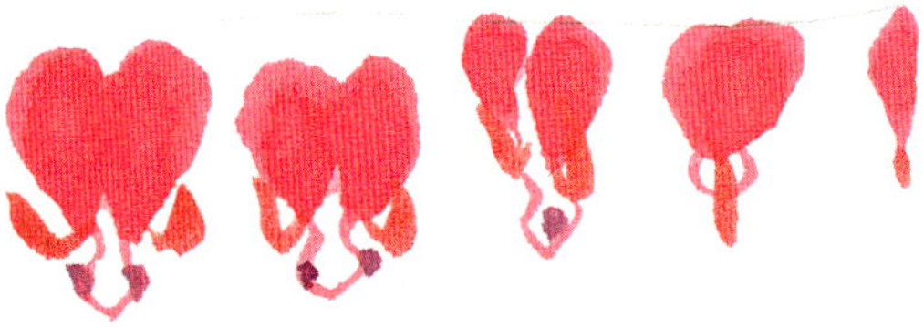

Step 4

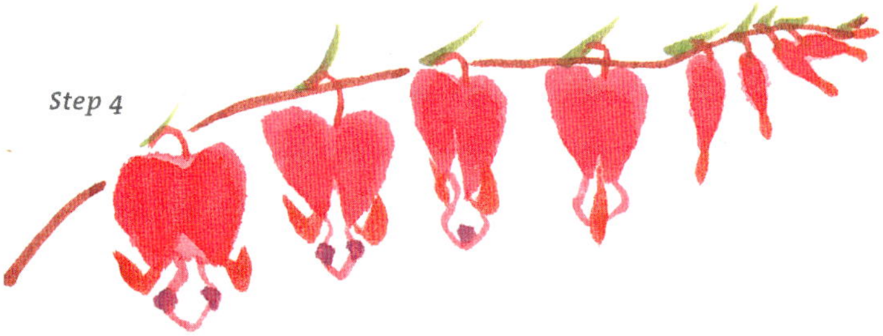

Brushes to use: B1, B3

Step 1 Load **B1** with permanent rose. Hold the brush at an angle of 45 degrees to the surface and paint a long dot for a petal. Each petal has a tail on the outer side. Load **B3** with alizarin crimson and paint a long dot for the tail by the outer side of the petal and connect it to the petal with a short line. Paint two petals with tails for each flower. Clean **B3** and dip it into permanent rose. Draw lines to represent the inner white petals and add a short, thin stalk to each flower. Clean **B3** again and dip it into mauve. Add one dot to each side of the white petals.

Step 2 Practise painting flowers in different postures. Note that the two red petals are apart when the flower is opened. They are close together when the flower is not opened. Paint two small long dots for each bud.

Step 3 Use a clean, damp **B3** to paint a water line for the flower stalk. I use a thin pencil line to indicate the position of the water line. Paint flowers along the long stalk, with opened flowers towards its lower end and buds along the other end. Paint flowers of different postures.

Step 4 Mix one part of sap green with one part of permanent rose. Load **B3** with this new colour and fill in the sections of the long stalk where it is visible. Clean **B3** and dip it into permanent rose and add the short stems connecting the flowers to the long stalk. Clean **B3** again and dip it into sap green. Add a tiny thin leaf with a short line at the joint of each flower stalk to the main stalk.

See also

leaves p79
finished painting p141

HYDRANGEA FLOWER HEADS

Colour Palette

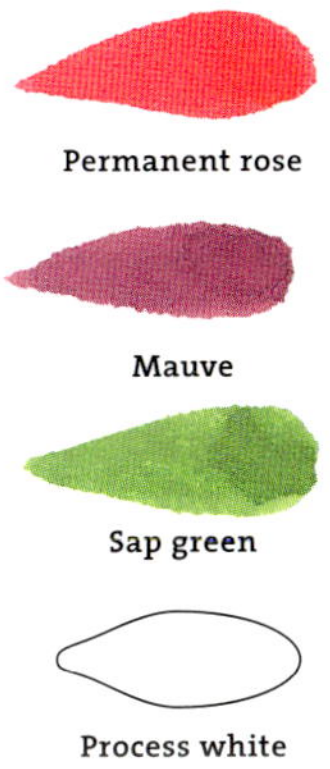

Technical information: The petals of a hydrangea flower are small, wide and pointed. You need a medium size brush to control the size of the petals and to be able to paint a sharp point. **B2** is a perfect brush for this. To make the petals short you have to paint the long dots with the brush at a high angle to the paper. The petals, though small, are wide. You need two long dots side by side for each petal. Each flower has four petals, each pointing in a different direction, so make sure that you point the handle of the brush in the right direction for painting each petal.

To paint a flower head, always start with the flowers at the front. Use the front flowers to sketch out the shape and the size of the flower head. Then use a darker colour to fill in the spaces for background flowers to finish the flower head. The darker colour enables the front flowers to stand out. This technique adds a three-dimensional effect to the flower head.

Brushes to use: B2, B3, B4

Step 1 Load **B2** with permanent rose. Hold the brush at a high angle to the paper and paint a long dot. Use two long dots side by side to make a pointed petal. Each flower has four petals pointing in different directions. So practise painting petals pointing in different directions.

Step 2 Paint four petals for each flower. Paint some flowers with the back of the petals facing. Use diluted permanent rose for the back of the petal. Mix a tiny bit of mauve with permanent rose to make a darker colour. Use this darker colour to paint flowers in the background.

Step 3 Start to paint the flower head with the flowers in the front. Use permanent rose for the front flowers. Position them to mark out the size and the shape of the flower head. Mix a little bit of mauve into the permanent rose to make it darker. Use this darker colour to add flowers to the background. Load **B3** with sap green. Paint the main stalk. Clean **B3** and load it with permanent rose. Paint the short stalks connecting the flowers to the main stalk. Load **B4** with mauve and paint a few tiny markings on the main stem.
Clean **B4** and dip it into process white. Paint a white dot at the centre of each of the front flowers.

Step 1

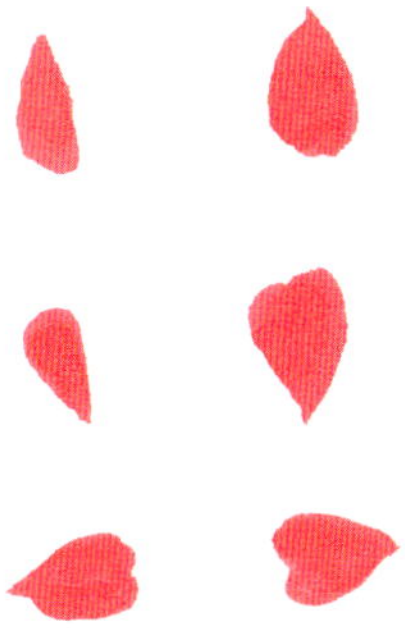

Step 2

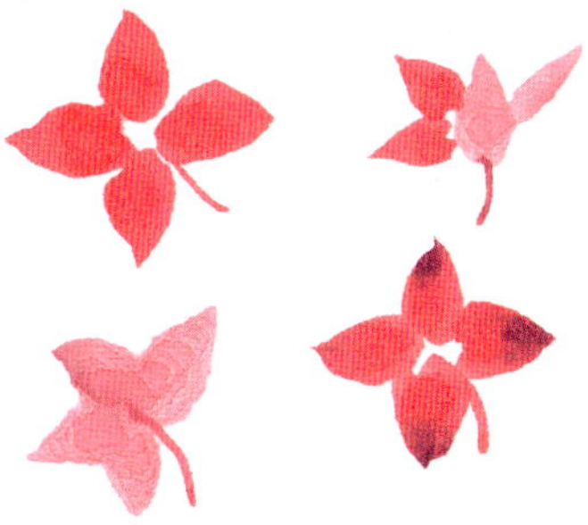

Step 3

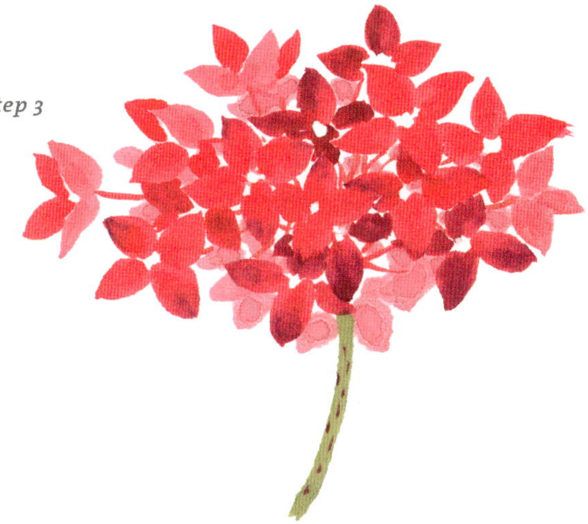

See also
leaves p86
finished painting p91

DAFFODIL FLOWERS

Colour Palette

Lemon yellow

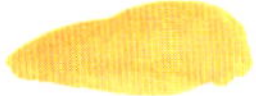

Gamboge

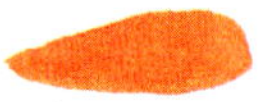

Cadmium orange

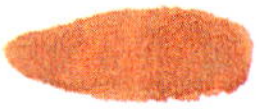

Burnt sienna

Technical information: There are many types of daffodils with different shapes and with different combinations of colours. The more common yellow one has short wide petals and long trumpets tinted with orange on the edge. Load the brush with two colours of lemon yellow and gamboge to paint the petals. Use two long dots for each petal. The trumpets are made up of extra long dots painted close together. Use three colour loadings of lemon yellow, gamboge and cadmium orange for the extra long dots.

Step 1

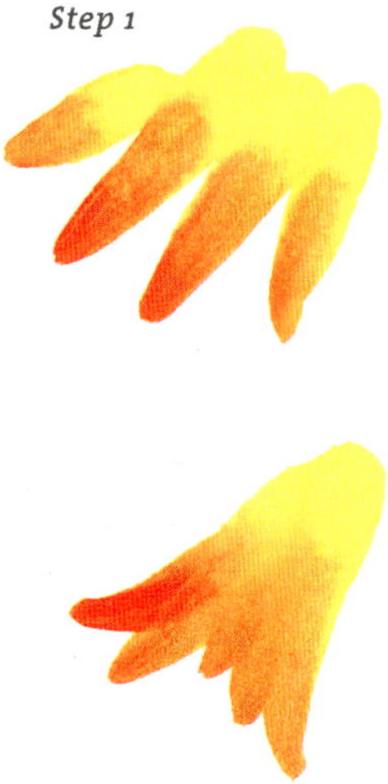

Step 2

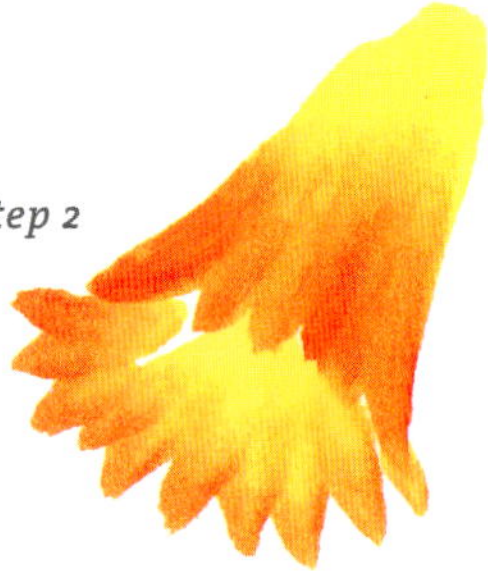

Step 3

Step 4

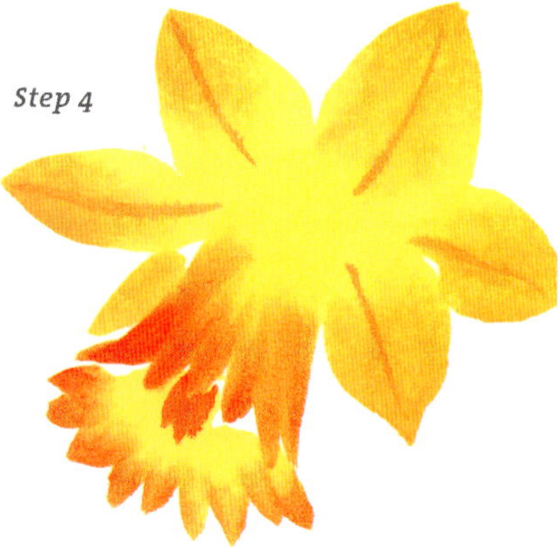

Brushes to use: B2, B4

Step 1 Load **B2** with lemon yellow, then half-load with gamboge and, finally, dip the nib of the brush into cadmium orange. Practise long dots and extra long dots. Use these dots to paint one side of the trumpet.

Step 2 Load **B2** again exactly as in step 1 and use more long dots to paint the other side of the trumpet.

Step 3 Clean **B2**. Load it with lemon yellow and dip the tip of the brush into gamboge. Hold the brush at a high angle to the paper and paint two long dots to form a single petal. Practise more petals, each pointing in a different direction.

Step 4 Add the petals around the trumpet to form a flower. Each flower has six petals. Dip **B4** into cadmium orange and draw a central vein on each petal. Mix a little bit of burnt sienna into the cadmium orange. Dip **B4** into this mixture and draw three or four short lines at the centre of the flower as stamens.

LILAC LEAVES

See also

flowers p46
finished painting p59

Technical information: Lilac leaves are heart-shaped. Each leaf is painted with two long dots close together. Use **B1** and press hard for each long dot in order to make big leaves. Use sap green for most of the leaves but paint some with edges of indigo or burnt sienna.

Colour Palette

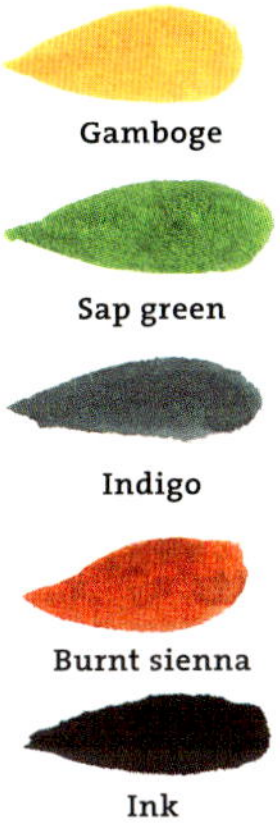

Step 1

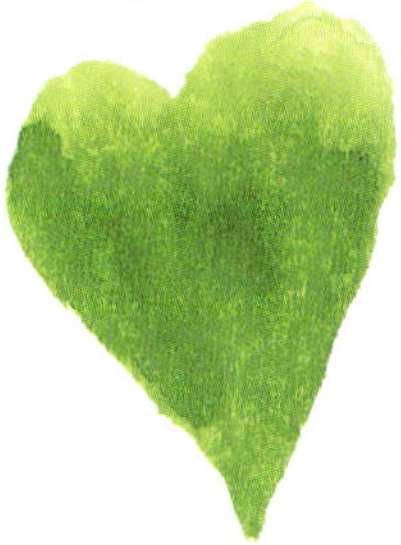

Step 2

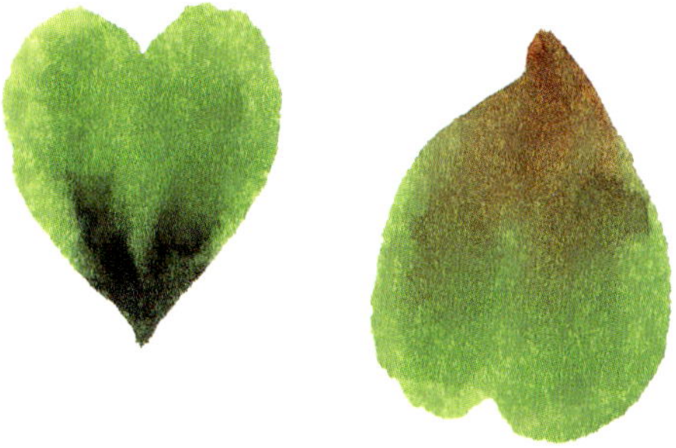

Step 3

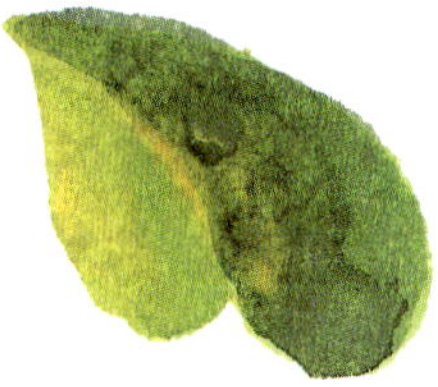

Step 4

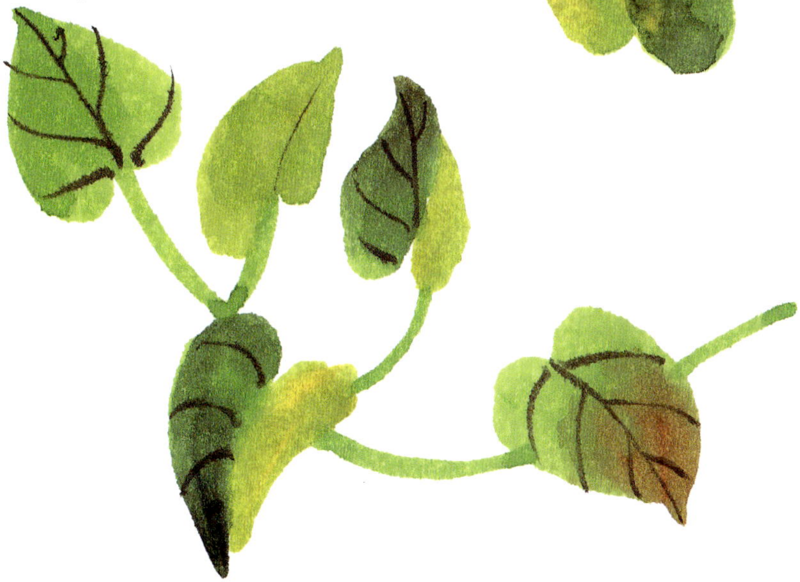

Brushes to use: B1, B3, B4

Step 1 Load **B1** with sap green. Hold the brush at a low angle to the paper and paint a long dot. Press the brush hard during painting to make bigger dots. Paint two long dots to make a leaf.

Step 2 Practise more leaves. Dip the nib of the brush into indigo to paint leaves with darker edges. Also dip the nib into burnt sienna to paint leaves with brown edges.

Step 3 Make a lighter green by mixing one part of sap green with one part of gamboge. Use this lighter green to paint the leaf backs. Paint a folding leaf with one light green long dot close to a darker green long dot.

Step 4 Paint a few lilac leaves. Lilac leaves are arranged in pairs. Two consecutive pairs are at right angles to each other. Make a brownish green by mixing one part of sap green with one part of burnt sienna. Load **B3** with this green and paint the main branch. Add shorter branches connecting the leaves to the main branch. Load **B4** with ink. Draw lines to represent the veins on the front of the leaves.

See also

flowers p114
finished painting p151
water line p155

MORNING GLORY LEAVES

Technical information: Morning glory leaves are also heart-shaped but are longer than lilac leaves. Slide the long dots to make extra long dots when you paint the leaves. The leaves are arranged singly along the long, thin stem of this climber. Use the water line technique to help with positioning the long stem before painting the leaves.

Colour Palette

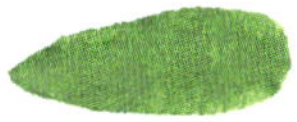

Sap green

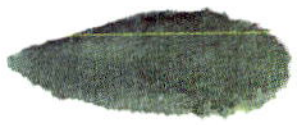

Indigo

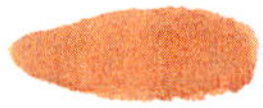

Burnt sienna

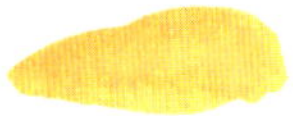

Gamboge

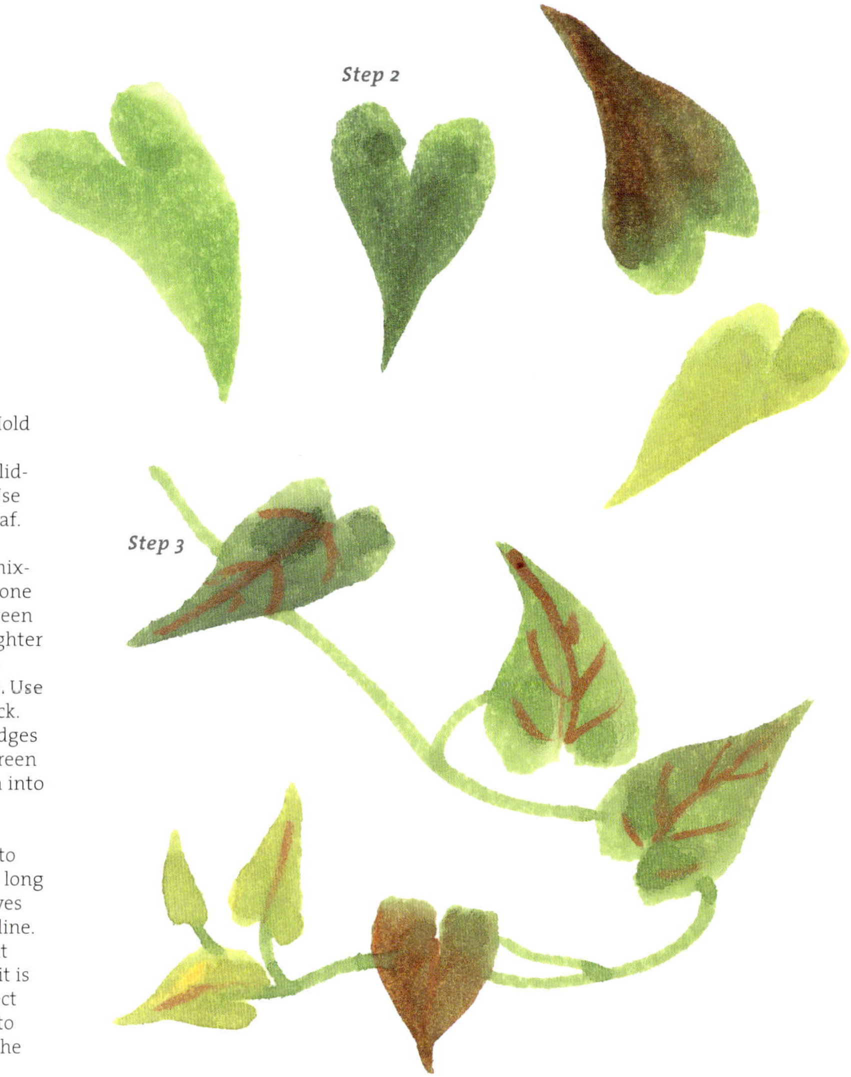

Brushes to use: B1, B3, B4

Step 1 Load **B1** with sap green. Hold the brush at a low angle to the paper. Paint extra long dots by sliding the brush during painting. Use two extra long dots to make a leaf.

Step 2 Make a darker green by mixing two parts of sap green with one part of indigo. Use this darker green to paint darker leaves. Make a lighter green by mixing one part of sap green with one part of gamboge. Use this lighter green for the leaf back. Paint some leaves with brown edges by loading the brush with sap green and dipping the nib of the brush into burnt sienna.

Step 3 Use a clean and damp **B3** to draw a water line to indicate the long stem of morning glory. Paint leaves with different colours along the line. Load **B3** with sap green and paint sections of the long stem where it is visible. Add short stalks to connect the leaves to the stem. Dip **B4** into burnt sienna and draw lines on the leaves to represent the veins.

See also
flowers p65
finished painting p149

WATER LILY LEAVES

Technical information: Water lily leaves are round with an opening on one side. You can use two big long dots to make up a leaf. The leaves are big so use **B1** and press hard during painting. Paint some leaves with two colour loadings of sap green, with the nib of the brush dipping into either indigo or burnt sienna.

Colour Palette

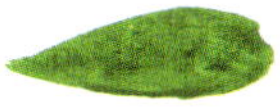
Sap green

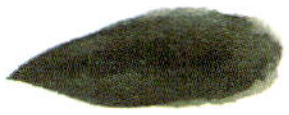
Indigo

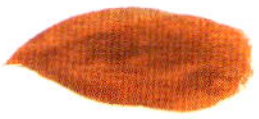
Burnt sienna

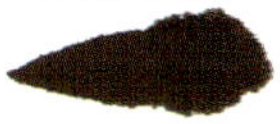
Ink

Step 1

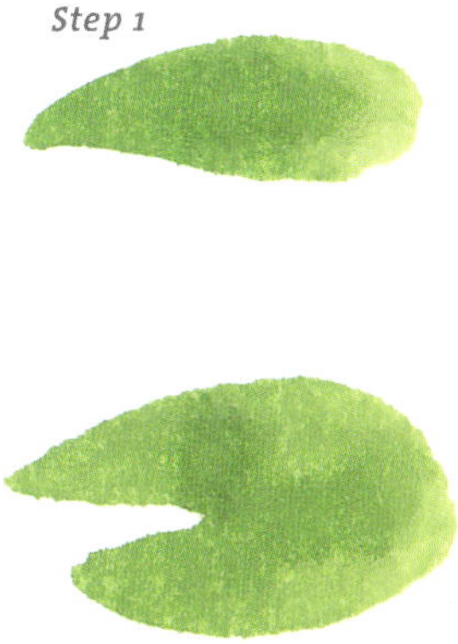

Step 2

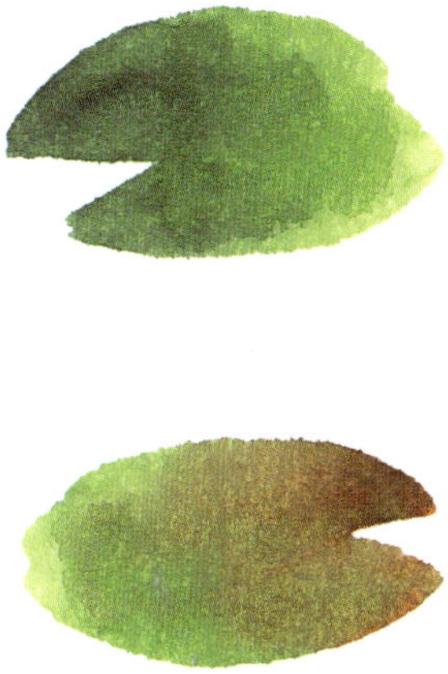

Step 3

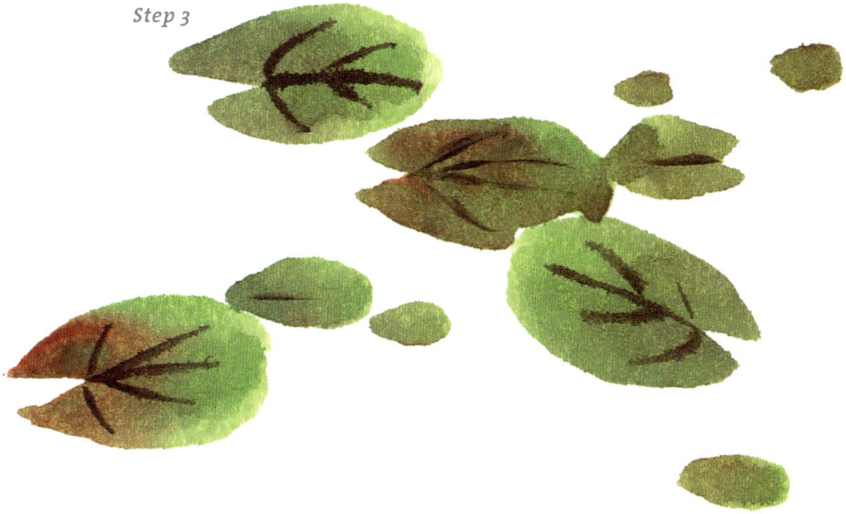

Brushes to use: B1, B4

Step 1 Fully load **B1** with sap green. Hold the brush at a low angle to the paper. Press hard to paint a long dot. Use two long dots to make a water lily leaf.

Step 2 Load **B1** with sap green and dip the nib of the brush into indigo. Paint some leaves with dark edges. Clean the brush and load it again with sap green and dip the nib of the brush into burnt sienna. Paint some leaves with brown edges.

Step 3 Paint a variety of leaves, some big, some small, some green and some with two colours. Dip **B4** into ink and paint the veins with dark lines on some of the bigger leaves.

See also
flowers p46
leaves p55

PROJECT 2
PAINTING LILAC

Colour Palette

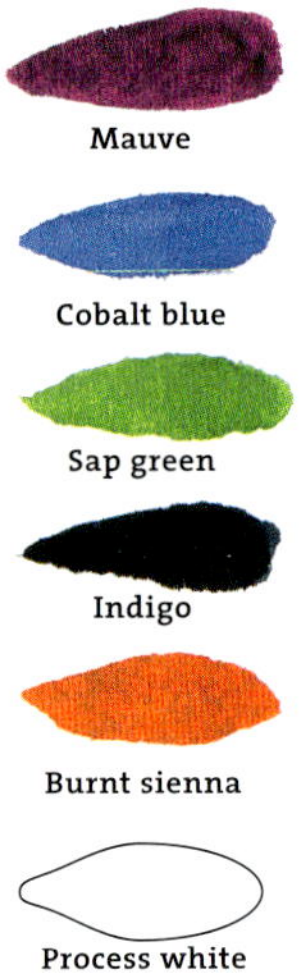

Technical information: I have shown you separately how to paint lilac flower heads and lilac leaves. Now it is time to bring both together to form a complete painting.

Let me start with the flower heads. Painting one flower head is different from painting many flower heads. I showed you how to achieve a three-dimensional effect in one flower head by painting mauve flowers in the front and adding flowers with a purple tone of mauve to the background. When painting many flower heads we have to stretch the palette so that some flower heads in the front stand out while others stay in the background. For those flower heads at the front, I use a dilute mauve for the flowers in the front and a darker tone of mauve for the flowers at the back. For the flower heads at the back, I mix one part of cobalt blue with two parts of mauve to make a purple. I add a little water to dilute this purple and use it for the flowers in the front, then add other flowers with the undiluted purple. In this way, I have expanded the palette to paint the front flower heads with lighter tones and the background flower heads with darker tones. Each flower head still has its light and dark flowers to maintain the three-dimensional effect.

You can use a variety of colour combinations for the leaves: sap green, light green made by mixing sap green with gamboge, dark green made by mixing sap green

Fig. 3

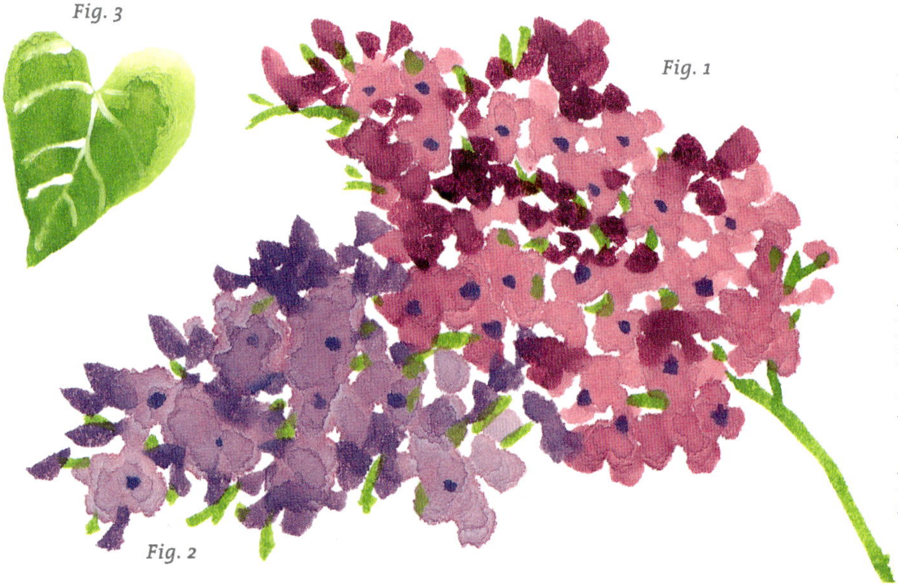

Fig. 1

Fig. 2

Brushes to use: B1, B2, B3, B4

Fig. 1 A flower head with diluted mauve for the flowers at the front and a darker tone of mauve for the flowers at the back. Purple has been used for the centres of flowers instead of ink this time.

Fig. 2 A flower head with diluted purple for the flowers at the front and a darker purple for the flowers at the back. Purple has been used for the centres of flowers instead of ink this time.

Fig. 3 Process white has been used to paint the veins of leaves instead of ink this time.

with indigo, sap green tinted with indigo or sap green tinted with burnt sienna. You can paint leaves facing outwards, leaves with the back facing, leaves showing the sides or folding leaves.

For the composition, paint some flower heads in front of the leaves and some behind the leaves. A common mistake is to paint all the flowers first and then add the leaves. This means that the flowers stand out above the leaves. In nature, not all flowers stand out. A safe rule is to start with the objects at the front, whether they are flowers or leaves, and build up the painting by adding objects towards the back in succession.

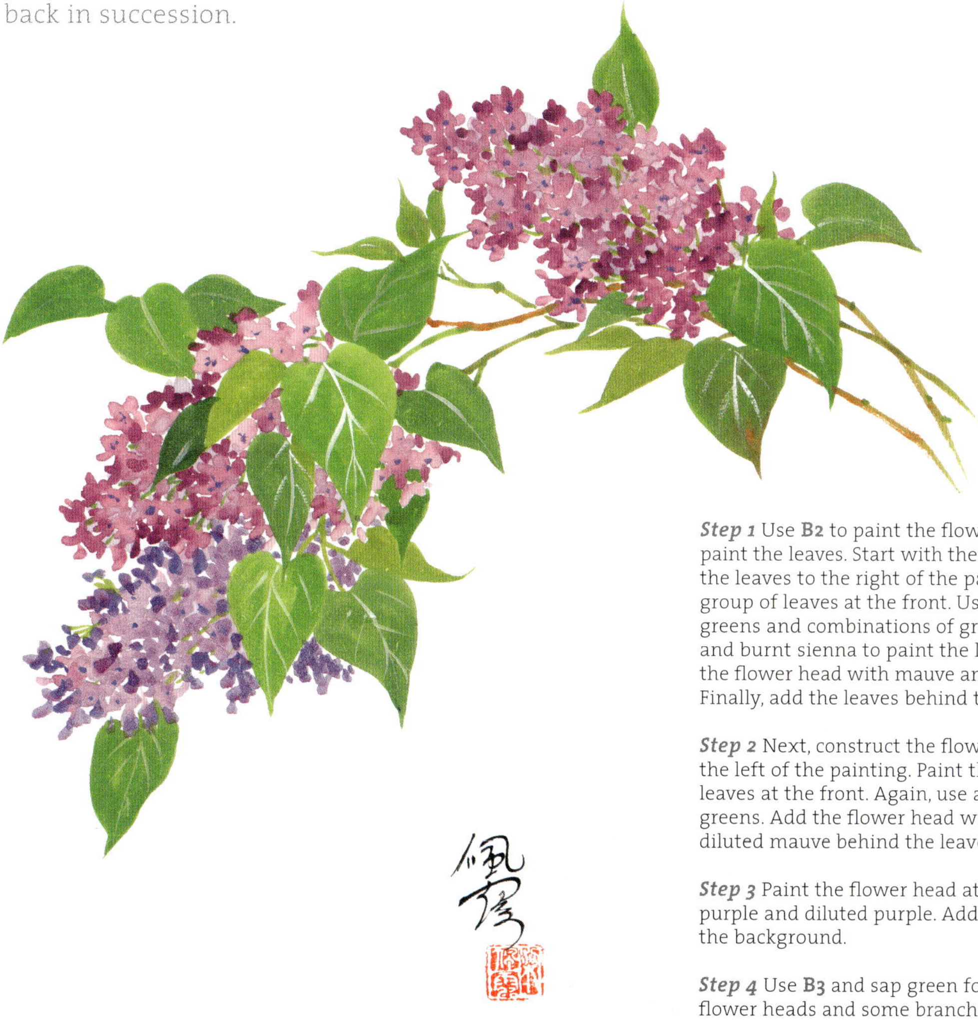

Step 1 Use **B2** to paint the flowers and **B1** to paint the leaves. Start with the flower head and the leaves to the right of the painting. Paint the group of leaves at the front. Use a variety of greens and combinations of greens with indigo and burnt sienna to paint the leaves. Then add the flower head with mauve and diluted mauve. Finally, add the leaves behind the flower head.

Step 2 Next, construct the flowers and leaves to the left of the painting. Paint the group of leaves at the front. Again, use a variety of greens. Add the flower head with mauve and diluted mauve behind the leaves.

Step 3 Paint the flower head at the back with purple and diluted purple. Add more leaves for the background.

Step 4 Use **B3** and sap green for the stalks of flower heads and some branches. Paint one or two mature branches with burnt sienna. Use **B4** and process white to paint the veins of leaves. Use **B4** and purple to paint a central dot in some of the flowers at the front.

See also
brush sizes p14
using the brush p28
wrist movement p32
press and lift p36

BRUSHSTROKE 3
SHORT BRUSHSTROKE

Fig. 1 Load **B2** with ink. A short brushstroke is painted with press and lift brushwork and wrist movement.

Fig. 2 A wet brush makes a bigger short brushstroke.

Fig. 3 Pressing the brush hard during painting will also result in a bigger brushstroke.

A short brushstroke is a simple press and lift brushwork using the wrist movement. The basic shape looks like a bamboo leaf. You can vary the shape of a short brushstroke by lengthening the lifting, or by delaying the pressing. You can also press more to the left or press more to the right.

The short brushstroke is one of the most frequently used brushstrokes in Chinese flower painting. It is used as a building block for many shapes, especially in the painting of leaves. A single short brushstroke forms petals of flowers such as daffodils, orchids, chrysanthemums or honeysuckle. It is also used to paint small leaves such as those of wisteria. For flowers with wider petals, such as those of the lily, azalea, water lily and lotus, each petal is painted with two or three short brushstrokes. To paint wider leaves like those of roses, camellia, lily and honeysuckle, you need two short brushstrokes for each leaf. The leaves of hydrangea, hibiscus, pansy, poppy and bleeding heart are more complicated. Multiple short brushstrokes are used to paint these shapes.

Leaves are important features in a flower painting. Properly placed leaves show off the flowers. By using the different shapes of short brushstrokes, we can vary the many different postures of leaves. We can also vary the colour of the leaves according to the time of the year and their stages of growth. A flower painting is livelier if we include all these variations in the composition. A section in this chapter on painting leaves shows you what you can achieve with short brushstrokes. Do read through it before you tackle painting the leaves of different plants.

Fig. 1

Fig. 2

Fig. 3

PRACTISING THE SHORT BRUSHSTROKE

Practise short brushstrokes of different shapes by following the instructions given below. Paint according to the direction indicated by the arrows.

Fig. 1 You can lengthen the lifting, making the short brushstroke longer.

Fig. 2 You can delay the pressing, making the short brushstroke longer at the beginning.

Fig. 3 The short brushstroke is wider to the left if you press more to the left.

Fig. 4 The short brushstroke is wider to the right if you press more to the right.

Fig. 5 A short brushstroke wider to the right plus a short brushstroke wider to the left makes a larger shape. This shape is useful for constructing larger petals and leaves.

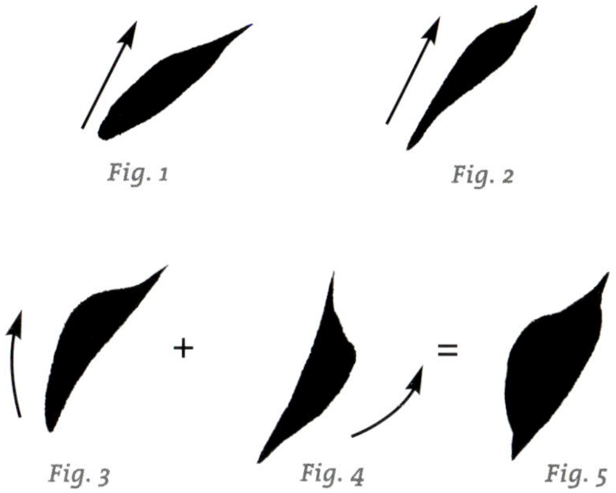

PRACTISING THE SHORT BRUSHSTROKE WITH COLOURS

You can load the brush with two tones of a colour, or two colours or three colours to paint a short brushstroke. You can vary the pressing and lifting during painting. A lot of shapes with different colour combinations can be created with just these basic techniques. The following are a few examples.

Fig. 1 A short brushstroke created with two tones of alizarin crimson.

Fig. 2 Load the brush with sap green and dip the nib of the brush into burnt sienna. Paint a short brushstroke.

Fig. 3 Load the brush with sap green and dip the nib of the brush into indigo. Press more to the right when you paint a short brushstroke.

Fig. 4 Load the brush with alizarin crimson and dip the nib of the brush into mauve. Paint a short brushstroke. Delay the pressing and, when you do, press more to the left.

Fig. 5 Load the brush with burnt sienna, dip half of the brush into sap green and, finally, dip the nib of the brush into indigo. Press hard to paint a short brushstroke and lengthen the lifting.

Fig. 6 Load the brush with permanent rose and dip the nib of the brush into mauve. Press lightly when you paint this short brushstroke and lengthen the lifting

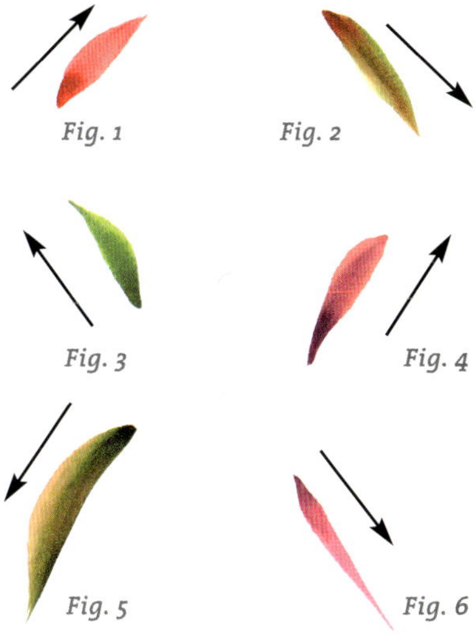

See also

leaves p107, p115
project 6 p116
finished painting p117

CHRYSANTHEMUM FLOWERS

Colour Palette

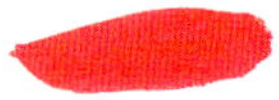

Permanent rose

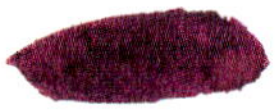

Mauve

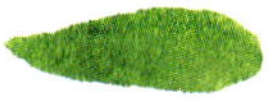

Sap green

Technical information: There are many types of chrysanthemum with a wide range of colours. We will concentrate on the common type with many petals. Use a short brushstroke for each petal. The petals at the centre of the flower are shorter and smaller. The outer petals are bigger and longer. Lengthen the lifting part of the short brushstroke for a longer petal.

Brushes to use: B1, B3, B4

Step 1 Practise painting the petals. Fully load **B1** with permanent rose and dip the nib generously into mauve. Begin with the shorter and smaller petals. Use a small short brushstroke for each. Press lightly with the tip of the brush. Practise a few . Without reloading, continue to paint a few bigger petals. Lengthen the lifting parts of the short brushstrokes for the bigger petals.

Step 2 There is a traditional way of painting a chrysanthemum flower. Use a big brush so that you can load a lot of colours. Press lightly when painting the petals so that the colours in the brush will go a long way. Load **B1** with permanent rose and dip the nib generously into mauve. Start at the centre of the flower with small short brushstrokes. You will notice that these petals are darker because you are using the mauve at the nib of the brush. Without reloading, add bigger and longer petals outwards. Now the petals have two colours because some of the mauve is used up. The more you move outwards, the bigger and longer the petals will be. By now the mauve will be used up, so the petals on the outside will be of the permanent rose colour. Let some petals cross each other. It makes the flower look more natural. If you need more petals on the outside and your brush runs out of colours, reload **B1** with permanent rose and continue to paint. The advantage of this traditional method is that the colours change slowly from dark to light as you paint the flower from the inside to the outside. The resulting flower has a darker centre.

Step 3 Load **B3** with mauve and highlight the flower with a few small short brushstrokes. Clean **B3** and dip it into sap green. Paint the stalk. Dip **B4** into mauve. Paint central veins on some of the bigger petals.

Step 1

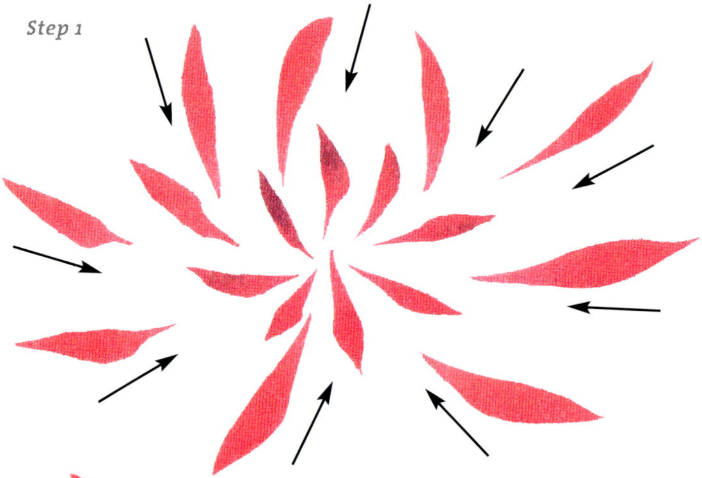

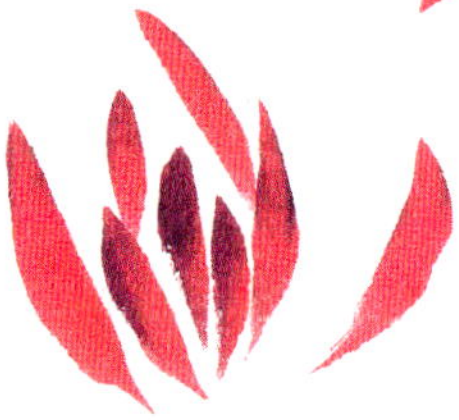

Step 2

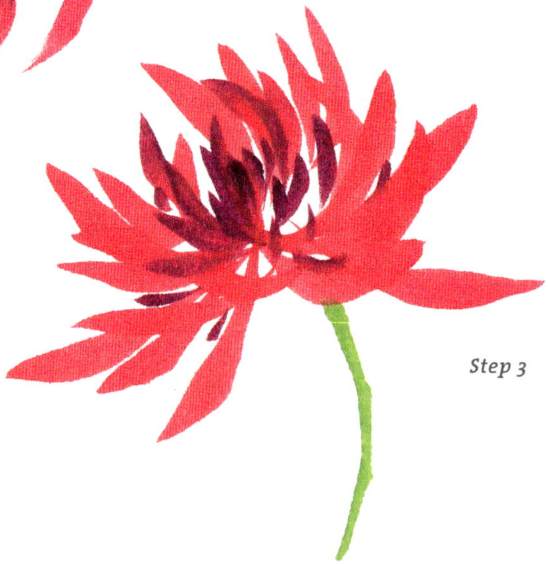

Step 3

See also
leaves p77
finished painting p134

HONEYSUCKLE FLOWER HEAD

Colour Palette

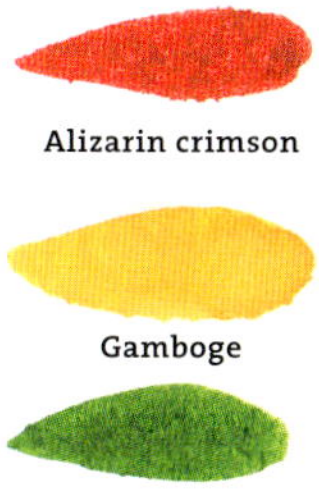

Technical information: The flowers of this honeysuckle are red on the outside and orange on the inside. A honeysuckle flower head is made up of buds and opened flowers. There are three sizes of bud in one flower head. Buds at the centre are shorter and smaller and have a darker colour. The buds on the outer part are bigger and longer and their colour is lighter. Buds that are about to open swell at the top. Each opened flower has five petals and long thin stamens. You can use a variety of short brushstrokes to paint all the buds and opened flowers. The flower head sits on the middle of a broad leaf.

Step 1

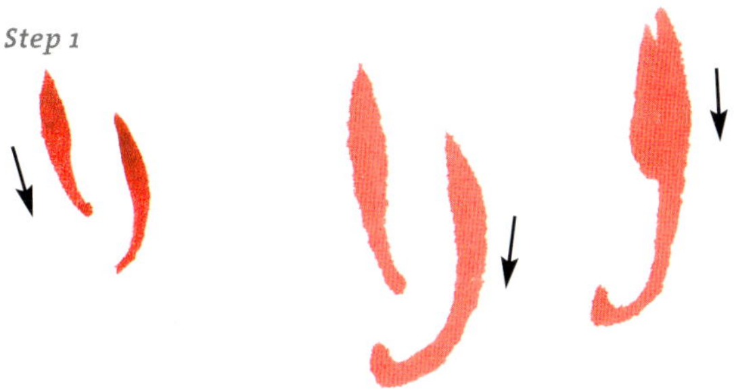

Step 2

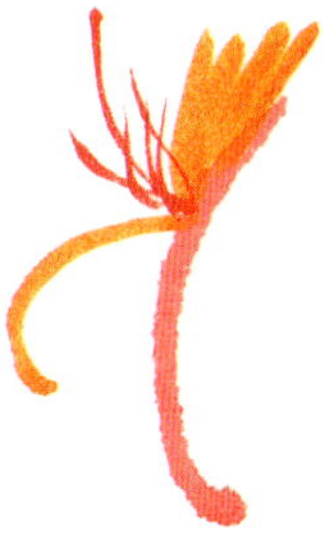

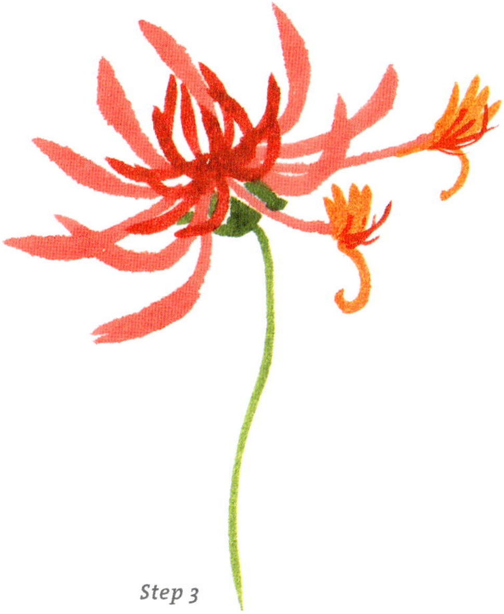

Step 3

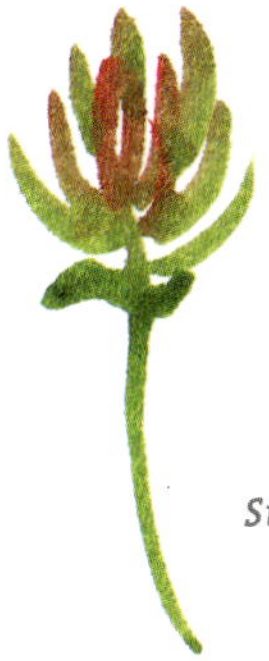

Step 4

Brushes to use: B2, B3, B4

Step 1 Use **B2** to paint the buds. Use alizarin crimson for each bud in the centre. Press lightly to paint a short brushstroke for each small bud. For a bigger and longer bud, use a short brushstroke with the lifting stage lengthened. Use diluted alizarin crimson for the bigger buds. For a bud about to open, add an extra small short brushstroke to the head to make it bigger.

Step 2 Paint an opened flower. Load **B2** with diluted alizarin crimson. Paint a short brushstroke. Make an orange colour by mixing one part of alizarin crimson with one part of gamboge. Use this colour to paint five opened petals on each flower, with four on the upper part and one curving downwards. Load **B4** with alizarin crimson and add a long stigma and five stamens to the centre of each flower.

Step 3 Start a flower head with the small inner buds. Add bigger buds and buds about to open on the outside of the flower head. Add a few opened flowers. Load **B3** with sap green. Paint a broad leaf at the base of the flower and add a stalk.

Step 4 When it is very young a flower head is almost green. Load **B2** with sap green and dip the nib of the brush into alizarin crimson. Paint small short brushstrokes to represent the immature buds. Load **B3** with sap green. Add a leaf and a stalk at the base of the flower head.

See also
leaves p76
finished painting p136

LILY FLOWERS

Colour Palette

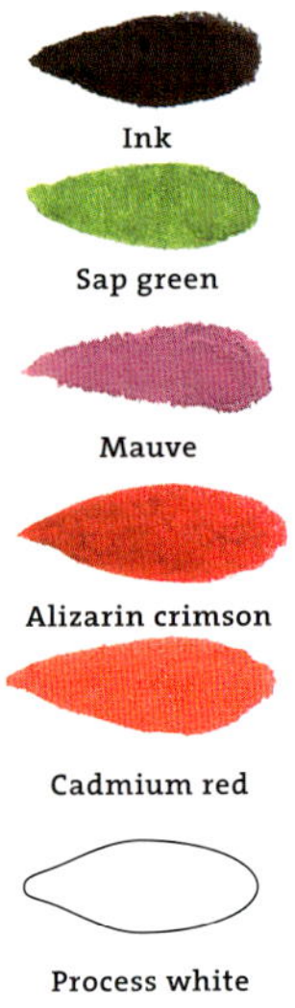

Technical information: Lily petals are big and wide. Use **B1** and press hard to paint two short brushstrokes for each petal. For wider petals, use three short brushstrokes for each, one in the middle and the other two at each side. Each flower has six petals, three at the front and three at the back. There are many varieties of lilies and the one here is the oriental type. You can apply the same techniques to painting other types of lily.

Brushes to use: B1, B3, B4

Step 1 Load **B1** with cadmium red and dip the nib of the brush into alizarin crimson. Practise a short brushstroke. Press hard during painting. Each petal is made up of two short brushstrokes. Paint the short brushstrokes from the outer tip of the petal so that the outer tip is darker.

Step 2 A wider petal is made up of three short brushstrokes. Start with the one in the middle and add the other two, one on each side. Load **B4** with mauve and draw the veins. Then dip **B4** into ink and add some dots on each petal to represent the markings.

Step 3 Dip **B4** into process white and paint a stigma and six stamens for the centre of the flower. Dip **B4** into ink and add a dot to each of the stigma and stamens.

Step 4 Start a flower with the three petals in the front. Space them evenly. Add a petal behind and between two front petals. Repeat with two more petals. Add veins and markings to each petal as described in step 2. Add the centre as described in step 3.

Step 5 You can use two long dots to paint a lily bud. Load **B1** with sap green and dip the nib of the brush into cadmium red. Place the nib at the upper tip of the bud so that the bud has a reddish tip and a green base. Use **B3** and sap green to add a stalk.

Step 1

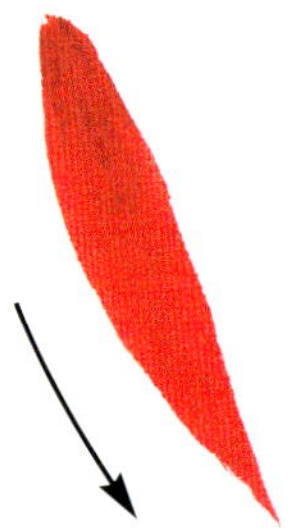

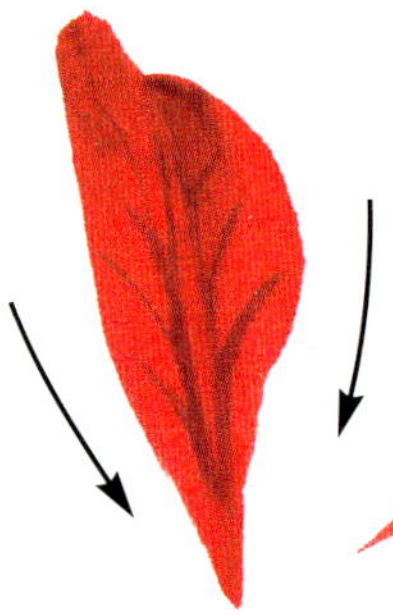

Step 2

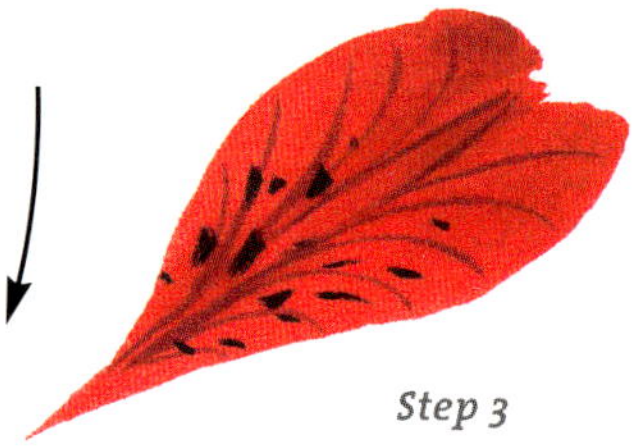

Step 3

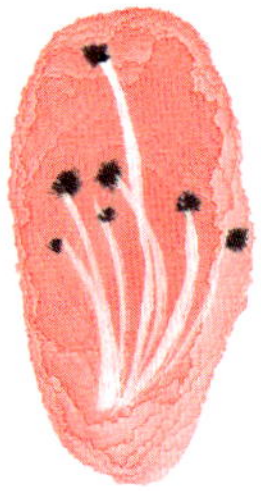

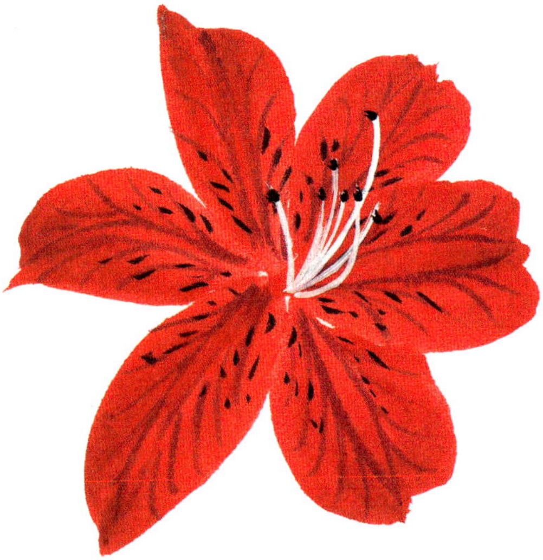

Step 4

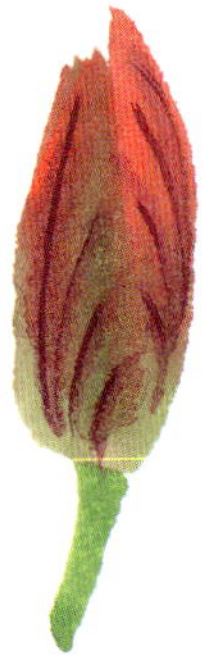

Step 5

WATER LILY FLOWERS

See also

leaves **p57**
finished painting **p149**

Technical information: A water lily flower has many petals. Each petal can be constructed with two short brushstrokes. Petals of an opened flower curl inward at the edges. Some of the outer petals sit on the water. It is better to use long dots for the petals that sit on the water.

Colour Palette

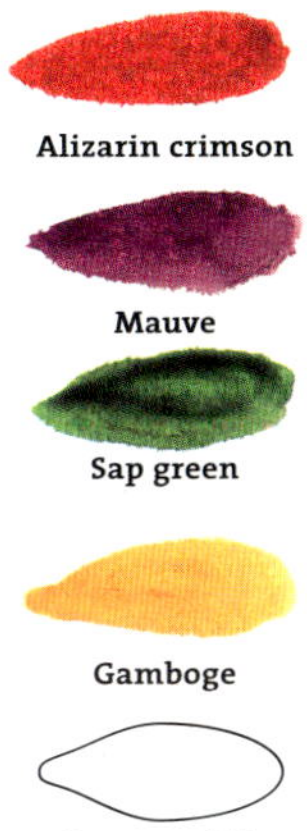

Alizarin crimson

Mauve

Sap green

Gamboge

Process white

Step 1

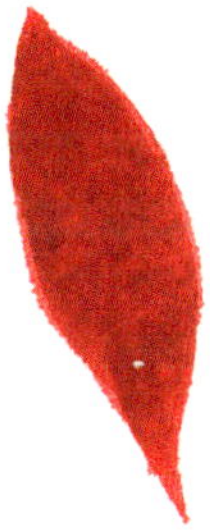

outside of petal

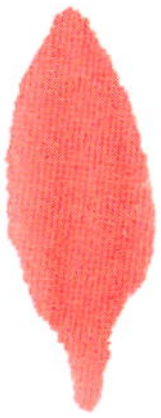

inside of petal

Step 2

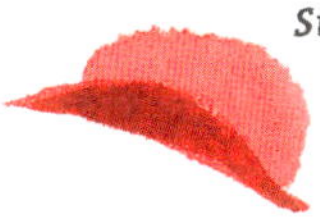

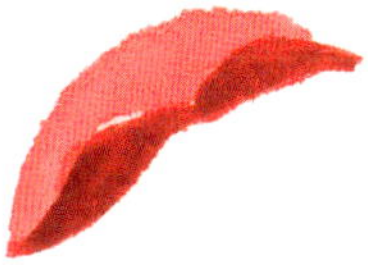

Step 3

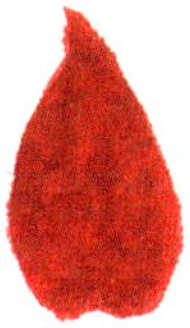

Step 4

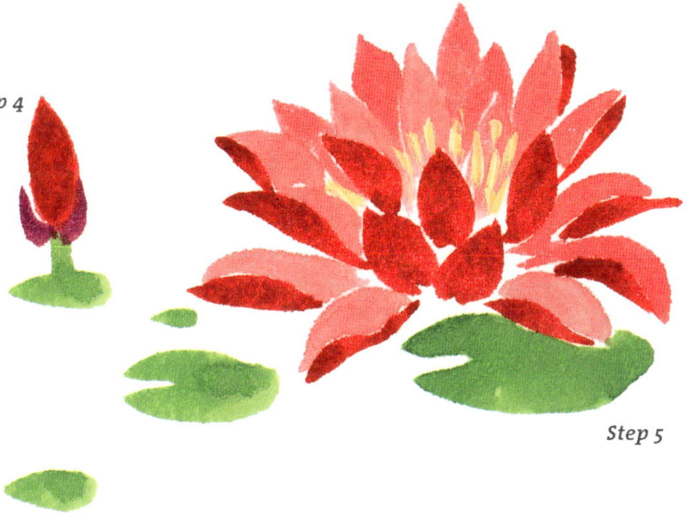

Step 5

Brushes to use: B2, B3, B4

Step 1 Load **B2** with alizarin crimson. Paint two short brushstrokes to make up a petal. Paint the outside of a petal with alizarin crimson and the inside with diluted alizarin crimson.

Step 2 Use **B2** and alizarin crimson to paint one or two small short brushstrokes for the curling edge of a petal. Clean **B2** and reload with diluted alizarin crimson to finish painting the petal.

Step 3 Use two long dots and alizarin crimson to paint a petal that sits on the water.

Step 4 To paint a bud, paint one or two small long dots for the outer bracts using **B2** and mauve. Then paint the closed petals using alizarin crimson with one or two long dots. Load **B3** with sap green and paint a short stalk.

Step 5 To paint a complete flower, start with the petals at the front. Add more petals towards the back. Remember to paint the inside of the petals with diluted alizarin crimson. Paint some petals with curling edges. Mix one part of gamboge with one part of process white. Load **B4** with this colour and add the stamens at the centre of the flower. Use **B2** and sap green to paint a few leaves with long dots.

See also

leaves **p127**
finished painting **p150**
water lily flowers **p65**

LOTUS FLOWERS

Colour Palette

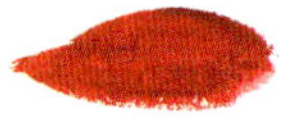

Alizarin crimson

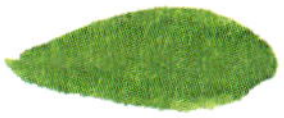

Sap green

Ink

Technical information: The lotus flowers are similar to water lily flowers, but a lotus flower is bigger. You can use the techniques for painting water lily flowers to paint the lotus flowers, but use the bigger brush **B1** instead of **B2**. A lotus flower has a large seedpod and a much longer stem than a water lily flower.

Step 1

Step 2

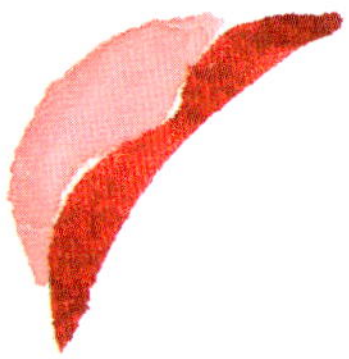

Step 3

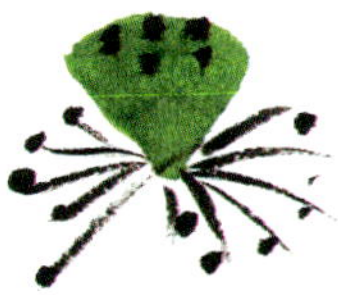

Step 4

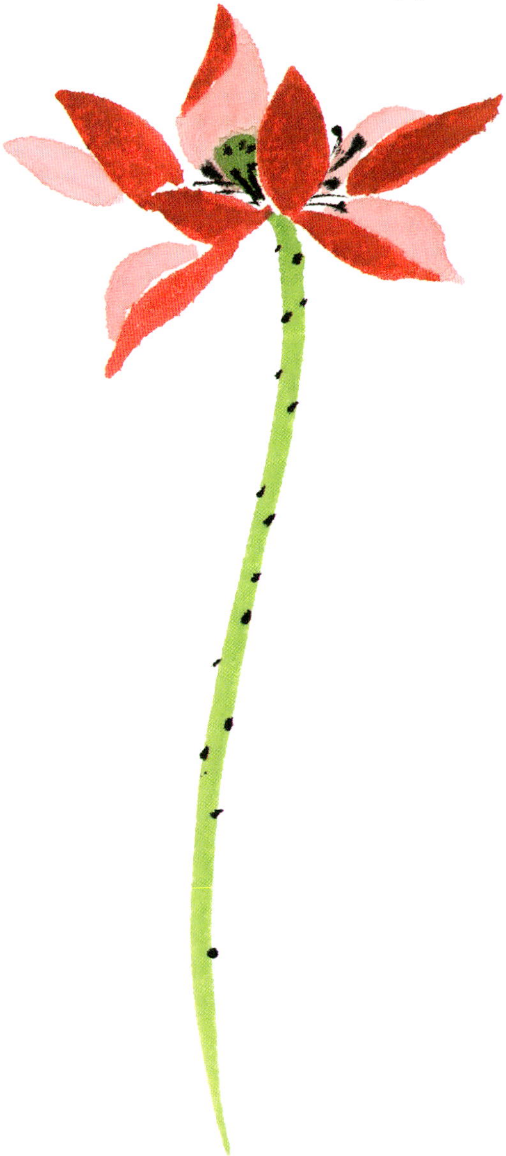

Brushes to use: B1, B2, B3, B4

Step 1 Load **B1** with alizarin crimson and paint two short brushstrokes to make up a petal. Use diluted alizarin crimson for the inside of the petals.

Step 2 Paint petals with curling edges. Use alizarin crimson and small short brushstrokes for the curling edge and finish the petal with diluted alizarin crimson.

Step 3 Each flower has a big seedpod in the shape of an inverted cone. Load **B3** with sap green and paint the seedpod. Dip **B4** into ink and paint a few dots on the seedpod as seeds. Add lines and tiny dots as stamens.

Step 4 To paint a lotus flower, start with the petals at the front. Add more petals towards the back until you finish painting the whole flower. Add the seedpod as described in step 3. Load **B2** with sap green and paint a thick, long stem. Add tiny dots along the stem with ink using **B4**.

AZALEA FLOWER HEADS WITH LEAVES

See also
finished painting **p148**

Technical information: The shapes of an azalea flower petal and an azalea leaf are very similar. You can use the same technique to paint either of them. Use two short brushstrokes for each petal or leaf. Each flower has five petals. A flower head is made up of many flowers in the middle with leaves surrounding the flowers.

Step 1

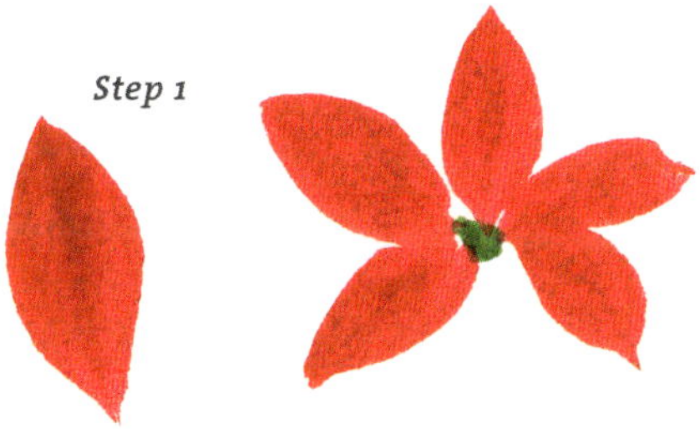

Step 2

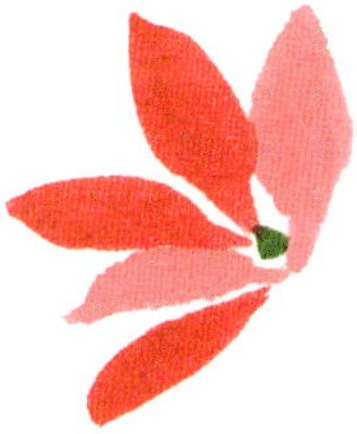

Step 3

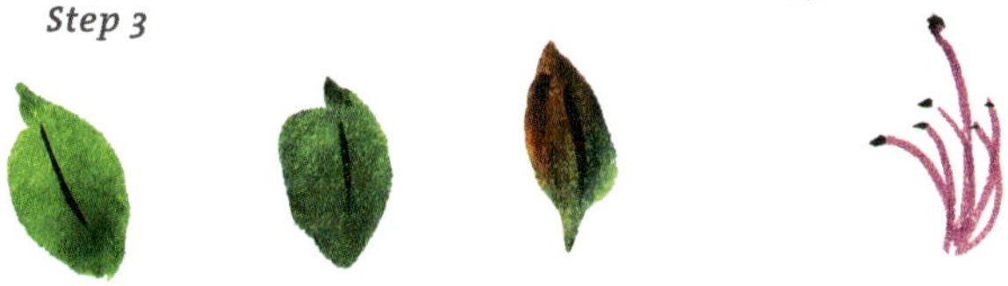

Step 4

Colour Palette

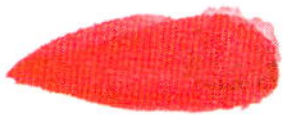

Permanent rose

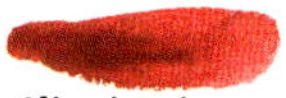

Alizarin crimson

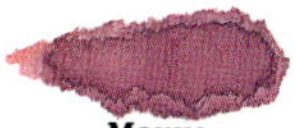

Mauve

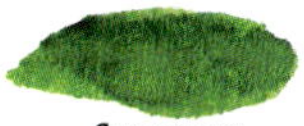

Sap green

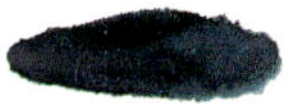

Indigo

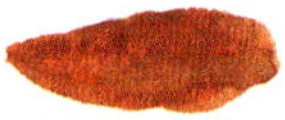

Burnt sienna

Ink

Brushes to use: B2, B3, B4

Step 1 Mix one part of alizarin crimson with one part of permanent rose. Load **B2** with this colour to paint the petals. Use two short brushstrokes to paint a petal. Paint five petals for a flower. Add a dot of sap green with **B3** to the centre of each flower.

Step 2 Paint a flower with the backs of one or two petals. Use diluted colour for the backs of the petals. The centre of each flower has a long stigma and five shorter stamens. Load **B4** with mauve to draw the centre. Dip **B4** into ink and add tiny dots to the stigma and each stamen.

Step 3 Each leaf is made up of two short brushstrokes. Prepare sap green. Prepare a darker green by mixing two parts of sap green with one part of indigo. Paint a leaf with sap green and one with the darker green using **B2**. Paint a leaf with a brown tip by dipping the nib of **B2** loaded with sap green into burnt sienna. Dip **B4** into ink and add a central vein to each leaf.

Step 4 Start the flower head with the flowers at the front. Add more flowers towards the back. Remember to use diluted colour for the backs of the petals. Add leaves around the flowers, some with sap green, some with darker green and some with brown edges. Mix sap green with a little bit of alizarin crimson. Load **B3** with this colour and paint the stalks and branches connecting the different parts of the flower head.

See also
short brushstroke p60
water line p155

PAINTING LEAVES WITH SHORT BRUSHSTROKES

Colour Palette

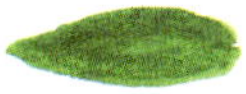
Sap green

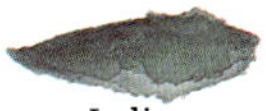
Indigo

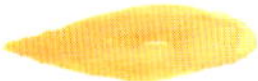
Gamboge

Lemon yellow

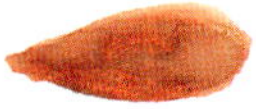
Burnt sienna

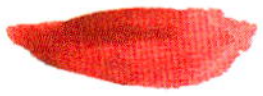
Alizarin crimson

Technical information: Short brushstrokes can be used to paint a variety of leaves. In general, use one short brushstroke for a small leaf and two short brushstrokes for a wider leaf. You can vary the pressing and lifting of the short brushstrokes. Many leaves with complicated shapes can be painted with multiple short brushstrokes.

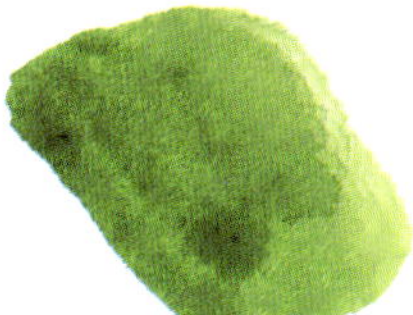
Sap green

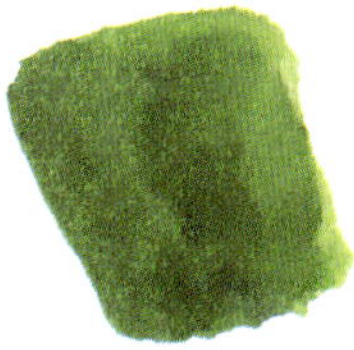
Dark green

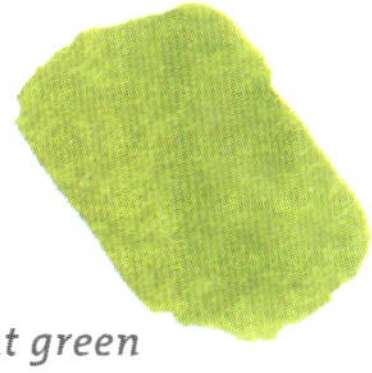
Light green

Lemon green

Olive green

Brushes to use: B2, B3

Greens

Not all leaves have the same colour, even on one single plant. The colour of a plant changes at different stages of growth and also in different seasons. Green is the main ingredient for painting leaves, but there are many tones of green. You can mix sap green with other colours to create a wide range of greens. The following are those used in this chapter. I will refer to each one when we come to paint leaves of different plants.

Sap green

This green is the basic green for general painting.

Dark green

Mix two parts of sap green with one part of indigo. This green is used for painting mature leaves.

Light green

Mix one part of sap green with one part of gamboge. This green is used for painting young leaves.

Lemon green

Mix one part of sap green with one part of lemon yellow. Use this green to paint young leaves in early spring. The light green made by using gamboge is too warm for this time of the year.

Olive green

Mix two parts of sap green with one part of burnt sienna. This green is used for painting older leaves.

The notes on when to use each green provide a general guideline. Many plants do not fall within this guideline. For example, a golden jasmine has golden coloured leaves and some astilbe has reddish leaves. So be flexible in your use of greens.

SMALL LEAVES

Paint a small leaf with a single short brushstroke. Try the following exercises. Paint in the directions indicated by the arrows. I used **B2** to paint all the leaves. You can create bigger leaves using **B1**.

Fig. 1 Use sap green and a short brushstroke to paint a small leaf.

Fig. 2 Use dark green and a short brushstroke to paint a small leaf.

Fig. 3 Use light green and a short brushstroke to paint a small leaf. Lengthen the lifting so that the leaf is longer.

Fig. 4 Use olive green and a short brushstroke to paint a small leaf. Delay the pressing so that the leaf has a longer base.

Fig. 5 Some leaves are darker at the base. Load **B2** with sap green and dip the nib of the brush into indigo. Paint a small leaf, starting with the base of the leaf.

Fig. 6 Some leaves have darker tips. Load **B2** with light green and dip the nib of the brush into dark green. If you start the leaf from the tip, the leaf will have a darker tip.

Fig. 7 Older leaves tend to turn brown at the tips. Load **B2** with sap green and dip the nib of the brush into burnt sienna. Paint a small leaf, starting from the tip.

Fig. 8 Leaves like those of roses have crimson edges. Load **B2** with sap green and dip the nib of the brush into alizarin crimson. Paint a leaf, starting from the tip.

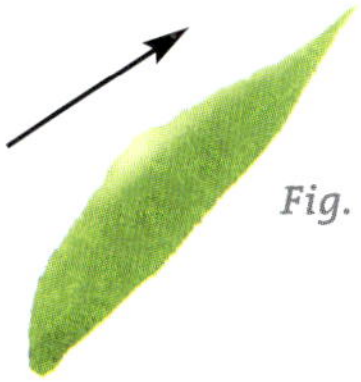
Fig. 1

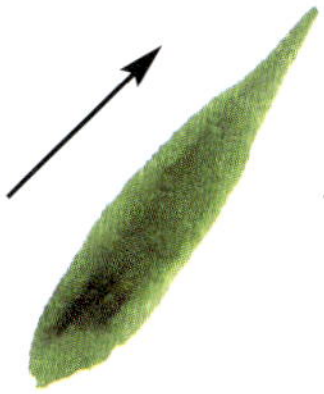
Fig. 2

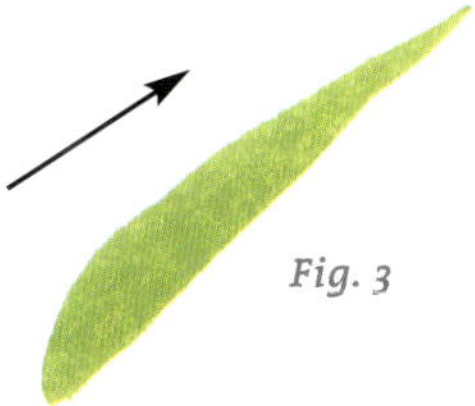
Fig. 3

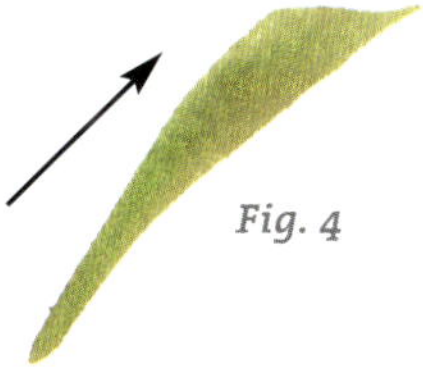
Fig. 4

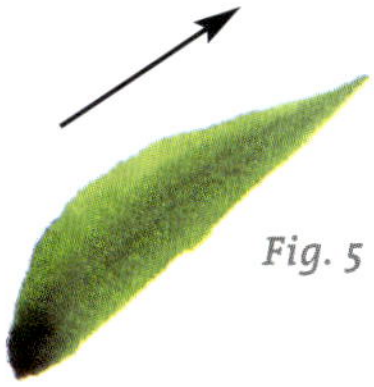
Fig. 5

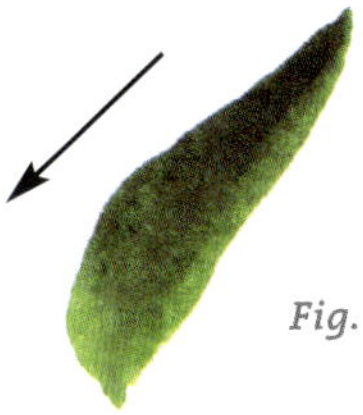
Fig. 6

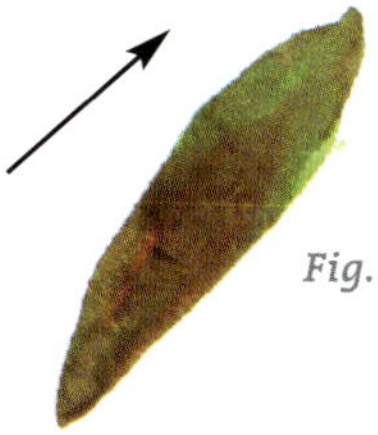
Fig. 7

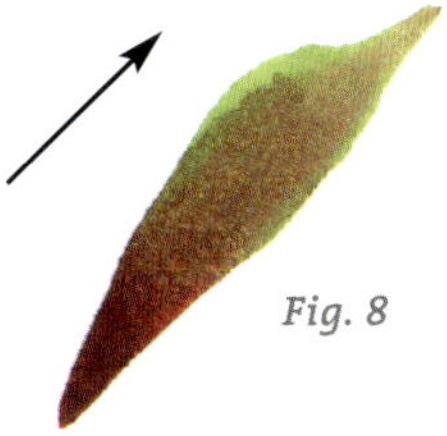
Fig. 8

WIDER LEAVES

Brushes to use: B2

Fig. 1 A leaf seen from the side is like a half leaf. You can use a single short brushstroke, pressing either more to the right or more to the left.

Fig. 2 You need two short brushstrokes to paint a wider leaf. Press one of them more to the right and the other more to the left.

Fig. 3 Paint a wider leaf in dark green.

Fig. 4 Paint a wider leaf with a brown edge.

Fig. 5 Paint a wider leaf with a crimson tip.

Fig. 6 You can lengthen the lifting parts of the two short brushstrokes. The result will be a longer leaf with a wide base and slender tip.

Fig. 7 You can also delay the pressing parts of the two short brushstrokes. The result will be a leaf with a wide tip but a slender base.

Fig. 1

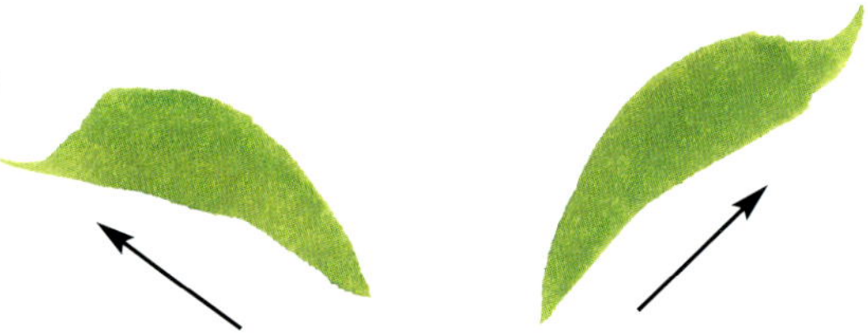

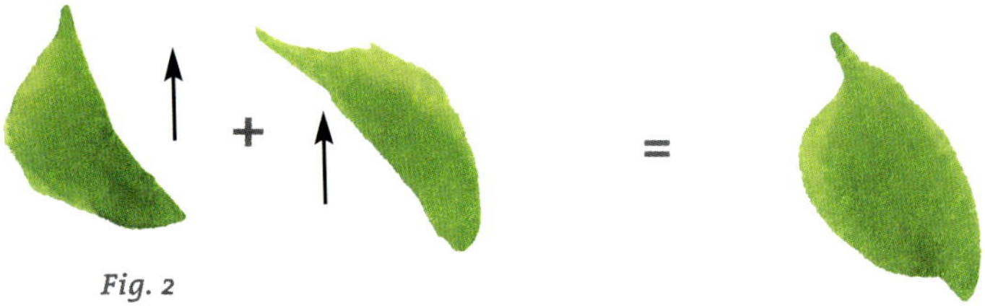

Fig. 2

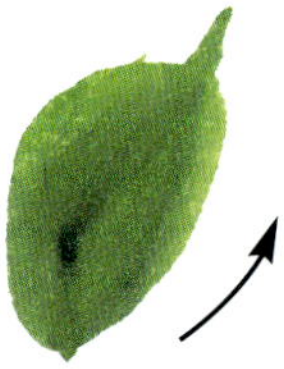

Fig. 3

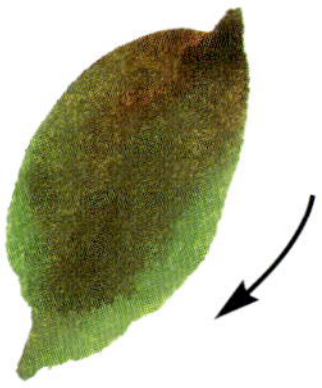

Fig. 4

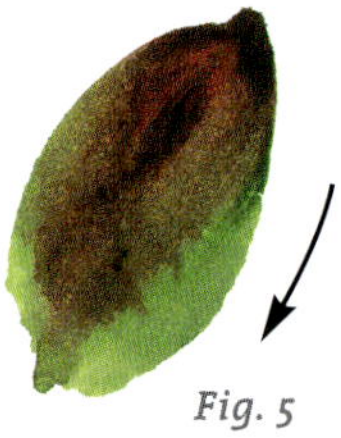

Fig. 5

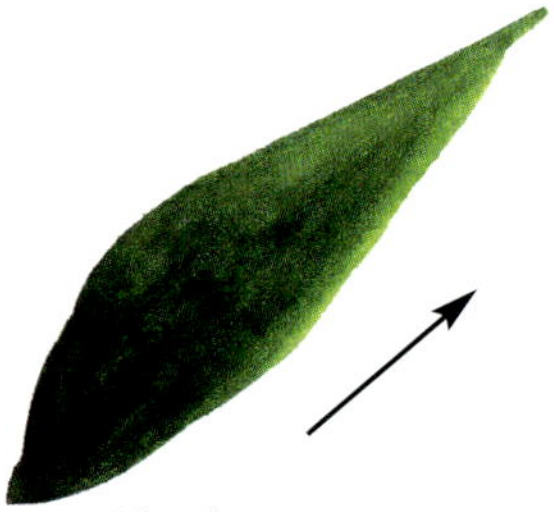

Fig. 6

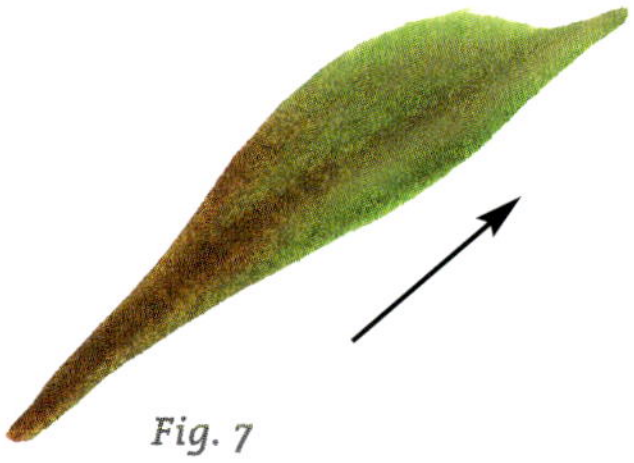

Fig. 7

LEAVES WITH MORE THAN ONE POINT

Leaves of plants like bleeding heart, and some clematis, have more than one point in each leaf. To paint a leaf with more than one point, start with a small leaf or a wide leaf. Then add a small short brushstroke for each additional point.

Fig. 1 Two big short brushstrokes plus a small short brushstroke make a two-pointed leaf.

Fig. 2 Two small short brushstrokes plus two big short brushstrokes make a three-pointed leaf.

Fig. 3 Five short brushstrokes make a five-pointed leaf.

Fig. 4 Six short brushstrokes make a three-pointed wide leaf.

Fig. 5 Ten short brushstrokes make a five-pointed wide leaf.

Fig. 1

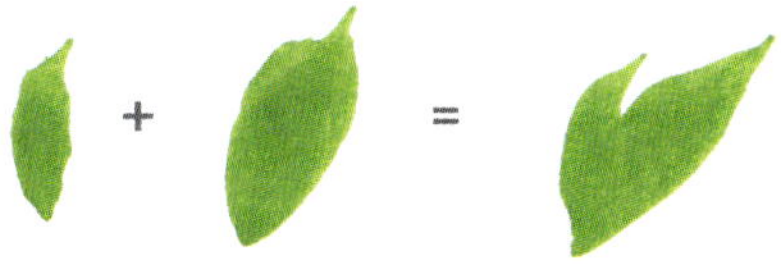

Fig. 2

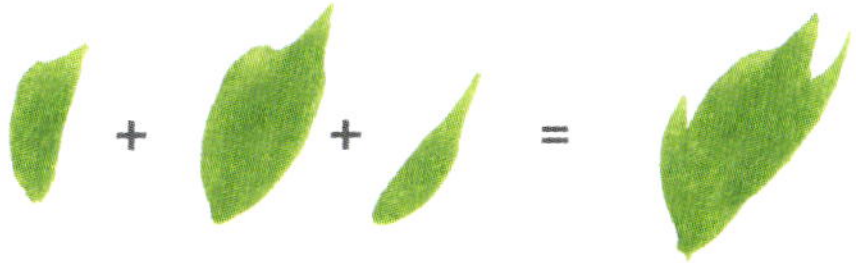

Fig. 3

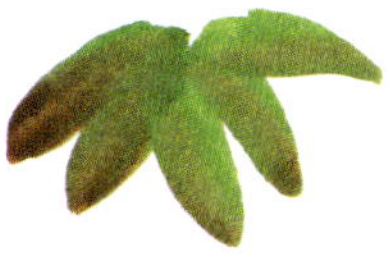

Fig. 4

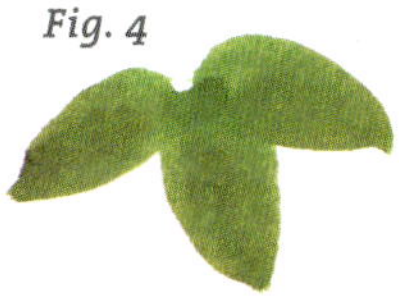

Fig. 5

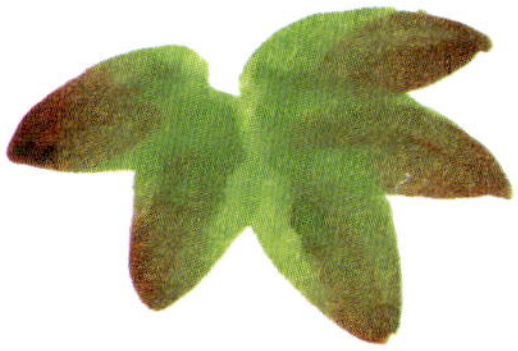

A LONG LEAF STALK

To paint a long leaf stalk, always start with a water line to indicate the long stalk. The following four steps provide a general guideline for painting a stalk with many leaves.

Step 1 Use a clean and damp **B3** to draw a water line to represent the long stalk. I used a pencil line here to indicate the water line.

Step 2 Paint the leaves at the front.

Step 3 Paint the sections of the stalk where it is visible.

Step 4 Add more leaves to the back of the stalk.

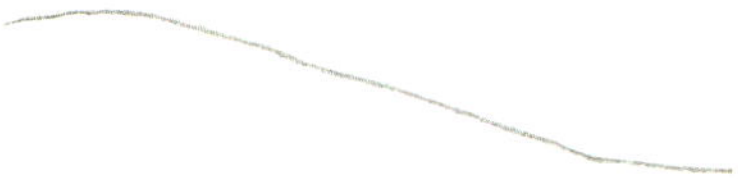

Step 1

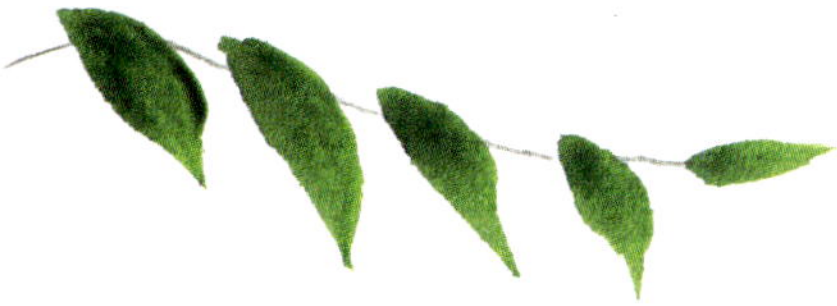

Step 2

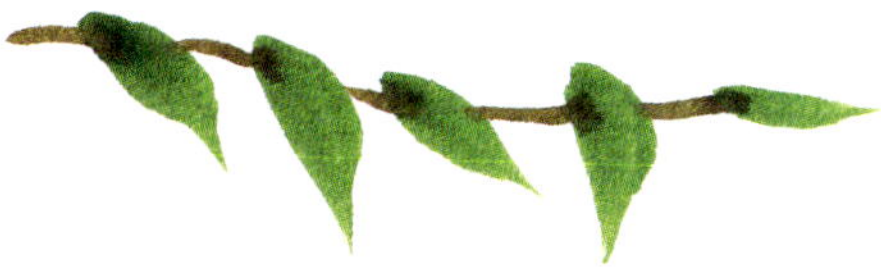

Step 3

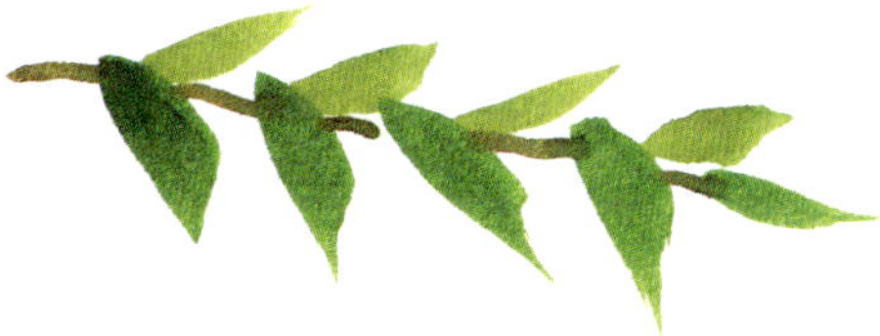

Step 4

See also

flowers p104
finished painting p137
branches p95
painting leaves p68

WISTERIA LEAVES

Colour Palette

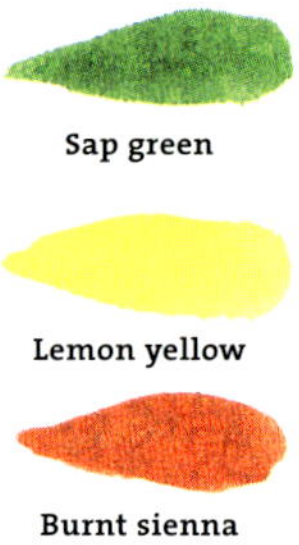

Technical information: Wisteria leaves begin to come out very early in the spring. They don't have the warm colour of summer yet, so use lemon green for the young leaves. Sprouting leaves usually have brownish tips. A leaf stalk bears many leaves. Leaves are small. New shoots are like tendrils when they first come out and wrap themselves around old branches. These tendril-like shoots will become woody in the next year. New shoots are green and thin. Old shoots are brown, hard and dry.

Brushes to use: B2, B3, B4

Step 1 Load **B3** with sap green and paint a line to represent the shoot. Load **B2** with the lemon green. Dip the nib of the brush into burnt sienna and paint short brushstrokes along the shoot as leaves. Leaves are arranged opposite each other. Load **B4** with burnt sienna and paint a central vein along each leaf.

Step 2 Load **B3** with sap green and paint twisting thin lines to represent new shoots. Dip the nib of the brush into burnt sienna and paint tiny sprouting leaves at the ends of each shoot.

Step 3 Paint a group of leaves. Start with the shoot in the front and add leaves along the shoot. Add the next shoot and then leaves. Work towards the back. Dip **B4** into burnt sienna and add veins to the leaves at the front.

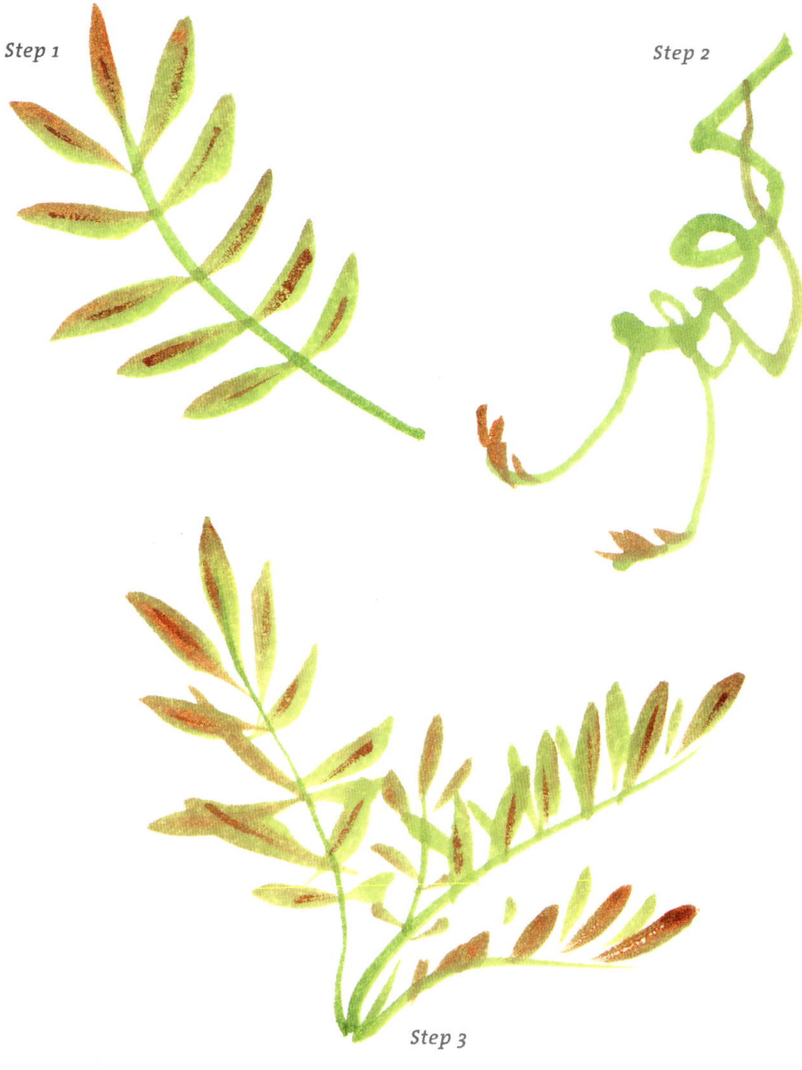

See also

trunks p94
finished painting p99
painting leaves p68

BAMBOO LEAVES

Technical information: Use a short brushstroke with the lifting extended to paint a bamboo leaf. Younger leaves are sap green. Mature leaves are darker green. Older leaves have brown edges. Leaves grow in groups of three, four or five.

Colour Palette

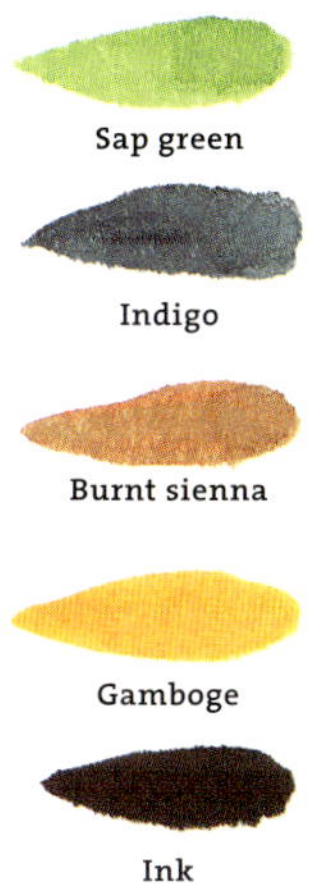

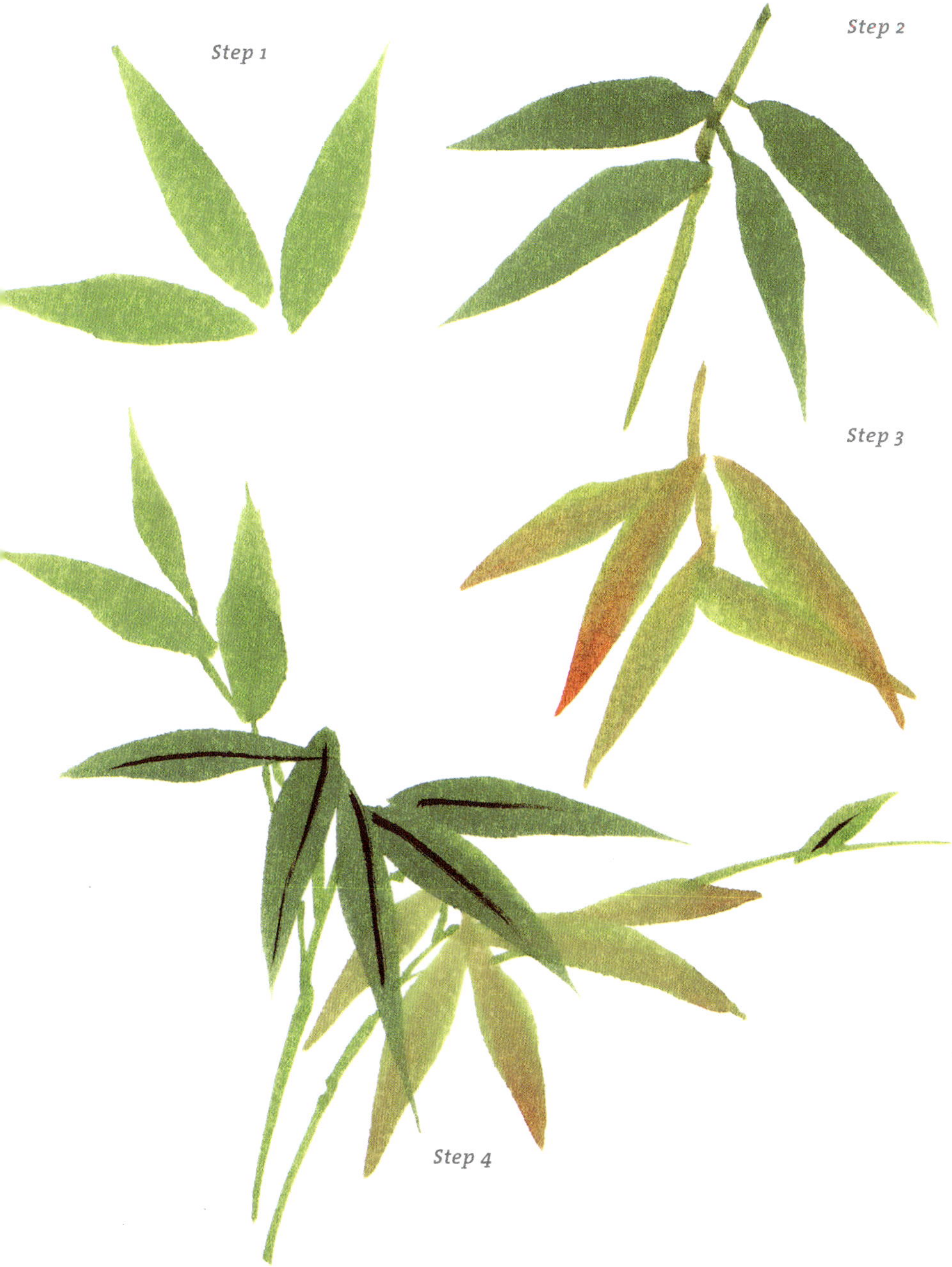

Brushes to use: B1, B3, B4

Step 1 Load **B1** with sap green and paint a short brushstroke for each bamboo leaf. Lengthen the lifting part of the short brushstroke so that the leaf is longer. A group sometimes has three leaves.

Step 2 Load **B1** with dark green to paint more bamboo leaves. A group may also have four leaves.

Step 3 Load **B1** with olive green to paint more bamboo leaves. A group sometimes has five leaves. One or two leaves may have brown tips.

Step 4 Paint a group of dark leaves. Add groups of lighter leaves. Finish with groups of old leaves. Load **B3** with sap green and paint shoots to connect the leaves. Dip **B4** into ink and paint central veins on a few front leaves.

See also

flowers	p121
finished painting	p140
water line	p155
painting leaves	p68

CAMELLIA LEAVES

Technical information: Camellia leaves are big and wide. You need two short brushstrokes painted with **B1** for each leaf. The leaves are usually very dark. Young leaves are light green and have crimson edges. Older leaves have brown tips.

Colour Palette

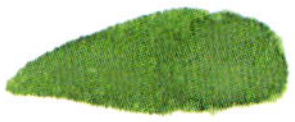

Sap green

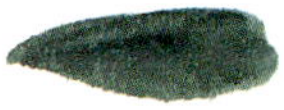

Indigo

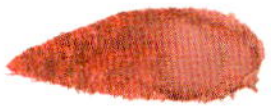

Alizarin crimson

Brushes to use: B1, B2, B3, B4

Step 1 Load **B1** with sap green. Paint one short brushstroke pressing more to the right and another pressing more to the left. Use two such brush-strokes to make up a leaf. Paint another leaf with dark green.

Step 2 Paint a folded leaf with two short brushstrokes. Use sap green to paint the back of the leaf.

Step 3 Young leaves at the top of the branch are smaller and have crimson edges. Load **B2** with sap green and dip the nib of the brush into alizarin crimson to paint the young leaves. Use single short brushstrokes for the small leaves at the very top of the branch.

Step 4 Use a clean and damp **B3** to paint a water line to represent the main branch. Paint a few leaves along the water line, some dark and some light. Paint the new leaves at the top with crimson edges. Load **B3** with sap green and dip the nib of the brush into alizarin crimson and fill in the sections of the main branch where it is visible. Add short stalks to connect the leaves to the main branch. Dip **B4** into crimson and paint veins on the leaves.

Step 1

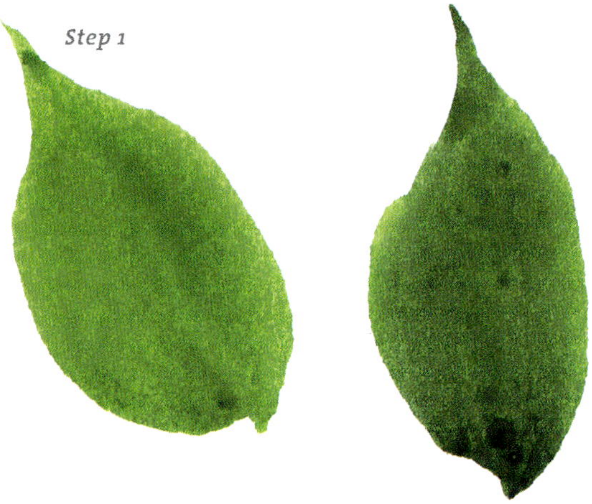

Step 2

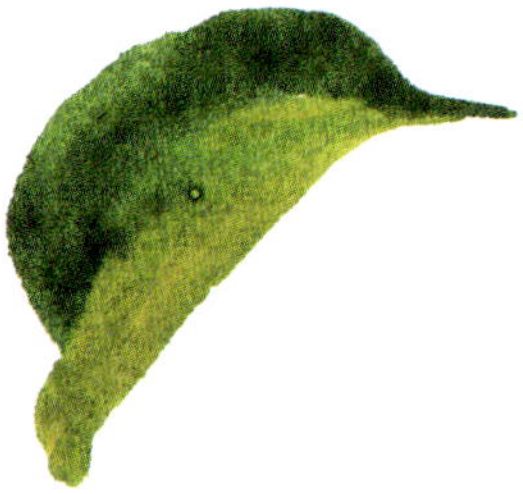

Step 3

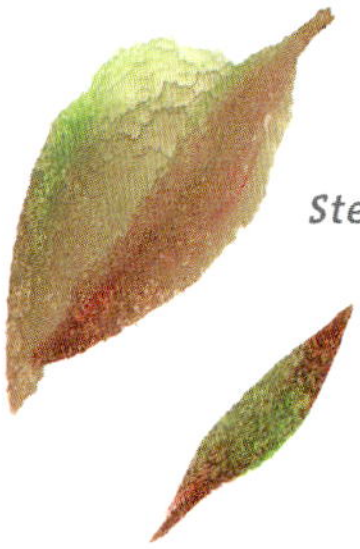

Step 4

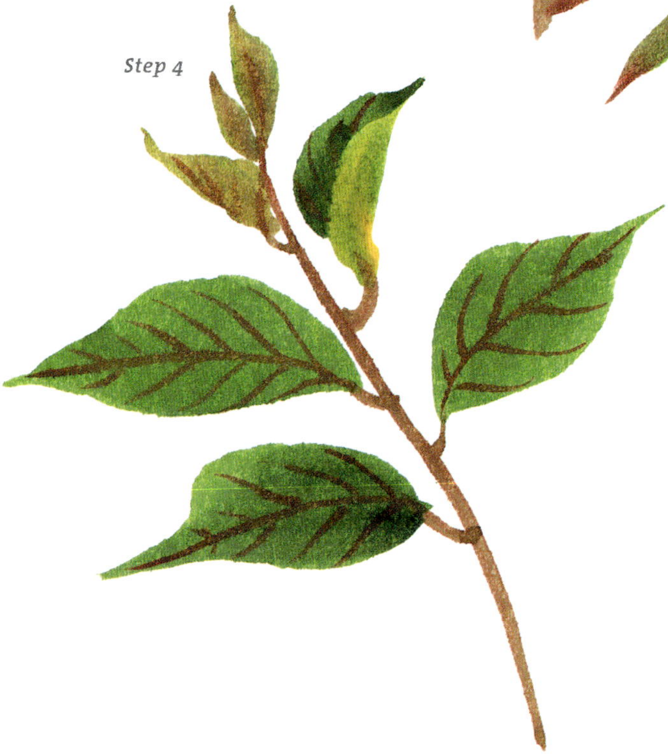

See also

flowers	p113
finished painting	p143
water line	p155
painting leaves	p68

ROSE LEAVES

Technical information: Rose leaves vary in sizes and colour even within one plant. Use **B1** for big leaves and **B2** for smaller leaves. Use two short brushstrokes to make up a leaf. Mature leaves are dark green while younger leaves are sap green. Leaves can have crimson edges. Older leaves have brown edges. There are usually five leaves to a stalk.

Colour Palette

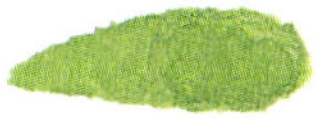

Sap green

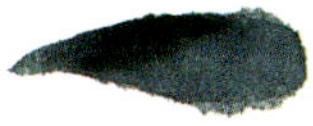

Indigo

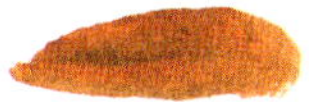

Burnt sienna

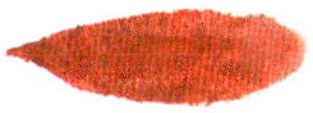

Alizarin crimson

Step 1

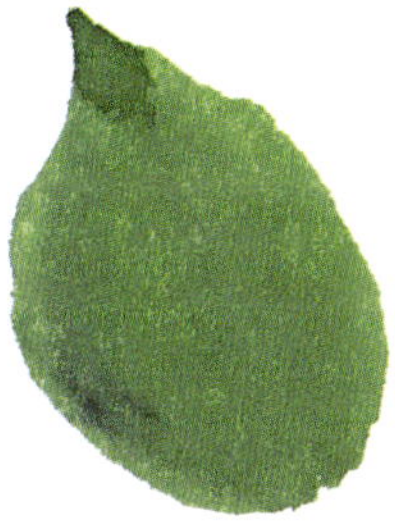

Step 2

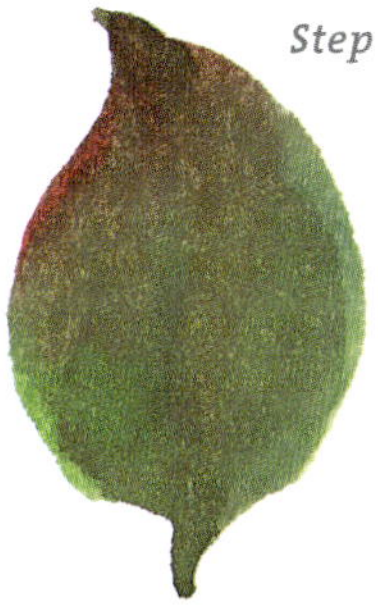

Step 3

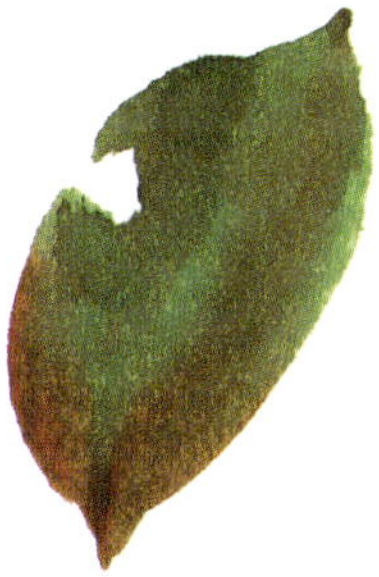

Step 4

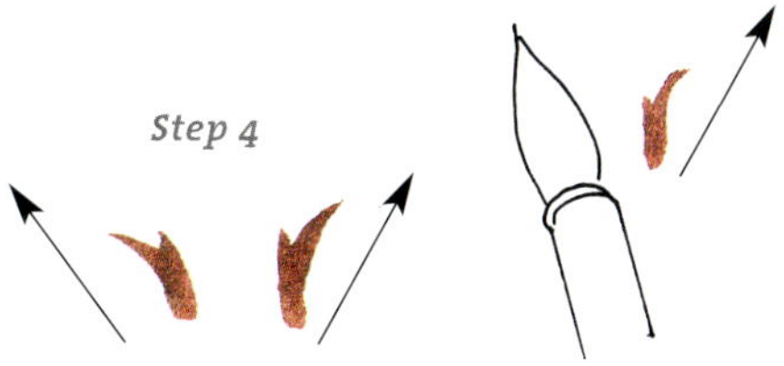

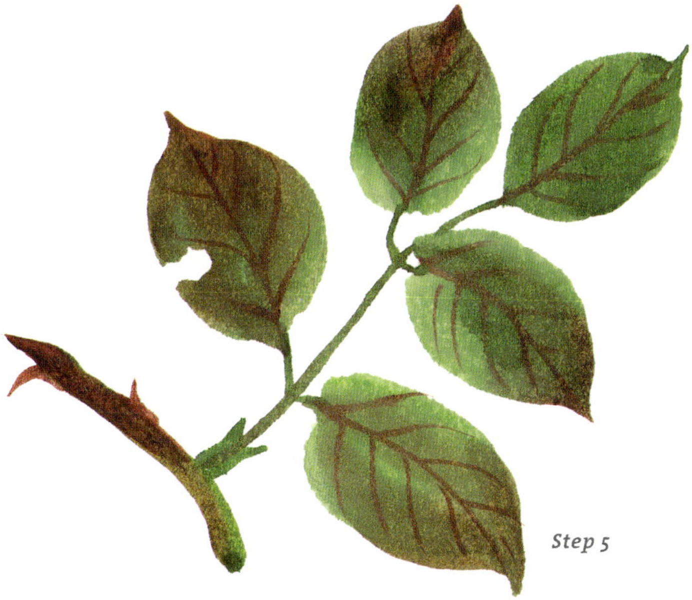

Step 5

Brushes to use: B1, B2, B3, B4

Step 1 Load **B1** with dark green. Paint two short brushstrokes for a leaf.

Step 2 Load **B1** with dark green and dip the nib of the brush into alizarin crimson. Paint a leaf with a crimson edge.

Step 3 Load **B1** with sap green and dip the nib of the brush into burnt sienna. Paint a leaf with a brown edge and a broken edge.

Step 4 Dip **B4** into alizarin crimson. Position the brush as indicated. Press and lift the brush upwards to paint a thorn as indicated in the diagram.

Step 5 Use a clean and damp **B3** and paint a water line to represent the leaf stalk. Paint a variety of leaves along the water line. Mix one part of sap green with one part of alizarin crimson. Load **B2** with this mixture and paint a section of a branch. Load **B3** with this mixture and paint the leaf stalk connected to the branch and the short stalks connecting the leaves to the leaf stalk. Clean **B3** and dip it into sap green. Add two leaf bracts to the base of the stalk. Load **B4** with alizarin crimson. Place the brush along the side of the branch and paint some thorns. Use **B4** and alizarin crimson to paint the leaf veins.

See also

flowers p64
finished painting p136
water line p155
painting leaves p68

LILY LEAVES

Colour Palette

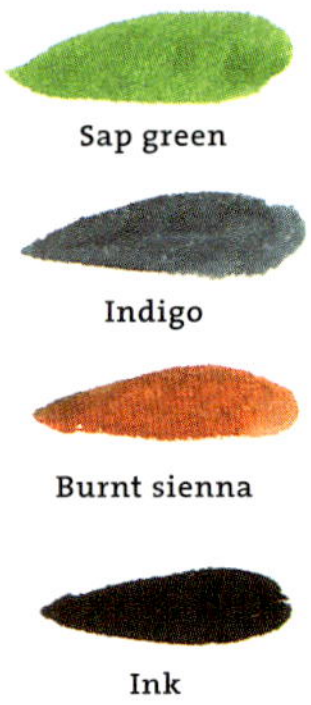

Technical information: There are many types of lily. Some have big broad leaves and can be painted using short brushstrokes with **B1**. Some have long slender leaves. The leaves of the lily plant grow along a long stem. Use a water line to position the stem.

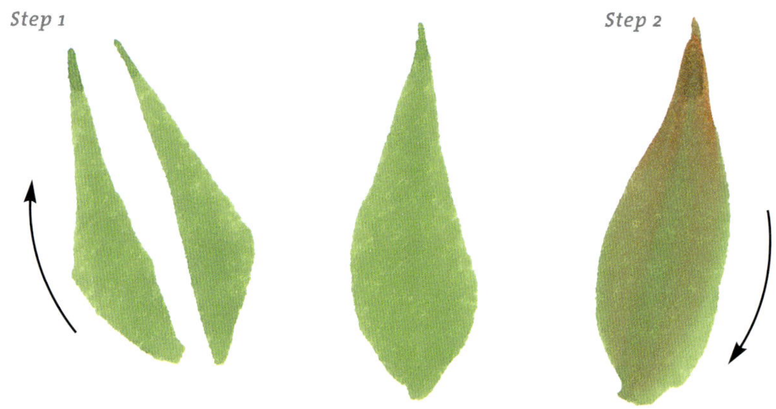

Brushes to use: B1, B2, B3, B4

Step 1 Load **B1** with dark green. Use two short brushstrokes to paint a leaf. Lengthen the lifting parts of the short brushstrokes.

Step 2 Load **B1** with dark green and dip the nib of the brush into burnt sienna. Paint a leaf with a brown edge. Start the short brushstrokes from the tips and delay the pressing.

Step 3 Paint a folding leaf with sap green on the back.

Step 4 Use a clean and damp **B3** to draw a water line to represent the position of the stem. Use **B1** to paint some leaves along the line at the front. Use a variety of greens. Mix one part sap green with one part burnt sienna. Load **B2** with this mixture and paint sections of the stem where it is visible. Add more leaves to the back of the stem. Dip **B4** into ink and draw the veins on the leaves at the front.

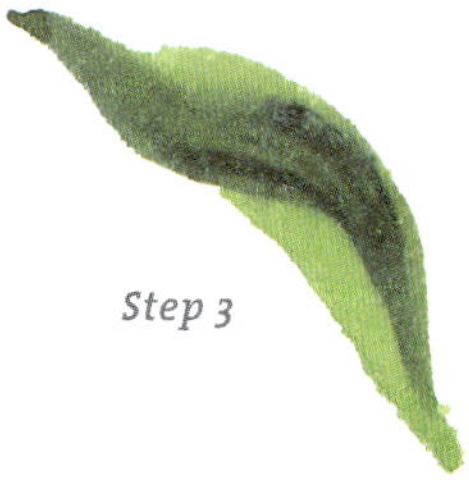

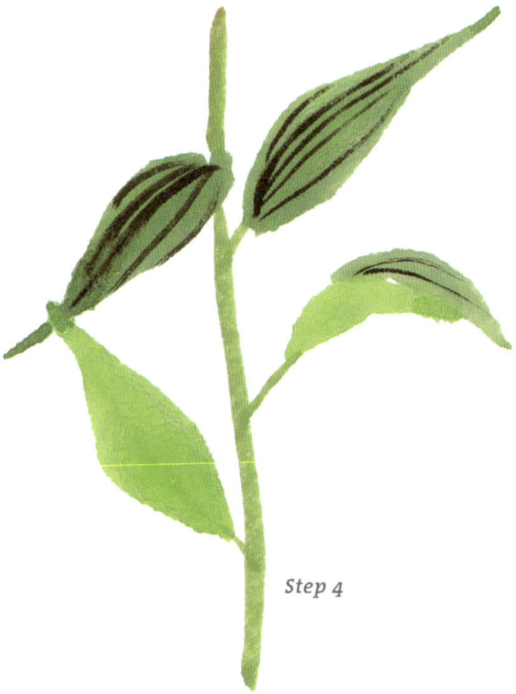

See also

flowers p63
finished painting p134
water line p155
painting leaves p68

HONEYSUCKLE LEAVES

Technical information: Honeysuckle is a climber. The young shoots wrap around anything they can get hold of. Pairs of leaves joined at the base appear along the shoot. The flower heads sprout from the leaf base.

Use a water line to mark out the young shoot before painting the leaves. Paint the leaves with sap green or dark green, some of them with brown or crimson edges. Use light green with a crimson tip for young leaves at the tip of the shoot.

Colour Palette

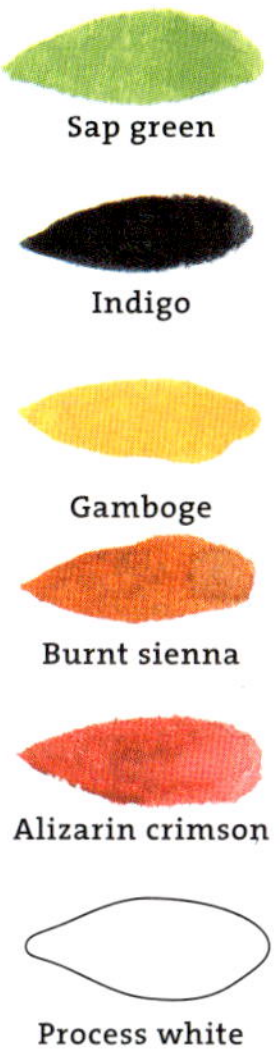

Brushes to use: B1, B2, B3, B4

Step 1 Load **B1** with sap green. Paint two short brushstrokes to make up a leaf.

Step 2 Load **B1** with dark green and dip the nib of the brush into burnt sienna. Paint a dark green leaf with a brown edge.

Step 3 The small leaves at the top of the shoot are light green and some have crimson edges. Load **B2** with light green and dip the nib of the brush into alizarin crimson to paint these smaller leaves. Use a single short brushstroke for each of the very small leaves at the tip of the branch.

Step 4 Paint a pair of leaves joined at the base. The shoot passes through the central point where the two leaves join. Begin with the leaf at the front. Add the section of the shoot and then the leaf at the back.

Step 5 Use a clean and damp **B3** to paint a water line. Paint the leaves at the front in a variety of colours described in steps 1 to 3. Mix two parts of sap green with one part of alizarin crimson. Load **B3** with this colour to paint the sections of the shoot where it is visible. Add more leaves to the back of the shoot. Dip **B4** into process white and add veins to the leaves.

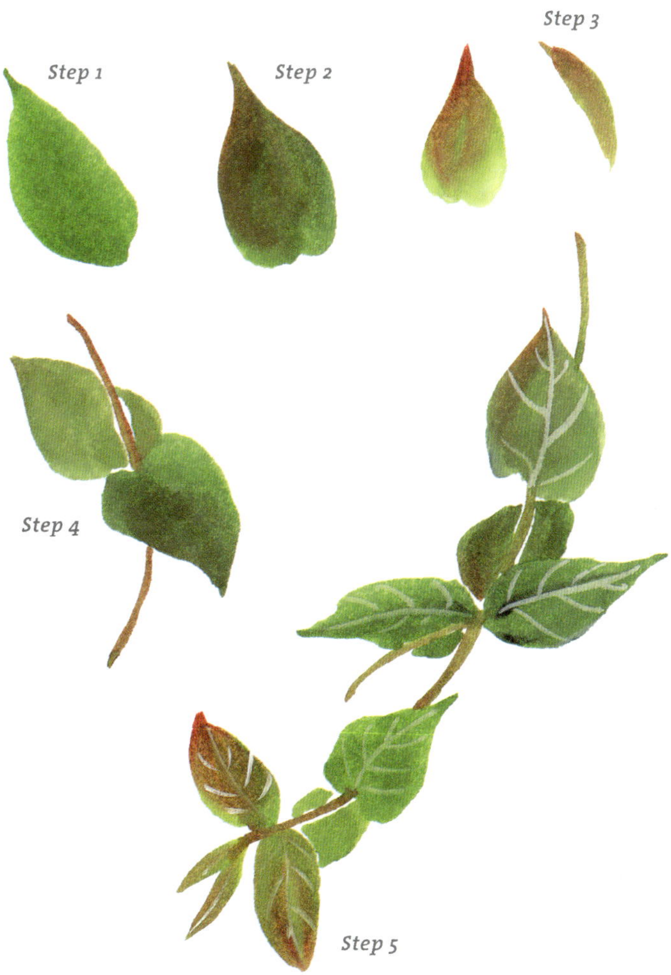

See also

flowers p120
finished painting p133
water line p155
painting leaves p68

CLEMATIS LEAVES

Technical information: Young clematis shoots wrap around anything they come into contact with. The shape of the leaf is variable. It can be a simple leaf or have one or two extra points. Most leaves are sap green and dark green, though some have crimson edges.

Colour Palette

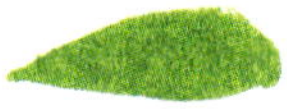

Sap green

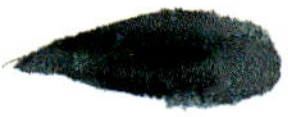

Indigo

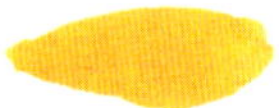

Gamboge

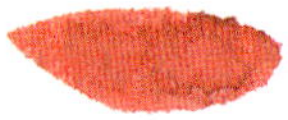

Alizarin crimson

Step 1

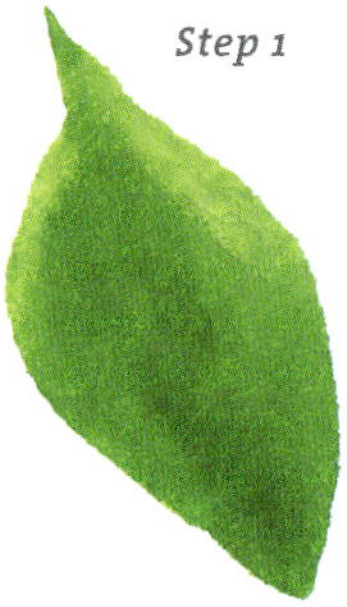

Step 2

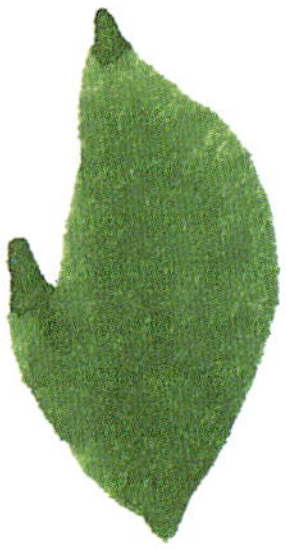

Step 3

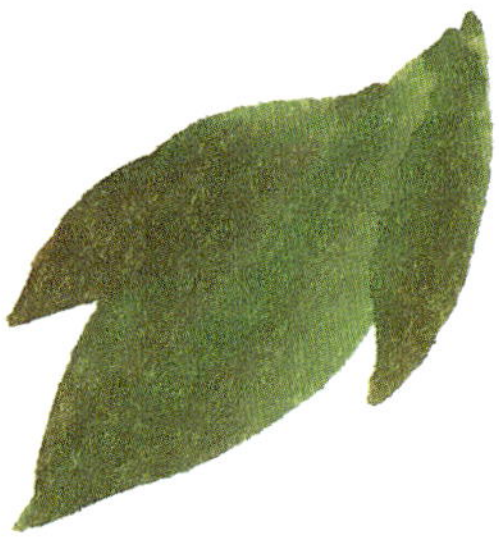

Step 4

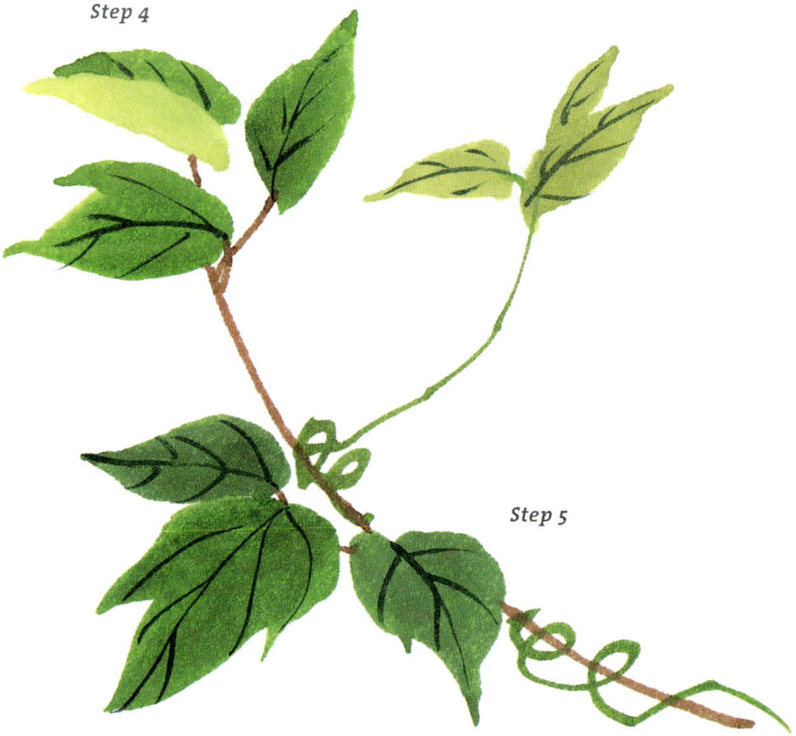

Step 5

Brushes to use: B1, B2, B3, B4

Step 1 Load **B1** with sap green and paint a leaf with two short brushstrokes.

Step 2 Load **B1** with dark green. Use three short brushstrokes to paint a leaf with one extra point.

Step 3 Load **B1** with dark green and dip the nib of the brush into burnt sienna. Paint a leaf with two extra points and a brown edge.

Step 4 Paint a folding leaf. Use light green for the underside of the leaves. Add two more leaves to make a group.

Step 5 Use a clean damp **B3** to paint a water line to represent the main stem. Use **B1** to paint a few leaves, some in dark green and some in sap green along the water line. Use **B2** to paint a few smaller leaves, some in dark green and some in sap green. Mix one part of sap green with one part of alizarin crimson. Load **B3** with this colour to paint the main stem and the leaf stalks where they are visible. Clean **B3** and reload with sap green. Add a new shoot wrapping around the stem. Add new leaves in light green to the new shoot. Load **B4** with indigo and add veins to the leaves.

See also

flowers p53
finished painting p141
painting leaves p68

HYDRANGEA LEAVES

Technical information: Hydrangea leaves have many points. Paint a short brushstroke for each point. A leaf is built up with many short brushstrokes so it is better to use **B2**. **B1** will make the leaf too big, unless you are doing a very big painting with big leaves.

Colour Palette

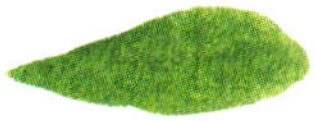

Sap green

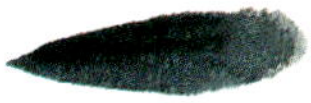

Indigo

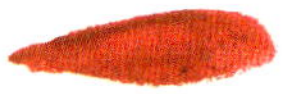

Alizarin crimson

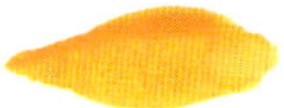

Gamboge

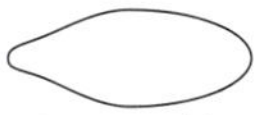

Process white

Step 1

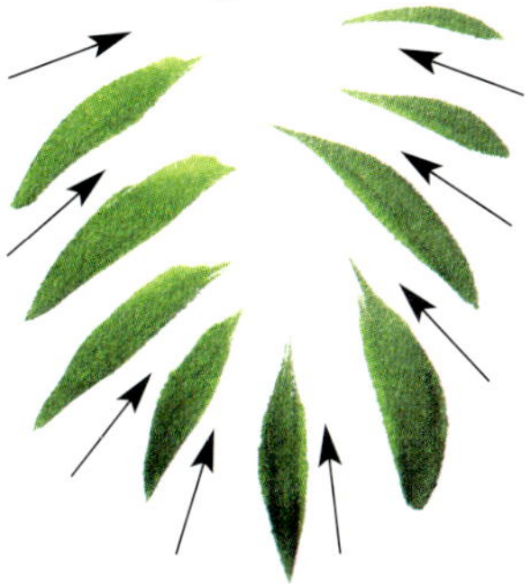

Step 2

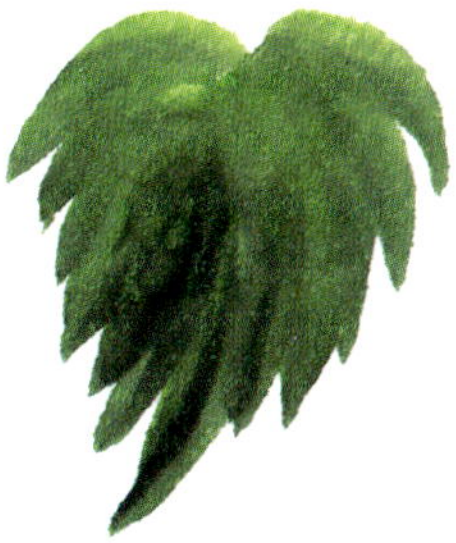

Step 3

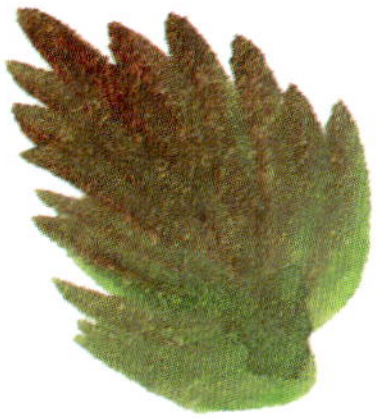

Step 4

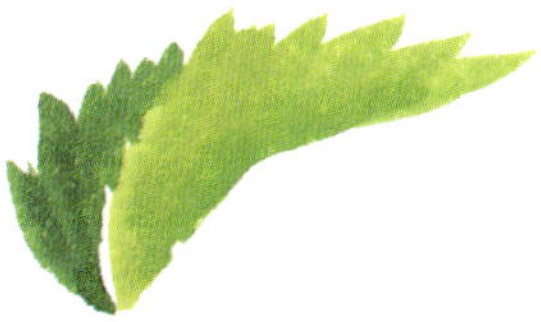

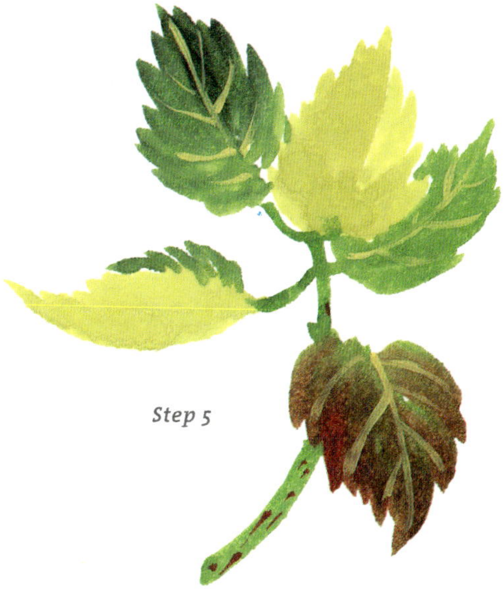

Step 5

Brushes to use: B2, B3, B4

Step 1 Load **B2** with sap green and dip the nib of the brush into indigo. Practise short brushstrokes with this two-colour loading. Paint short brushstrokes in the direction indicated by the arrows.

Step 2 Start a leaf with a short brushstroke at the tip. Add short brushstrokes along one side. Bear in mind the shape of the leaf, then add short brushstrokes along the other side to complete the leaf.

Step 3 Load **B2** with sap green and dip the nib of the brush into alizarin crimson. Paint a leaf with a crimson edge. A hydrangea leaf turns crimson at the edge when it gets old.

Step 4 Use light green for the underside of a leaf. Paint a leaf viewed from the side.

Step 5 Paint some leaves with dark green and some with sap green. Load **B3** with sap green and paint the main stalk. Paint shorter stalks to join the leaves to the main stalk. Mix one part of process white with one part of gamboge. Dip **B4** into this mixture and add veins to the leaves. Clean **B4** and dip it into alizarin crimson. Paint some marks on the main stem.

See also

flowers p105
finished painting p138
water line p155
painting leaves p68

HIBISCUS LEAVES

Colour Palette

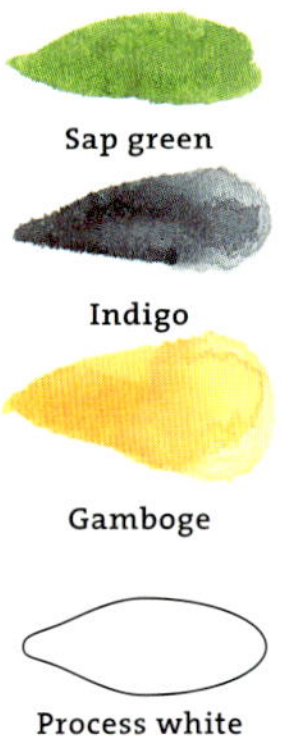

Technical information: Hibiscus leaves also have many points, but these are irregular. Some points are large and some are small. Use single short brushstrokes for the small points and two short brushstrokes for each of the larger ones.

The mature leaves of hibiscus are very dark. Only the very young leaves at the tops of the shoots are light green.

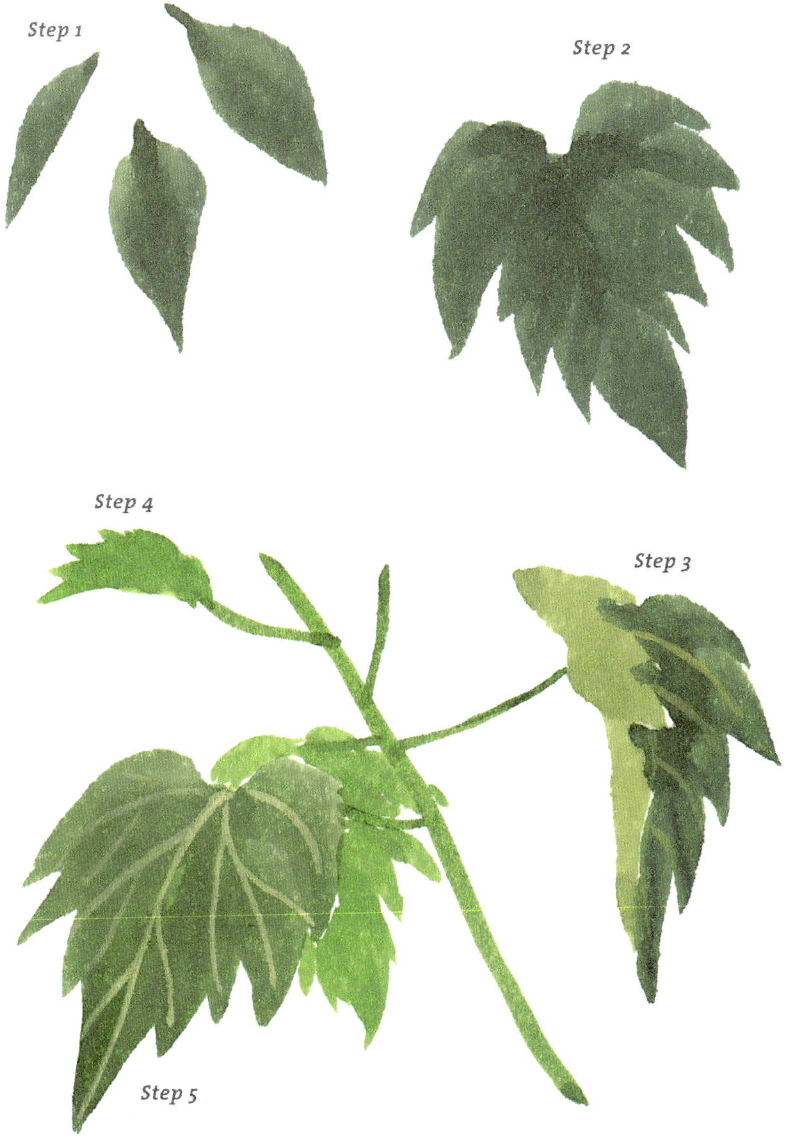

Brushes to use: B2, B3, B4

Step 1 Load **B2** with dark green and paint short brushstrokes. Paint some larger shapes with two short brushstrokes for each.

Step 2 Start at the tip of the leaf with a double short brushstroke. Build up one side of the leaf by painting single and double short brushstrokes close together. Finish the leaf by adding more single and double short brushstrokes on the other side.

Step 3 Paint a folding leaf. Use sap green for the underside of the leaf.

Step 4 Load **B2** with sap green and paint some young leaves.

Step 5 Use a clean and damp **B3** to paint a water line to represent the main shoot of the plant. Add the leaves at the front. Load **B2** with sap green and paint sections of the main stem where they are visible. Add more leaves at the back. Mix one part of gamboge with one part of process white. Dip **B4** into this mixture and add veins to the leaves.

See also	
flowers	**p126**
finished painting	**p145**
painting leaves	**p68**

PANSY LEAVES

Technical information: Pansy leaves have scallop-shaped edges. At the points where the stalks join the main stem, there are spider-like leaves. All the different leaves are built up with small short brushstrokes.

Colour Palette

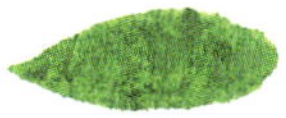

Sap Green

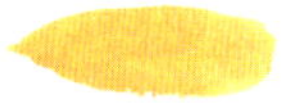

Gamboge

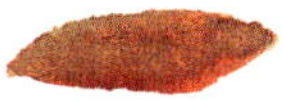

Burnt sienna

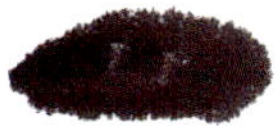

Ink

Step 1

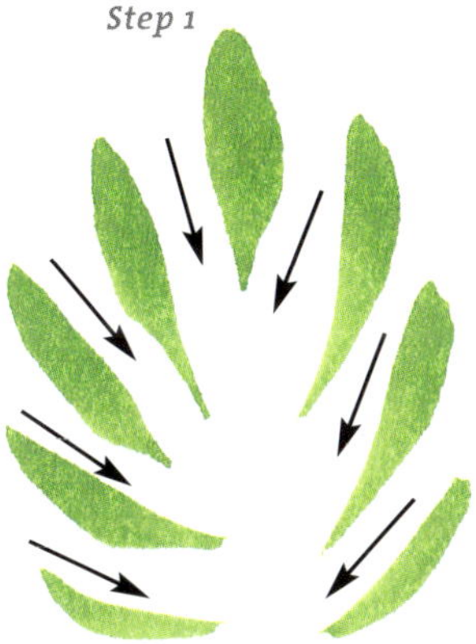

Step 2

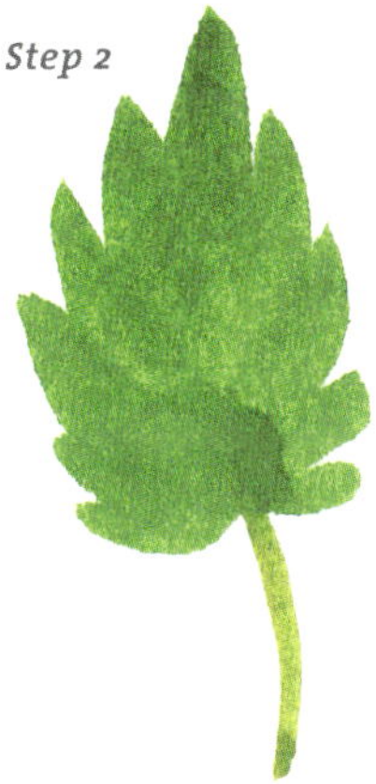

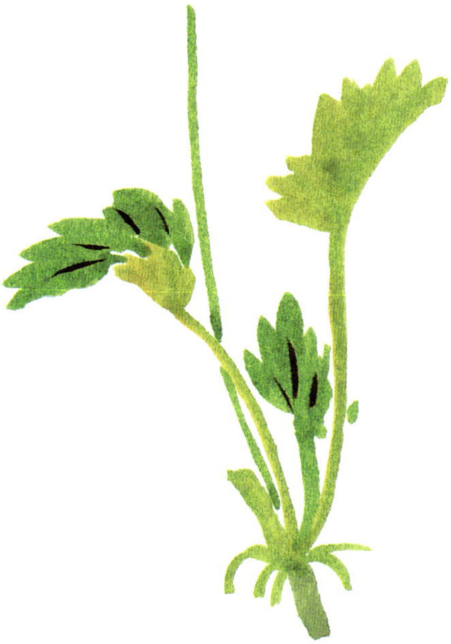

Step 3

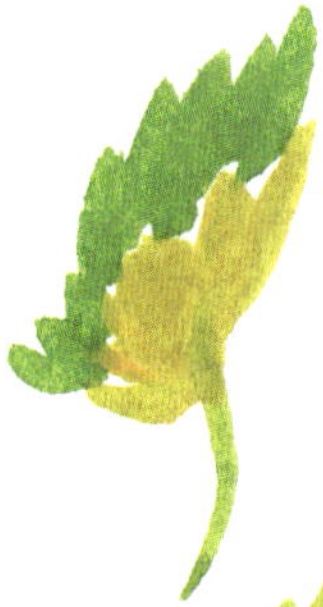

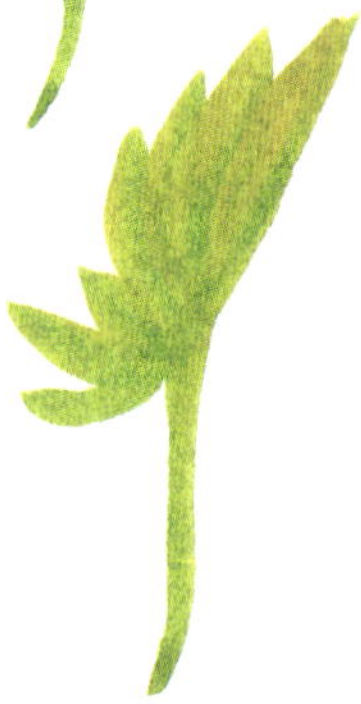

Step 4

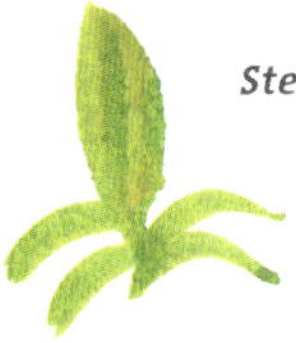

brushes to use: B2, B3, B4

Step 1 Load **B2** with sap green. Practise small short brushstrokes.

Step 2 Start a leaf at the tip with a small short brushstroke. Add more short brushstrokes on both sides to paint a leaf. Use **B3** and sap green to paint a stalk for the leaf.

Step 3 Use olive green for the backs of leaves. Paint a leaf showing the back. Paint a folding leaf. Remember to use olive green for the back. Use **B3** and olive green to add a stalk to each leaf.

Step 4 Use olive green to paint a spider-like leaf.

Step 5 Paint a group of leaves. Paint stalks for each leaf so that the bases of the stalks join together. Paint a spider-like leaf at the base of the stalks. Use **B3** and sap green to add the main stalk. Dip **B4** into ink and use thin lines for the veins of a few leaves.

See also

flowers p128
finished painting p146
painting leaves p68

POPPY LEAVES

Colour Palette

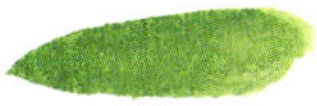

Sap green

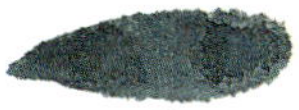

Indigo

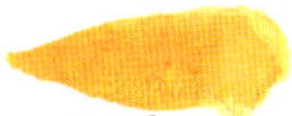

Gamboge

Ink

Technical information: A poppy leaf stalk has many leaflets on each side. Each leaflet is painted with a short brushstroke. Use sap green for the undersides of the leaves and dark green for their upper sides. Older leaves have brown edges.

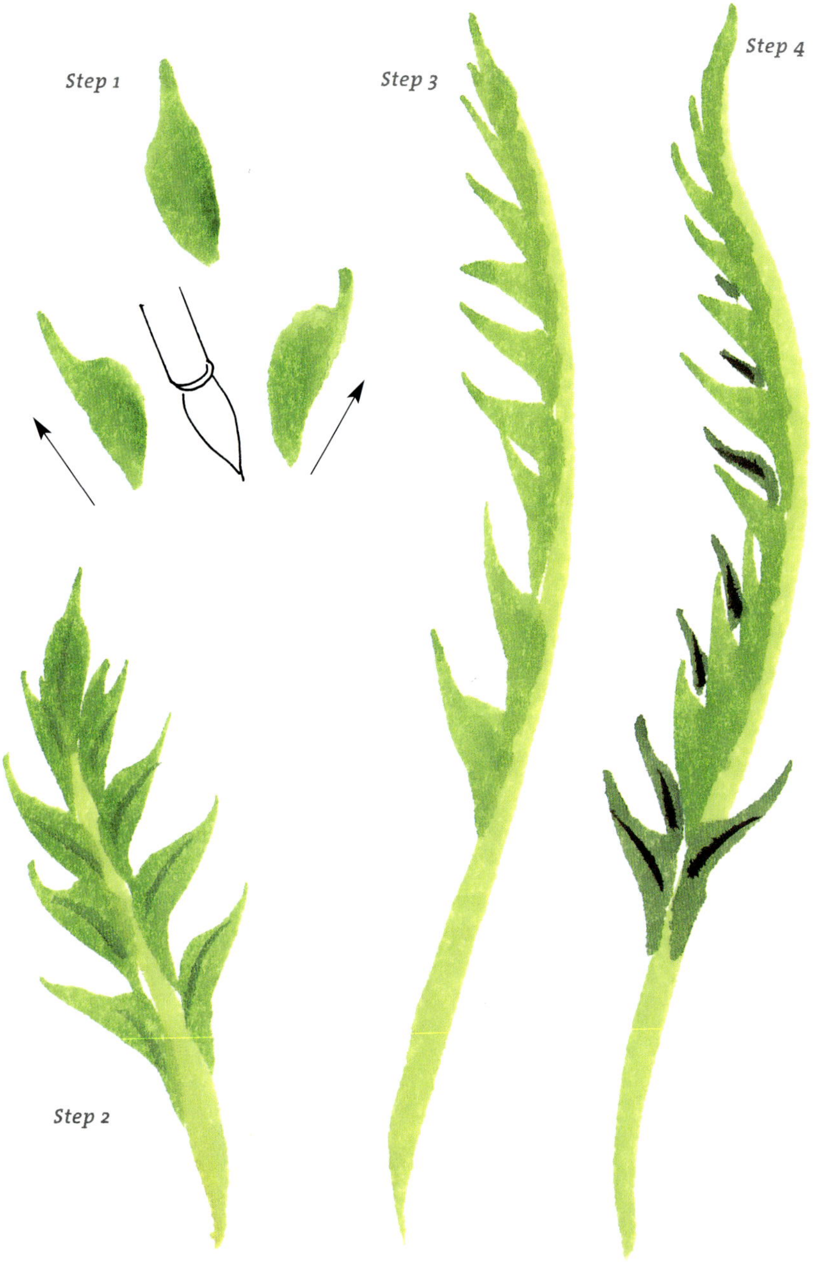

Brushes to use: B1, B2, B4

Step 1 Load **B1** with dark green. Paint a short brushstroke for the top of a leaf stalk, then practise a leaflet at each side of the stalk. Start each leaflet with the brush at an angle to the paper in the position indicated. in the diagram. Press the brush and lift in the direction indicated by the arrows.

Step 2 Load **B2** with light green and paint a long stalk. Paint a short brushstroke at the top of the stalk with dark green. Add leaves along both sides of the stalk with dark green.

Step 3 Paint a long stalk with **B2** and light green. Using sap green, add leaflets with the backs showing .

Step 4 Using dark green add some leaflets showing the upper sides of leaves. Dip **B4** into ink and add veins to the leaflets.

See also

flowers p52
finished painting p144
painting leaves p68

BLEEDING HEART LEAVES

Technical information: Each leaf stalk carries several leaves. The number of leaves is irregular. The shapes of the leaves are also irregular. Some are simple while some have two points and some have three points.

Colour Palette

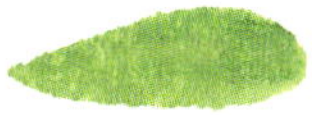

Sap green

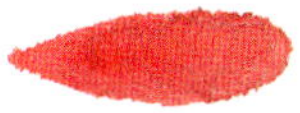

Alizarin crimson

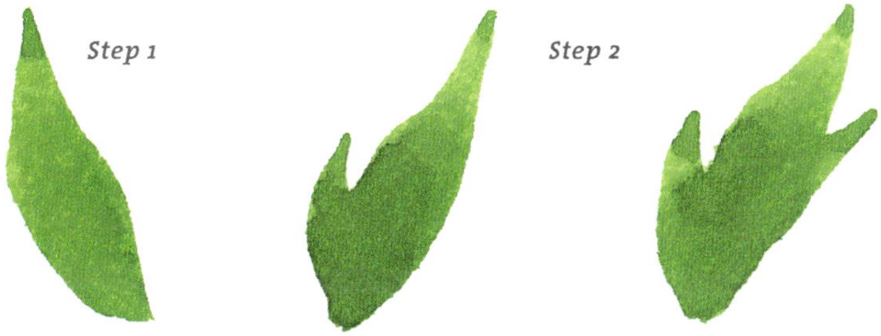

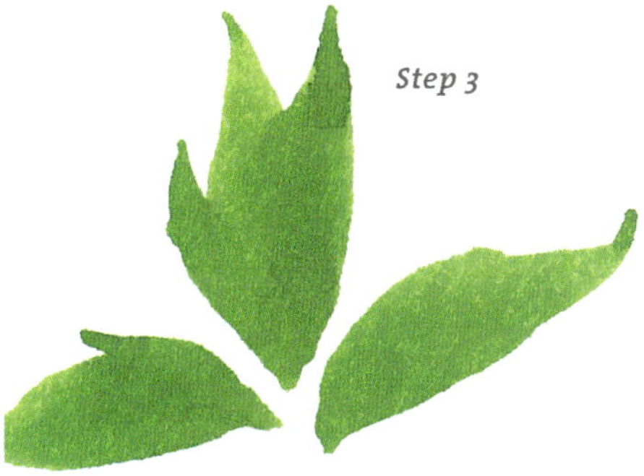

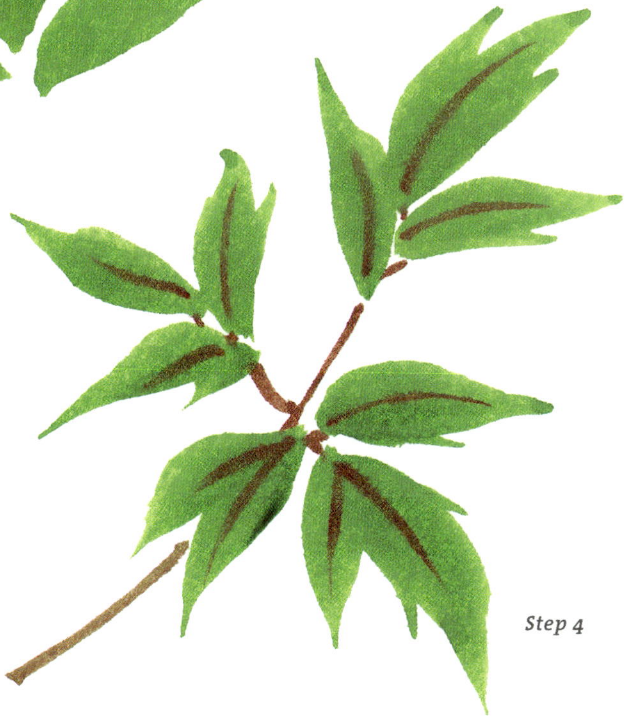

Brushes to use: B1, B3, B4

Step 1 Load **B1** with sap green. Paint a short brushstroke for a leaf.

Step 2 Paint a two-point leaf with one big short brushstroke and one small short brushstroke. Paint a three-point leaf with one big short brushstroke and two small short brushstrokes.

Step 3 Paint a group of leaves.

Step 4 Start with a few groups of leaves. Mix one part of sap green with one part of alizarin crimson. Dip **B3** into this mixture and add the stalks to connect the leaves. Dip **B4** into the mixture and paint veins on the leaves.

See also

press and lift p36
elbow movement p34
using brushes p28

BRUSHSTROKE 4 LONG BRUSHSTROKE

Step 1 Load **B1** with ink. Hold the brush at an angle to the paper with the handle pointing in the direction of the movement. Press.

Step 2 Move the brush with the elbow movement until the brushstroke is almost the desired length. Begin lifting the brush.

Step 3 Finish by moving your arm gradually and by rotating your wrist to lift the brush away from the paper. Do not rush the movement or the brushstroke will not end with a point.

Fig. 1 A long brushstroke with **B1** using ink and press and lift with the elbow movement.

Fig. 2 Use the bigger brushes for painting long brushstrokes because they carry sufficient moisture to sustain the brush-work. **B3** and **B4** carry too little moisture. You will find that they will run dry before you finish a brushstroke.

The long brushstroke is the press and lift brushstroke using the elbow movement. In flower painting, long brushstrokes are used to paint all long leaves such as those of the daffodil, the orchid, and the lily. Wider leaves such as those of tulip and iris require two or more long brush-strokes for each leaf. The leaves of the peony are painted with multi-ple long brushstrokes.

Step 1

Step 2

Step 3

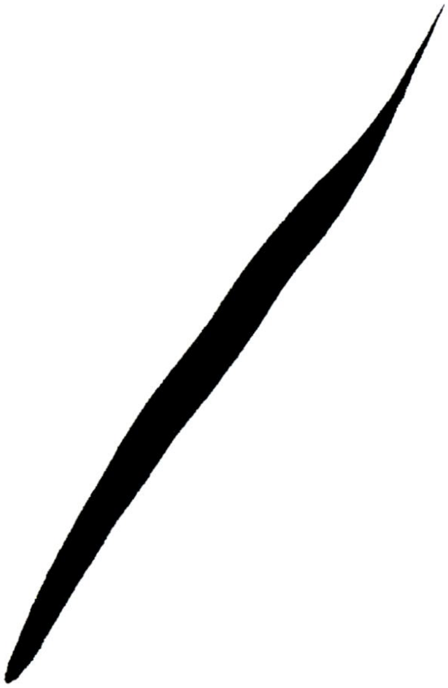

Fig. 1

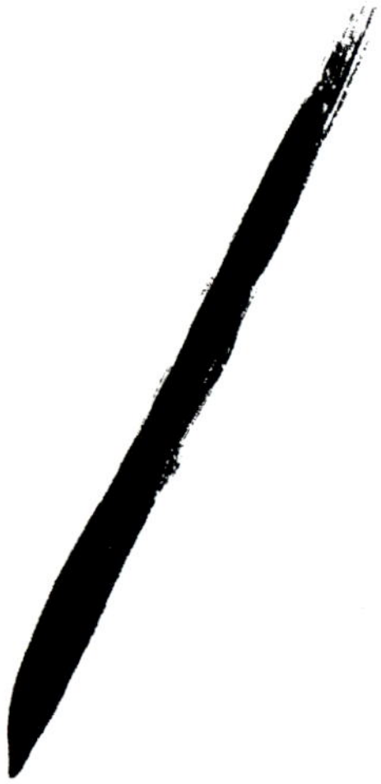

Fig. 2

PRACTISING LONG BRUSHSTROKE

In painting a long brushstroke, always point the handle of the brush in the direction of the brushwork. If the brushwork involves changing direction, change the direction of the handle of the brush also.

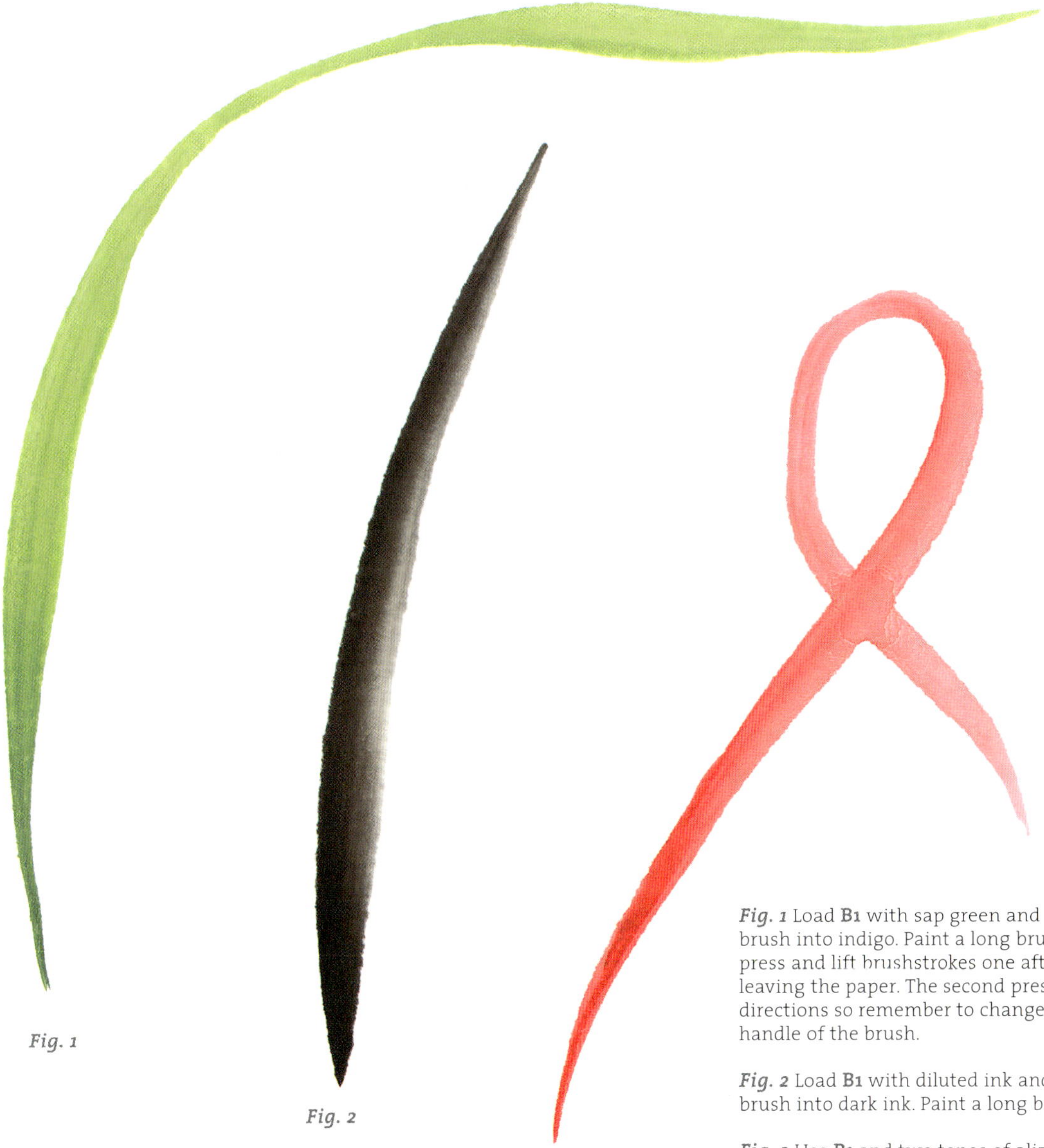

Fig. 1

Fig. 2

Fig. 3

Fig. 1 Load **B1** with sap green and dip the nib of the brush into indigo. Paint a long brushstroke with two press and lift brushstrokes one after another without leaving the paper. The second press and lift changes directions so remember to change the direction of the handle of the brush.

Fig. 2 Load **B1** with diluted ink and dip the nib of the brush into dark ink. Paint a long brushstroke.

Fig. 3 Use **B1** and two tones of alizarin crimson for this long brushstroke.

See also

orchid p40
greens p155

LONG SLENDER LEAVES

Colour Palette

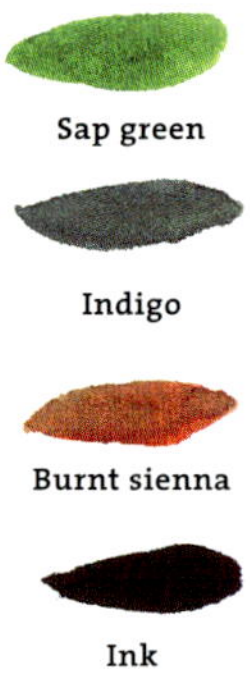

Technical information: Daffodils, orchids, Dutch irises and many other flowers have very long and slender leaves. Each one can be represented by a long brushstroke. Use a medium brush and press lightly to keep the brushstroke thin. You can use a variety of colour loadings.

Brushes to use: B2, B4

Step 1 Load **B2** with sap green. Paint a long thin leaf.

Step 2 Load **B2** with dark green. Paint a long thin leaf.

Step 3 Load **B2** with sap green and dip the nib of the brush into indigo. Paint a long leaf.

Step 4 Load **B2** with dark green and dip the nib of the brush into burnt sienna. Paint a long leaf. Dip **B4** into ink and add veins to some of the leaves.

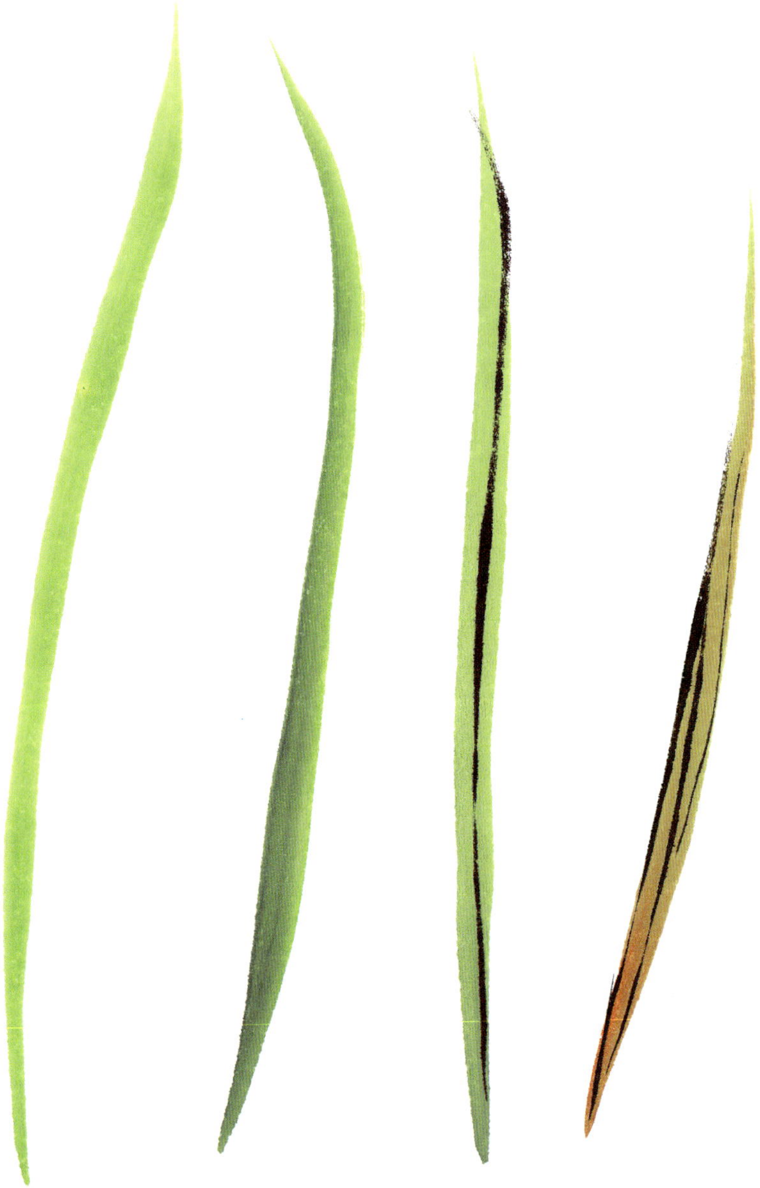

Step 1 *Step 2* *Step 3* *Step 4*

See also

flowers	p124
finished painting	p142
greens	p155

TULIP LEAVES

Technical information: Tulip leaves are broad. Use two or three long brush-strokes to paint a leaf. The leaves usually wrap around the stem. To paint a stem with leaves, you have to paint the stem in sections and add the leaves one at a time after each section of stem.

Colour Palette

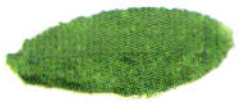

Sap green

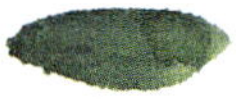

Indigo

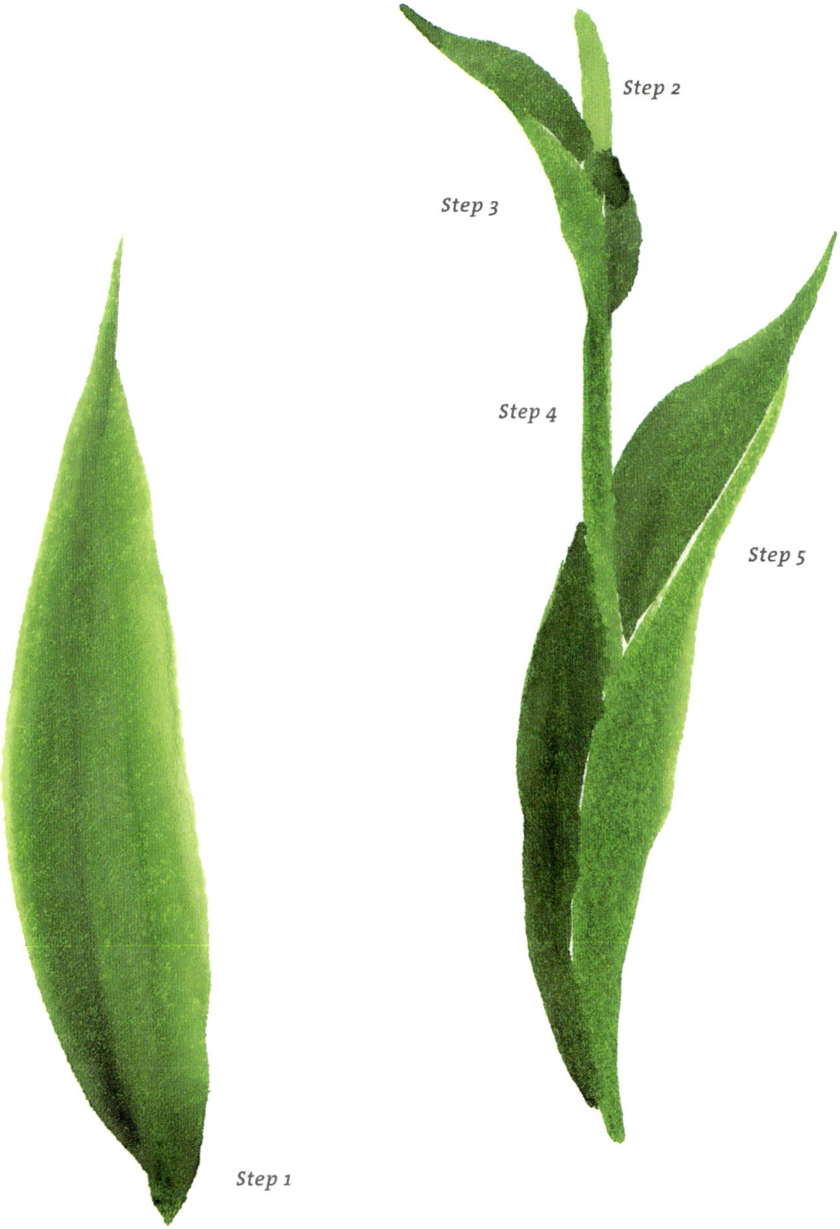

Brushes to use: B1, B2

Step 1 Load **B1** with sap green and dip the nib of the brush into indigo. Paint two long brush-strokes side by side to make up a leaf. Start the leaf from the base.

Step 2 Load **B2** with sap green. Paint the top section of the stem.

Step 3 Use **B1** to add a leaf wrapping around the stem. Use sap green for the back of the leaf.

Step 4 Use **B2** and sap green to add another section of stem under the first leaf.

Step 5 Paint the leaf at the base with **B1**.

See also

flowers p122
finished painting p135
greens p155

IRIS LEAVES

Colour Palette

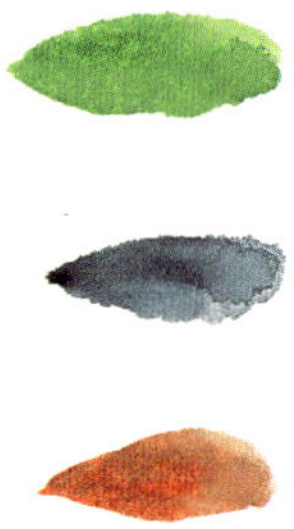

Technical information: Use two or three long brushstrokes to paint an iris leaf. Paint the leaf from the top. The base of a leaf wraps round the next leaf coming out. The new leaf usually points in the opposite direction to the one below it. When you paint a group of leaves, it is better to start with the lowest and oldest one and add successive leaves upwards. Many old leaves have brown tips.

Brushes to use: B1, B3, B4

Step 1 Load **B1** with sap green and dip the nib of the brush into indigo. Paint two long brushstrokes side by side to make an iris leaf. Begin the long brushstrokes from the top.

Step 2 Load **B1** with dark green and dip the nib of the brush into burnt sienna. Paint two long brushstrokes to make an iris leaf. Dip a dry **B3** into burnt sienna and extend the top of the leaf. The dry brush will add the effect of a broken tip.

Step 3 Clean **B1** and reload with sap green. Dip the nib of the brush into indigo and paint two long brush-strokes for a second leaf. This leaf points in the opposite direction to the first one. It comes out of the base of the first leaf.

Step 4 Mix one part of indigo with one part of burnt sienna. Dip **B4** into this mixture and add veins to the leaves.

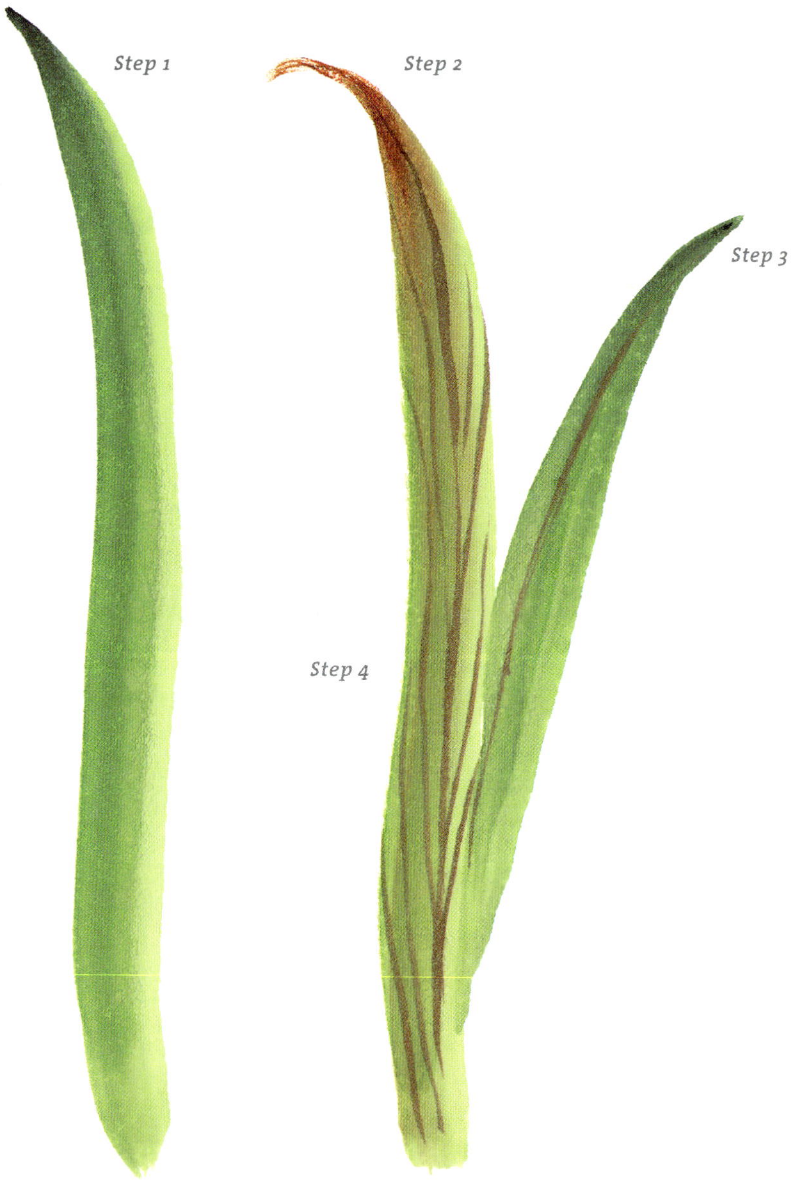

PEONY LEAVES

See also

flowers	p125
finished painting	p147
greens	p155
water line	p155

Technical information: The leaves of the perennial peony are long. A long leaf stalk carries a few groups of leaves. The number of leaves in each group is irregular. Use long brushstrokes to paint each leaf and paint a few leaves to form a group.

The upper side of the peony leaf is dark green. The underside is sap green.

Colour Palette

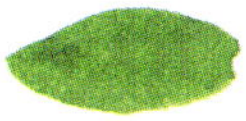

Sap green

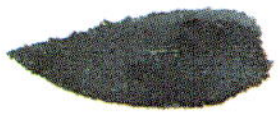

Indigo

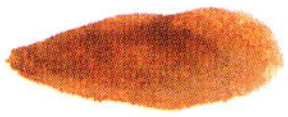

Burnt sienna

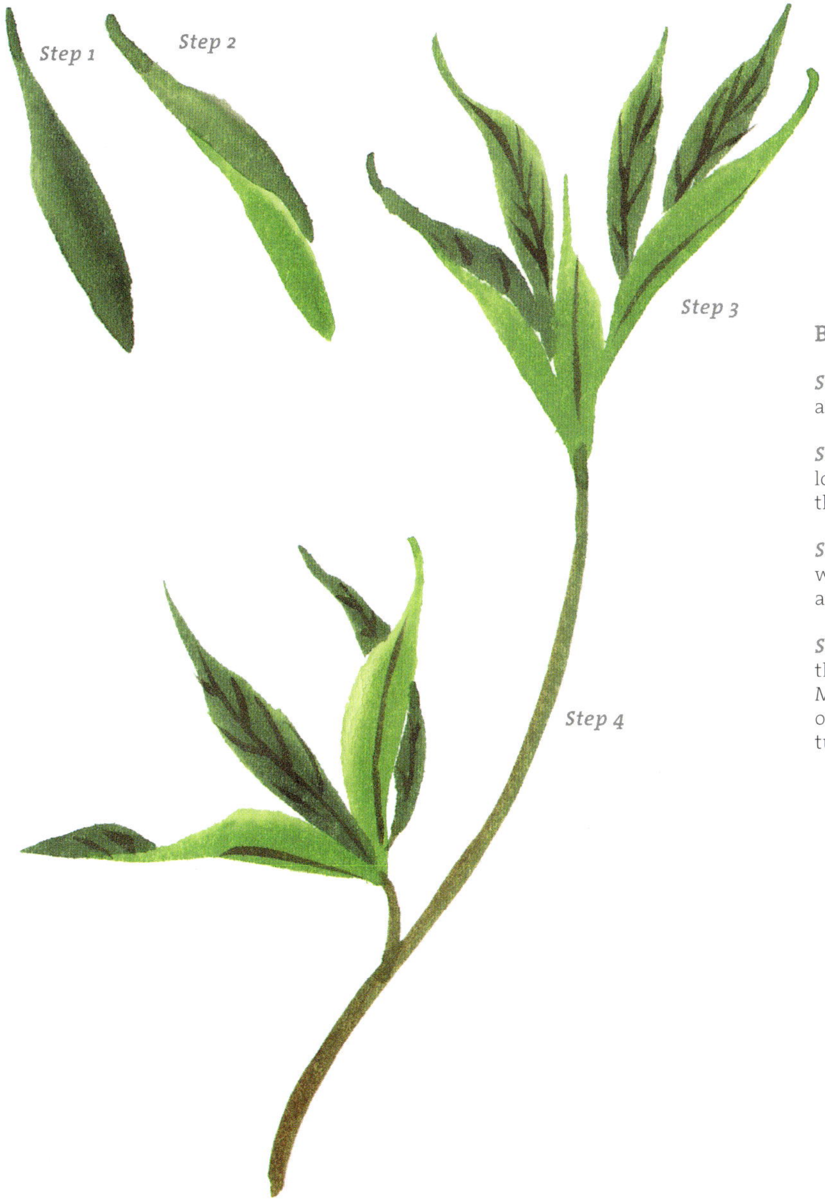

Brushes to use: B1, B2, B3, B4

Step 1 Load **B1** with dark green. Paint a peony leaf with a long brushstroke.

Step 2 Paint a folding leaf with two long brushstrokes. Use sap green for the underside.

Step 3 Use a clean damp **B3** to draw a water line. Paint groups of leaves along the water line.

Step 4 Use **B2** and olive green to add the long stalk and the short stalks. Mix one part of indigo with one part of burnt sienna. Dip **B4** into this mixture and paint the veins of the leaves.

See also

flowers p54
long slender leaves p86

PROJECT 3
PAINTING DAFFODILS

Technical information: We have seen how to paint the flowers and leaves of daffodils. In this project the daffodil flowers are painted with longer and pointed petals. Use a single short brushstroke for each petal. These daffodils with longer petals make a more expressive painting.

Colour Palette

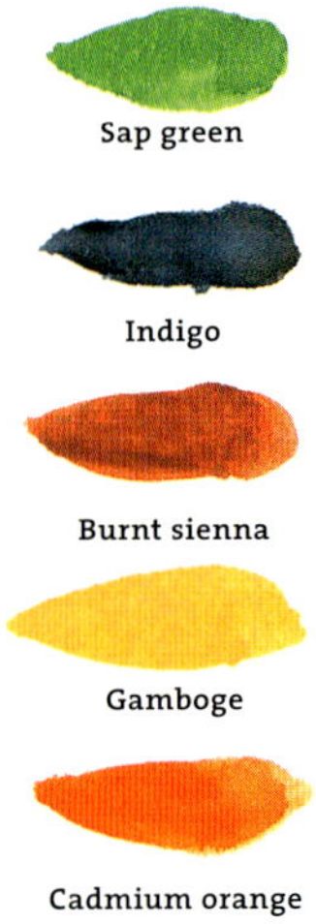

Step 1

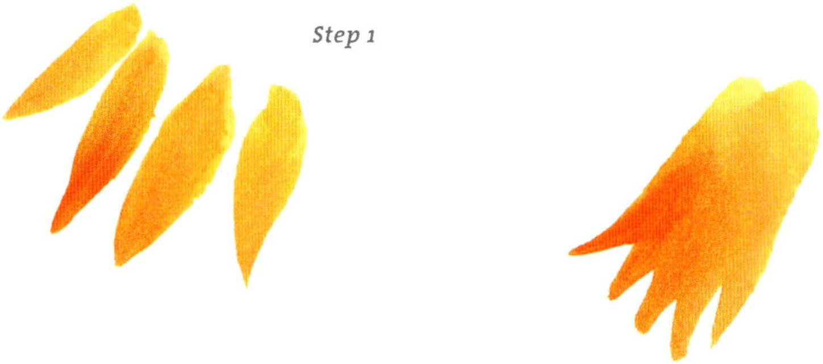

Brushes to use: B1, B2, B3, B4

Step 1 Load **B1** with gamboge and dip the nib of the brush into cadmium orange. Paint the trumpet of a flower using multiple long dots.

Step 2 Rinse the tip of **B1** to get rid of the cadmium orange. Reload with gamboge. Paint six petals to make up a flower. Use a single short brushstroke for each petal. Dip **B4** into cadmium orange. Paint a vein for each petal.

Step 3 A daffodil bud is made up of two short brushstrokes.

Step 2

Step 3

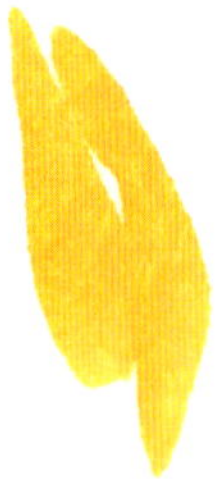

A finished painting of daffodils

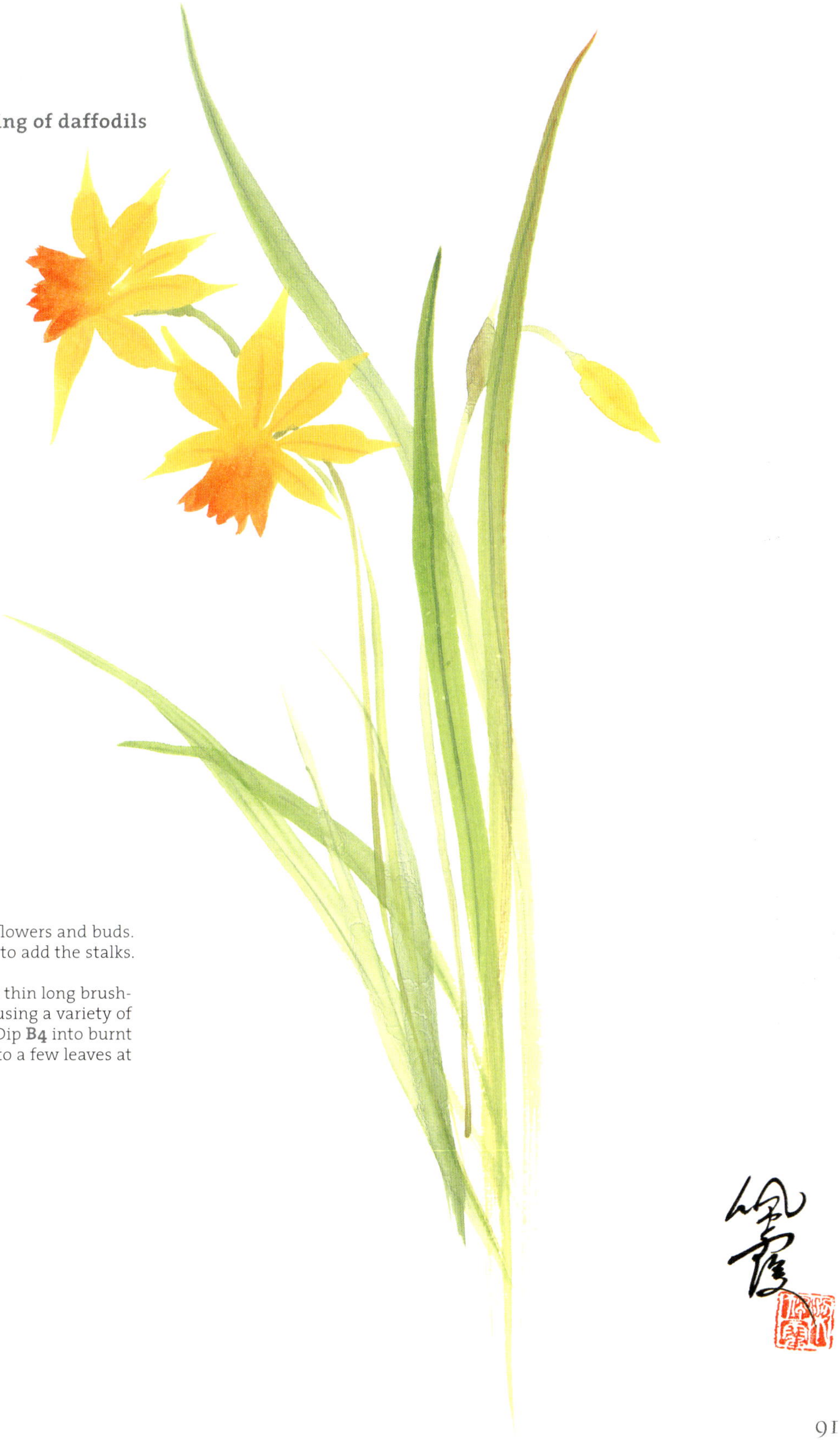

Step 1 Start with the flowers and buds. Use **B3** and sap green to add the stalks.

Step 2 Use **B2** to paint thin long brush-strokes for the leaves using a variety of colour combinations. Dip **B4** into burnt sienna and add veins to a few leaves at the front.

See also

elbow movement p34
using the brush p28

BRUSHSTROKE 5
SIDE BRUSHSTROKE

The side brushstroke is usually recognized as the brushstroke for painting the bamboo. Hold the brush with the handle pointing to your right. Press the brush and move up or down with elbow movement. The result is a brushwork that looks like a square or a rectangle. The angle of the brush to the paper affects the size of the brushwork – the lower the angle, the bigger the brush-stroke. The size of the brush also affects the size of the brushstroke – the bigger the size of the brush, the bigger the brushstroke.

A bamboo trunk is made up of a column of separate side brushstrokes. A tree trunk or a branch is made up of side brushstrokes made one after another without gaps in between. You can vary the thickness of this brushstroke to create thin stalks, or tree branches, or thick tree trunks.

Fig. 1 Load **B1** with ink. Hold the brush at an angle of 45 degrees to the paper. Press, then move downwards or upwards with elbow movement to paint a side brushstroke. A side brushstroke painted with elbow movement will have straight edges. Tree trunks formed with these brushstrokes will have strength. A side brushstroke using wrist movements will curve.

Fig. 2 A side brushstroke using **B2** at an angle of 45 degrees to the paper.

Fig. 3 Hold **B2** at an angle less than 45 degrees to the paper. The result is a bigger brushstroke.

Fig. 4 Hold **B2** at an angle more than 45 degrees to the paper. The result is a thinner brushstroke.

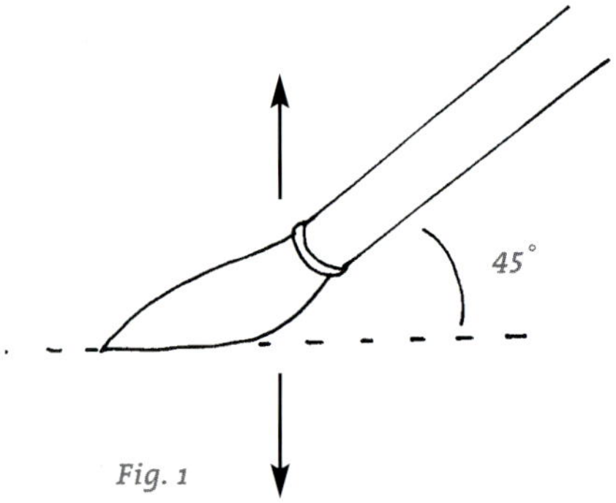

Fig. 1

Fig. 2

Fig. 3

Fig. 4

PRACTISING THE SIDE BRUSHSTROKE

A bigger brush creates bigger side brushstrokes. For really wide brush-works, you can paint two or three side brushstrokes next to each other. Try some side brushstrokes with two-tone and two-colour loadings on the brush.

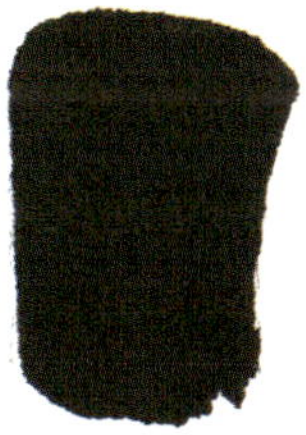

Fig. 1

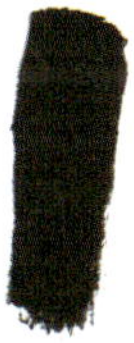

Fig. 2

Fig. 3

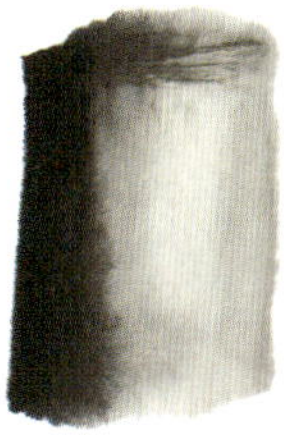

Fig. 4

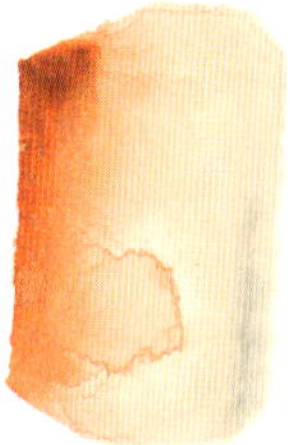

Fig. 5

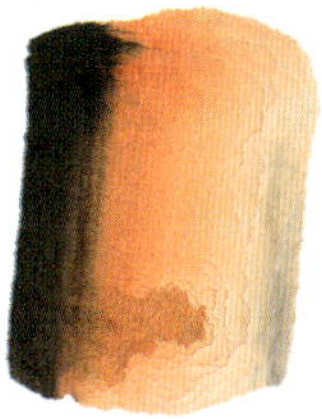

Fig. 6

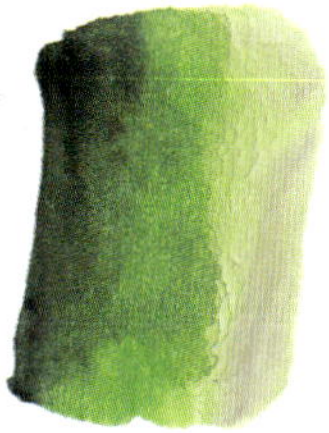

Fig. 7

Fig. 1 **B1** is a bigger brush. It makes a bigger side brushstroke.

Fig. 2 **B3** is a smaller brush. It makes a smaller side brushstroke.

Fig. 3 Use two side brushstrokes side by side to create an extra wide side brushstroke. This technique is used to paint big bamboo or big tree trunks. You can achieve the same result with a very big brush.

Fig. 4 Load **B2** with diluted ink and dip the nib of the brush into dark ink. Paint a side brushstroke with two tones of ink.

Fig. 5 Load **B2** with two tones of burnt sienna. Paint a side brush-stroke. This two-tone loading of burnt sienna is one of the ways of painting tree trunks and branches.

Fig. 6 Load **B2** with burnt sienna and dip the nib of the brush into ink. Paint a side brushstroke. This two-colour loading is another way of painting tree trunks and branches.

Fig. 7 Load **B2** with sap green and dip the nib of the brush into indigo. Paint a side brushstroke. This is one of the many two-colour loadings for painting bamboo trunks. Other ways include loading the brush with dark green and dipping the nib of the brush into ink, or loading the brush with burnt sienna and dipping the nib of the brush into sap green.

See also

leaves	p73
project 4	p98
finished painting	p99
greens	p155

BAMBOO TRUNKS

Colour Palette

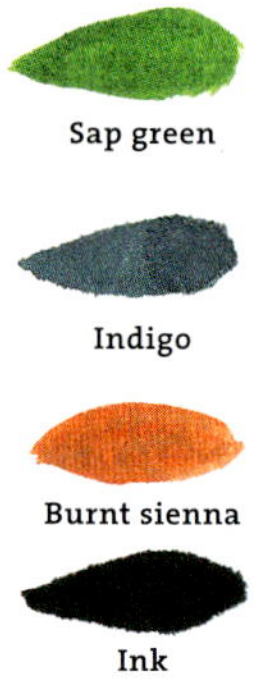

Technical information: A bamboo trunk is very upright. Use separate side brushstrokes one on top of another to build up a bamboo trunk. Leave a little space between two successive side brushstrokes and fill it in with a joint.

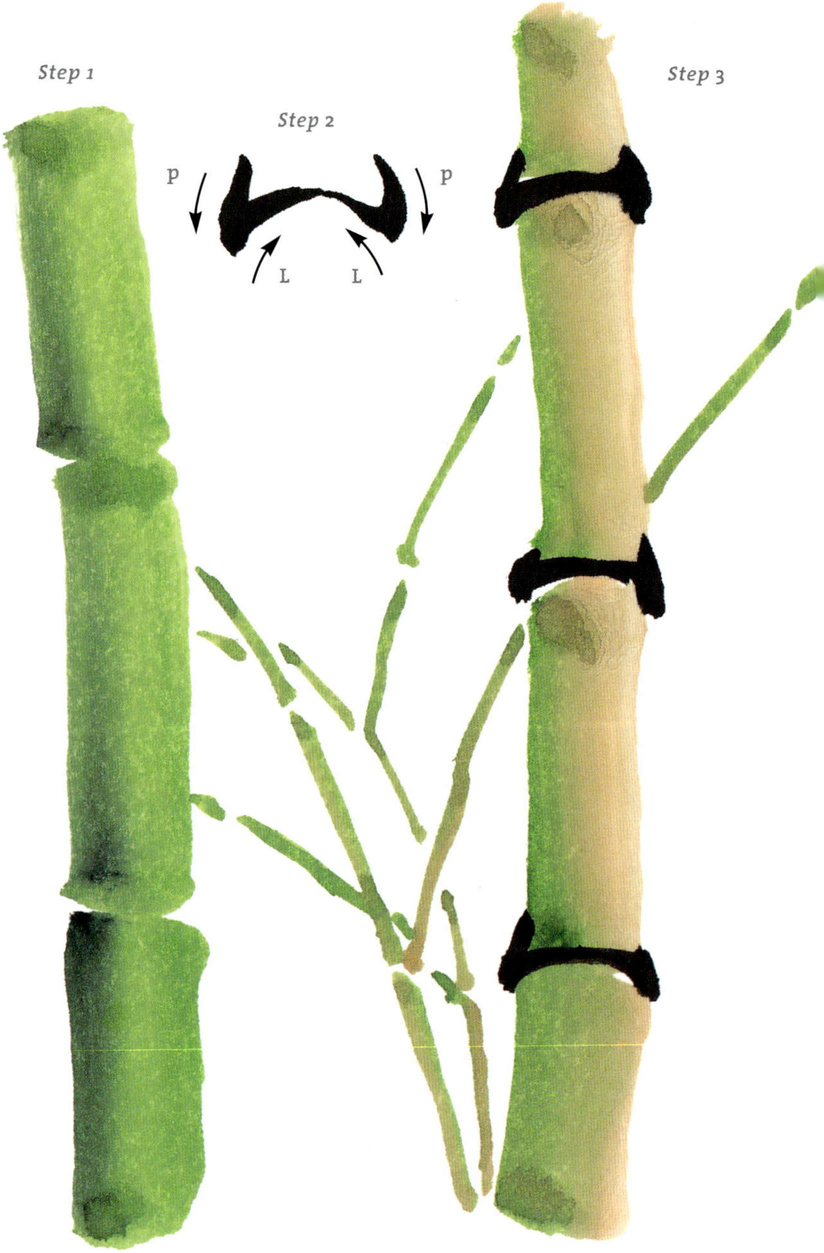

Brushes to use: B1, B2

Step 1 Load **B1** with sap green and dip the nib of the brush into indigo. Paint side brushstrokes in a column to represent the sections of a bamboo trunk. You can paint the side brushstroke upwards or downwards. Leave a little space between two successive side brushstrokes. Use this colour combination for young bamboos.

Step 2 Dip **B1** into ink and add the joints in between two successive sections. Each joint is made up of two press and lift brushworks, as illustrated.

Step 3 Load **B1** with burnt sienna and dip the nib of the brush into sap green. Paint side brushstrokes for the trunk of an old bamboo. Use ink to add the joints. Load **B2** with sap green and dip the nib of the brush into burnt sienna. Add some shoots to the trunk.

See also
using the brush p28
elbow movement p34

TRUNKS AND BRANCHES OF YOUNGER TREES

Technical information: You can paint a tree trunk or a branch with a continuous side brushstroke. Make regular short stops without lifting the brush away from the paper. The stops make the tree trunk more rugged looking. You can change the direction of the trunk at the stops. The stops also mark the places where branches come out.

Colour Palette

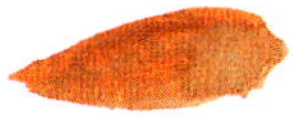

Burnt sienna

Ink

Step 1 *Step 2*

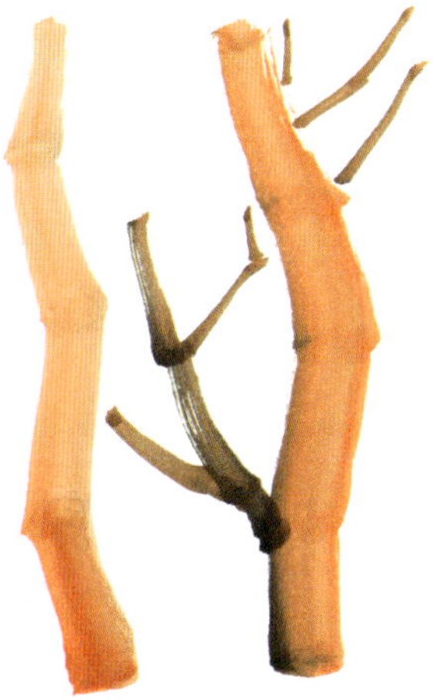

Short stop →

Brushes to use: B1, B2

Step 1 Load **B1** with two tones of burnt sienna. Hold the brush at an angle to the paper. Paint the tree trunk with a long side brushstroke with regular short stops. Do not stop for too long or the paper will absorb too much moisture at the stops, making the stops too big.

Step 2 Load **B1** with burnt sienna and dip the nib of the brush into ink. Paint a tree trunk. Add branches at the stops. You can paint the branches with **B2**, or **B1** held at a higher angle to the paper.

See also
using the brush p28
elbow movement p34

OLD TREE TRUNKS

Technical information: The texture of an old tree trunk is very rugged. You can use a dry brush to paint such a trunk. Alternatively, use the Mountain and Horse brush to paint it.

Colour Palette

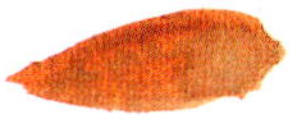

Burnt sienna

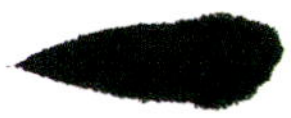

Ink

Brush to use: B1

Step 1 Wipe **B1** dry. Dip the brush into burnt sienna. Do not load the brush heavily with colour. Always wipe off excess moisture at the edge of the mixing dish if you are painting dry brushwork. Hold the brush at a low angle to the paper. Paint a tree trunk with a long side brushstroke. You can start the tree trunk from the base or from the top.

Step 2 Wipe **B1** dry. Dip the brush into diluted ink. Paint an old tree trunk. Dip the brush into dark ink. Holding the brush at a higher angle to the paper, Add some branches to the tree trunk. Add a few dots with dark ink to the trunk. These dots usually add more texture to an old tree.

Step 1

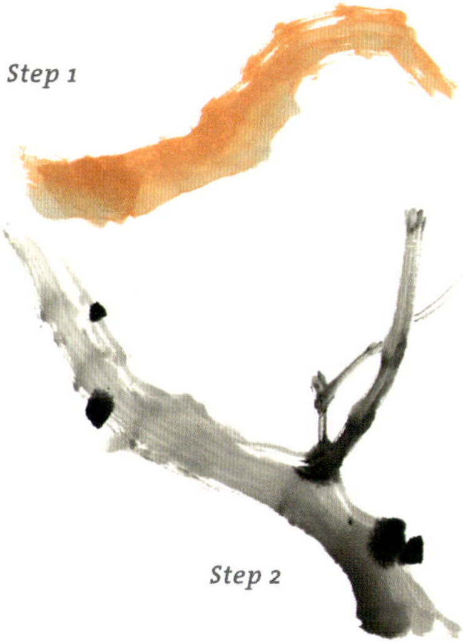

Step 2

See also

elbow movement p34
using the brush p28

STALKS

Colour Palette

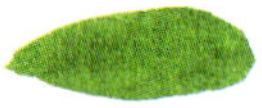

Sap green

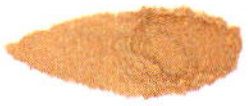

Burnt sienna

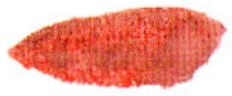

Alizarin crimson

To paint thin stalks, hold the brush in a vertical position and use the tip of the brush to paint. **B3** makes thinner stalks, **B2** makes thicker ones. If you hold **B3** at an angle, you can make thicker stalks with side brushstrokes.

Most flower stalks are smooth. Paint these smooth stalks with non-stopped brushwork using the elbow movement.

Other stalks have leaf joints, flower stalk joints or small branches along the sides. Paint these with elbow movements with regular short stops.

Colour adds character to the stalks. For example, a sap green geraniums flower stalk is almost crimson at the top. A brown chrysanthemum flower stalk is green near the flower head. Observing the flowers closely will give you ideas on how to load your brush with colour.

Brushes to use: B2, B3

Step 1 Load **B3** with sap green and dip the nib of the brush into alizarin crimson. Hold the brush in a vertical position. Paint a smooth geranium stalk from the top.

Step 2 Load **B2** with burnt sienna and dip the nib of the brush into sap green. Hold the brush in a vertical position. Paint a chrysanthemum flower stalk with regular short stops. Do not stop for too long or the paper will absorb too much moisture, making the stops too big.

Step 3 Load **B2** with sap green and dip the nib of the brush into alizarin crimson. Hold the brush at a high angle to the paper and use a long side brushstroke to paint a wider stalk with regular short stops. Lilies and phlox have stalks like this.

Step 4 Load **B2** with burnt sienna and dip the nib into sap green. Hold the brush at a high angle to the paper and paint a stalk with a long side brushstroke with regular short stops. The stops are places where the other little stalks come out. Hold **B2** vertically and add small thin stalks to the thicker one.

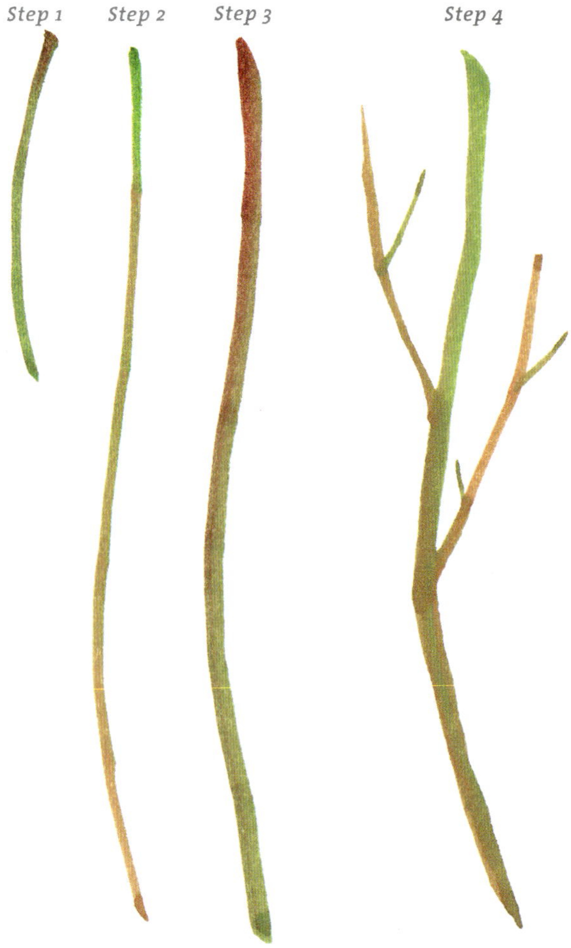

CLIMBERS

See also

elbow movement **p34**
wrist movement **p32**

Technical information: Flowers such as wisteria, honeysuckle and clematis are climbers. The young shoots of these climbers usually wrap around anything they come into contact with. They become woody in their second year of life. Old trunks are usually very rough in texture and braid with one another. Use a dry brush to paint old trunks with side brushstrokes.

Colour Palette

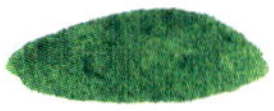

Sap green

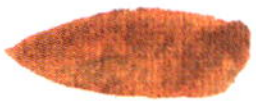

Burnt sienna

Ink

A young climber

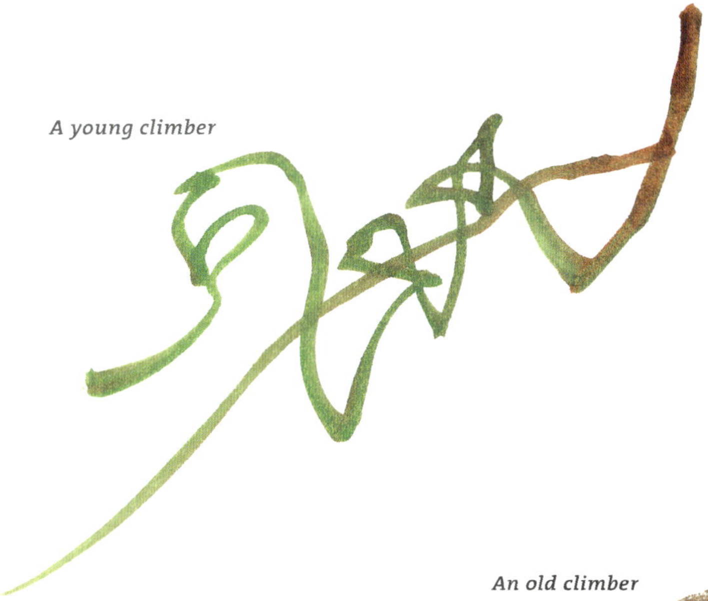

An old climber

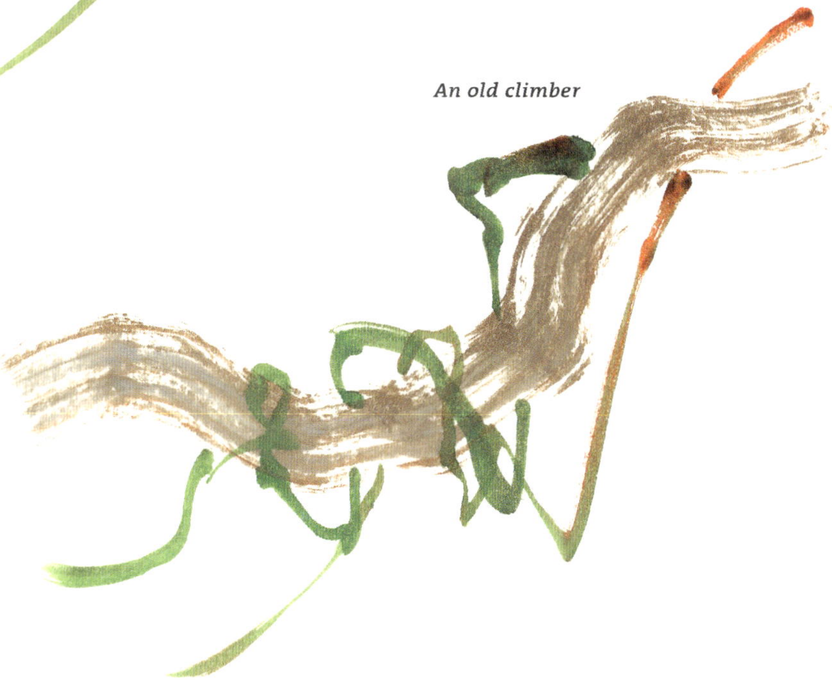

Brushes to use: B1, B2

A young climber

Load **B1** with sap green and dip the nib of the brush into burnt sienna. Hold the brush in a vertical position. Paint the curly shoots of a climber with combined elbow and wrist movement. Move with elbow movement and paint the curly bits by rotating the wrist.

An old climber

Mix burnt sienna with a tiny bit of ink to make it darker. Dilute part of the mixture with water. Wipe **B1** dry and dip into the diluted mixture. Paint an old trunk of a climber. Load **B2** with sap green and dip the nib of the brush into the undiluted mixture. Paint some young shoots on the old trunk.

See also

leaves p73
trunks p94

PROJECT 4 PAINTING BAMBOO

Colour Palette

Ink

A bamboo trunk is very upright and is hollow inside. Such characteristics make the bamboo a symbol of honesty. The Chinese use the bamboo to represent a respectable gentleman of great virtue, one who does not waver under the tremendous pressure of the world with all its corruptions and influences. Try to bear this in mind when you paint the bamboo. A trunk should be upright and strong. The composition should be simple.

You have seen the painting of bamboo leaves and trunks in colour. However, the most popular way of painting a bamboo is still using ink. In this project a bamboo is painted using ink.

Brushes to use: B1, B2, B3

Step 1 Load **B1** with diluted ink and dip the nib of the brush into dark ink. Practise painting some side brushstrokes to represent the sections of a bamboo trunk. Use dark ink to add the joints.

Step 2 Dip **B2** into ink and practise painting some thin shoots.

Step 3 Load **B1** with dark ink and practise painting bamboo leaves.

Step 4 Clean **B1** and load again with diluted ink. Practise painting leaves in diluted ink.

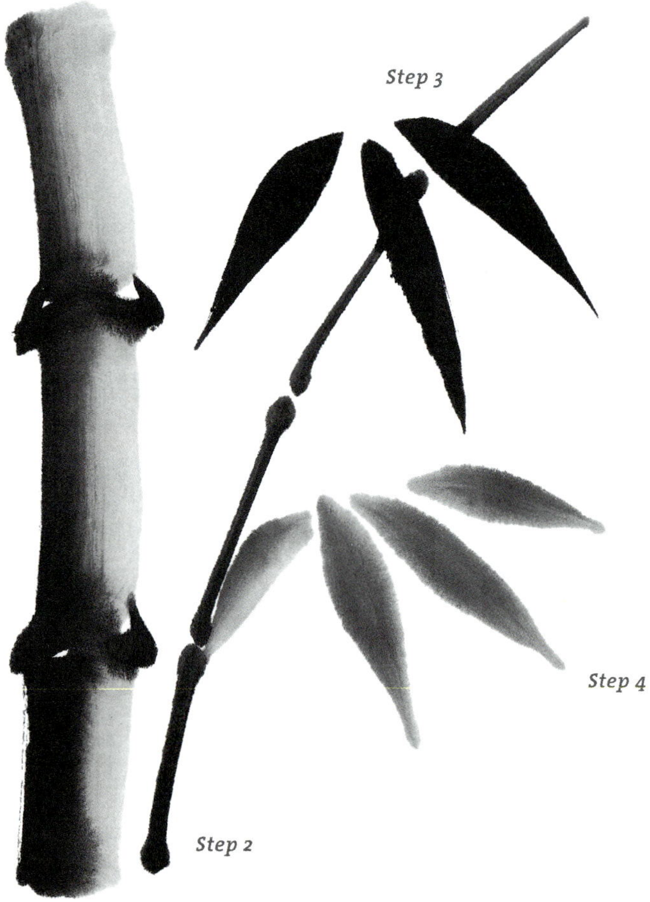

A PAINTING OF BAMBOO IN INK

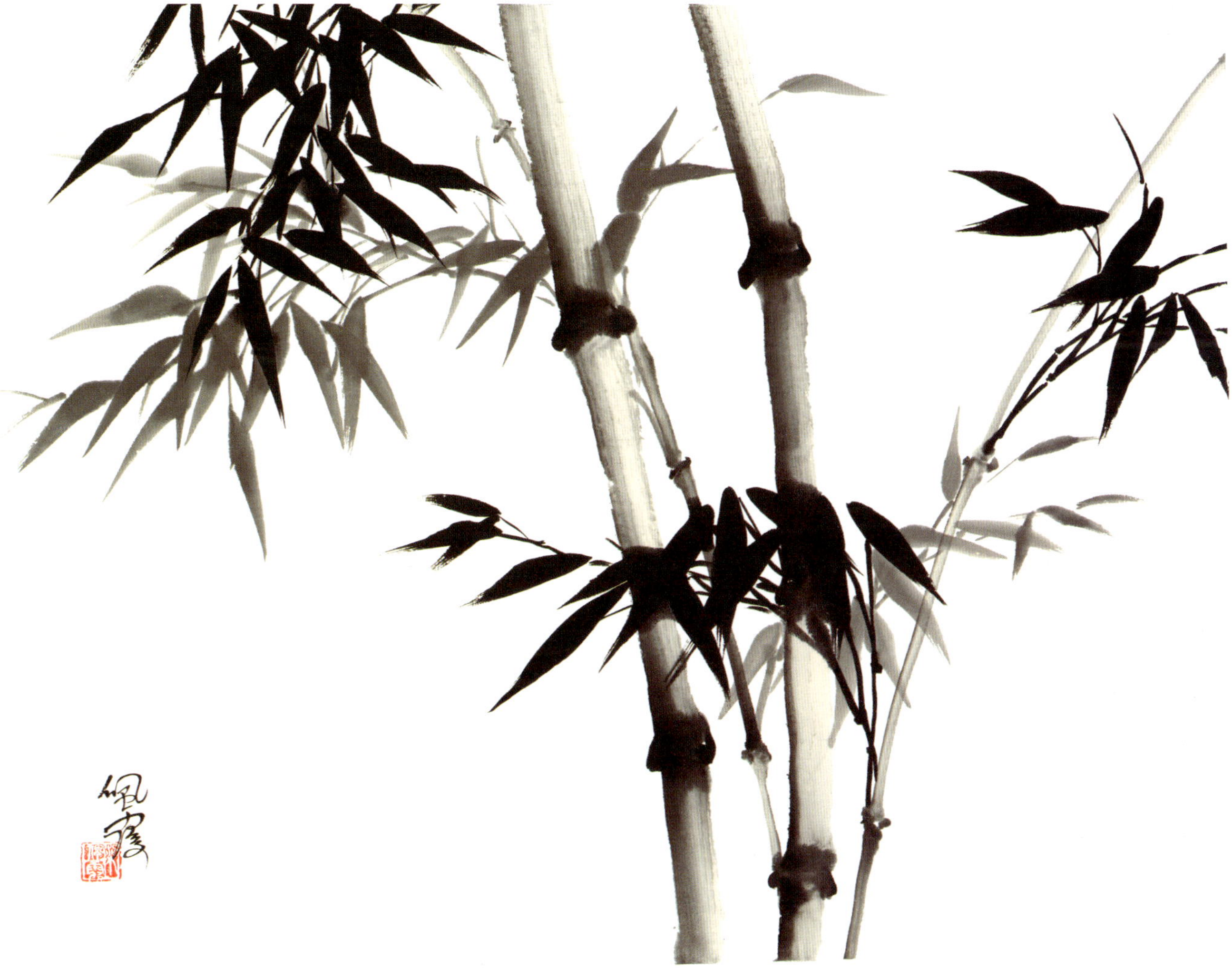

Step 1 Paint the two main trunks with **B1**.

Step 2 Paint some longer shoots with **B2**.

Step 3 Use **B1** to paint the leaves. Start with the dark leaves. Then add the leaves with diluted ink.

Step 4 Use **B3** and dark ink to add the short shoots connecting the leaves to the main shoots.

See also
wrist movement **p32**

BRUSHSTROKE 6
FAN BRUSHSTROKE

Fan brushstroke is the most popular brushstroke for painting flowers. For small flowers such as plum blossom, wisteria and geraniums, a single fan brushstroke makes a petal. Bigger flowers such as hibiscus require two fan brushstrokes to paint a petal. Leaves of geraniums are painted with multiple fan brushstrokes.

The size of a fan brushstroke varies according to the angle of the brush to the paper – the lower the angle, the bigger the brushwork. However, it is more effective to use different sizes of brush to create different sizes of brushwork.

Control the width of the brushstroke by how far you move the neck of the brush. A small movement results in a narrow brushstroke while a bigger movement makes a wider brushstroke.

Fig. 1 Fully load **B2** with ink or colour. Hold the brush at an angle to the paper as illustrated. Using wrist movement, move the neck of the brush only and keep the nib of the brush still. The resulting brush-work is fan shaped. I start the brushstroke from the left, but you can also start from the right and move to the left. The result will be the same.

Fig. 2 A fan brushstroke using **B2**.

Fig. 3 A smaller movement with the brush makes a narrow fan brushstroke.

Fig. 4 A bigger movement results in a wider fan brushstroke.

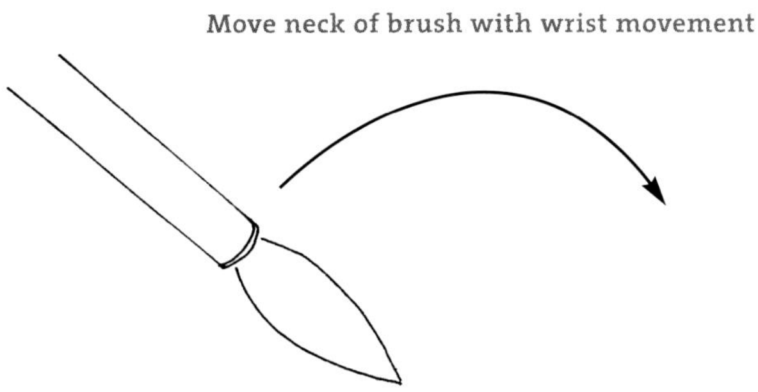

Fig. 1

Fig. 2

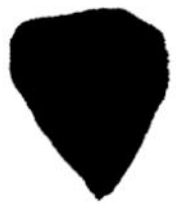

Fig. 3

Fig. 4

PRACTISING FAN BRUSHSTROKE

The size of the brush, the angle at which you hold it, the amount of movement you make on the neck of the brush and the number of brushstrokes you use to build up a shape, all contribute to the size of the final brushwork. Combined with two-tone and multi-colour loadings, you can achieve a variety of effects.

Fig. 1

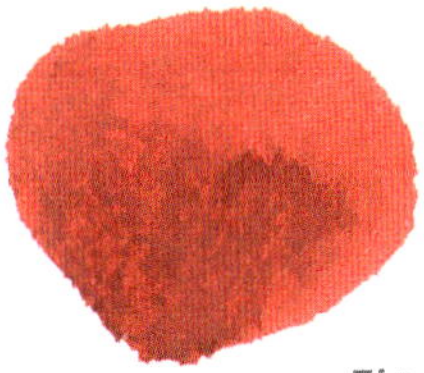

Fig. 2

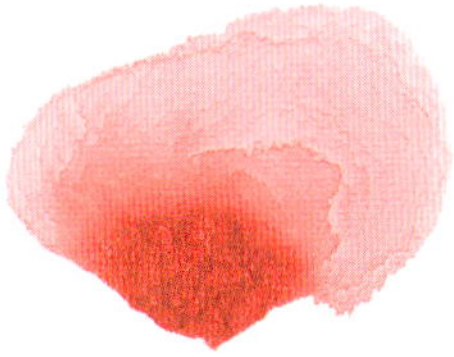

Fig. 3

Fig. 4

Fig. 5

Fig. 1 Load **B3** with ink and paint a fan brushstroke. **B3** makes a small fan brushstroke.

Fig. 2 Load **B1** with alizarin crimson. Paint a fan brushstroke. **B1** makes a big fan brushstroke.

Fig. 3 Load **B2** with two tones of alizarin crimson. Paint a fan brushstroke with a two-tone effect.

Fig. 4 Load **B2** with sap green and dip the nib of the brush into indigo. Paint a fan brushstroke with a two-colour effect.

Fig. 5 Load **B2** with sap green and dip the nib of the brush into indigo. Paint two fan brushstrokes side by side to make a bigger brushwork. Some bigger petals and leaves need more than one fan brushstroke to make up the shape.

See also

branches p95
project 5 p108
water line p155

PLUM BLOSSOM

Colour Palette

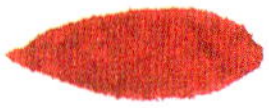

Alizarin crimson

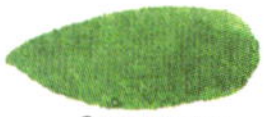

Sap green

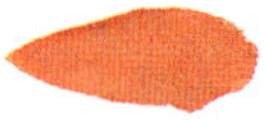

Burnt sienna

Ink

Technical Information: Use a single fan brushstroke to paint each petal. The petals are not wide so paint with a small movement. However, if you are creating a painting with a large number of blossoms, it will be more practical to use dots for the flowers instead.

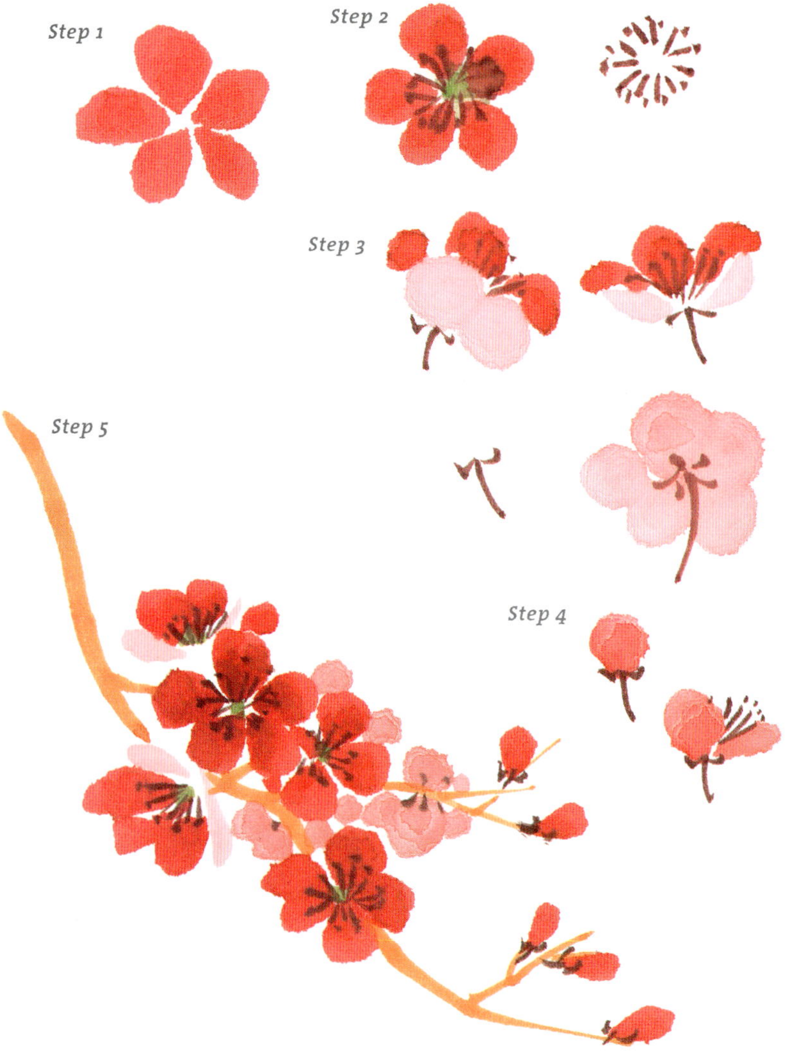

Brushes to use: B2, B3, B4

Step 1 Load **B2** with alizarin crimson. Paint a single fan brushstroke for a petal. Use a small movement so that the petal is not wide. Paint five petals for a flower.

Step 2 Mix a tiny bit of ink into alizarin crimson to make a dark red. Dip **B4** into this mixture and paint the centre of the flower. Dip **B3** into sap green and add a dot to the centre of the flower.

Step 3 Use diluted alizarin crimson to paint the backs of the petals. Paint flowers with the backs of some petals showing. Dip **B4** into the mixture in step 2 and paint the flower stalks, sepals and centres.

Step 4 Use a single fan brushstroke to paint a bud and two to paint a bud about to open. Add sepals and flower stalks to the buds.

Step 5 Use a clean damp **B3** to draw a water line to represent a branch of plum blossom. Paint some flowers at the front along the water line with **B2**. Remember to use diluted alizarin crimson for the backs of petals. Add the centres as described in step 2. Clean **B2** and reload with burnt sienna. Paint the sections of the main branch where it is visible. Use **B3** and burnt sienna to add shorter branches. Add some more flowers at the back.

GERANIUMS FLOWER HEADS

See also
leaves **p106**
finished painting **p132**

A single geraniums flower is very similar to a single plum blossom flower. Use a single fan brushstroke with a small movement to paint a petal.

Colour Palette

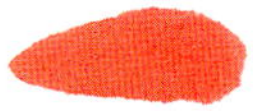

Cadmium red

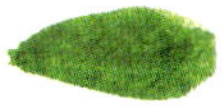

Sap green

Step 1

Step 2

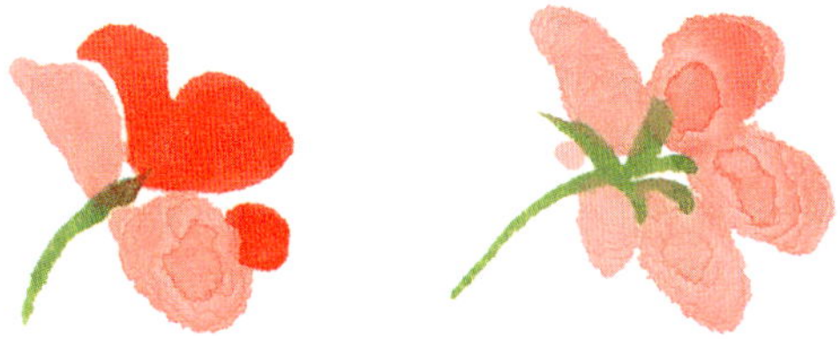

Step 3

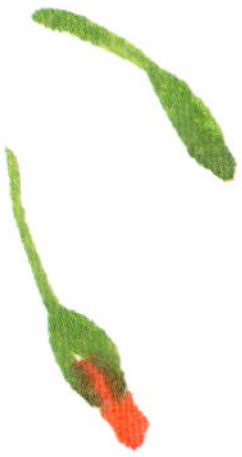

Step 4

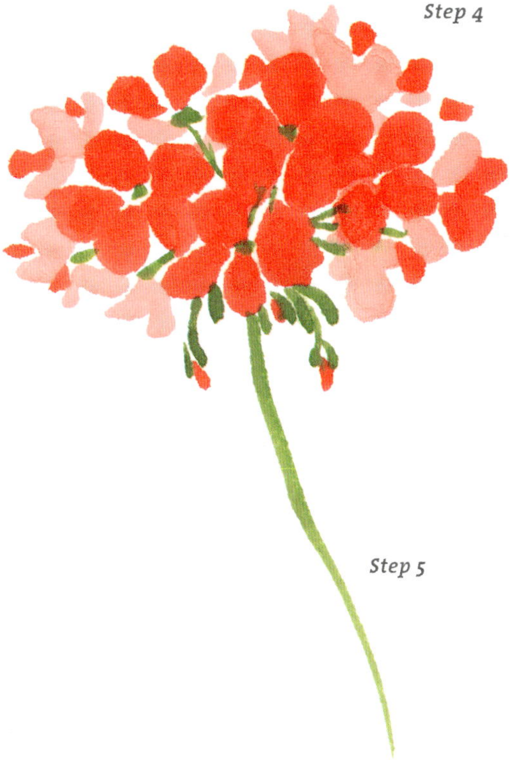

Step 5

Brushes to use: B2, B3

Step 1 Load **B2** with cadmium red and paint five fan brushstrokes to make up a single geraniums flower. Dip **B3** into sap green and paint a dot as centre.

Step 2 Paint flowers with the backs of some petals showing. Use diluted cadmium red for the backs of the petals. Dip **B3** into sap green and add the sepals and a short stalk to each flower.

Step 3 Dip **B3** into sap green and paint a closed bud with a small short brushstroke. Add a short stalk to the bud. Paint a short stalk and two sepals of a bud about to open. Dip **B3** into cadmium red and add the tip of the bud.

Step 4 Start a flower head with some flowers at the front. Keep the shape of the flower head round. Add some flowers at the back. Remember to use diluted cadmium red for the backs of petals. Use **B3** and sap green to add dots as centres to each flower facing the front. Each flower has a short stalk radiating from the centre of the flower head. Use **B3** and sap green to add the short stalks where they are visible.

Step 5 Buds are usually hanging down at the base of the flower head. Paint a few buds following the instructions given in step 3. Use **B3** and sap green to add the main stalk to the flower head.

See also

leaves p72
climbers p97
finished painting p137

WISTERIA FLOWER HEAD

Colour Palette

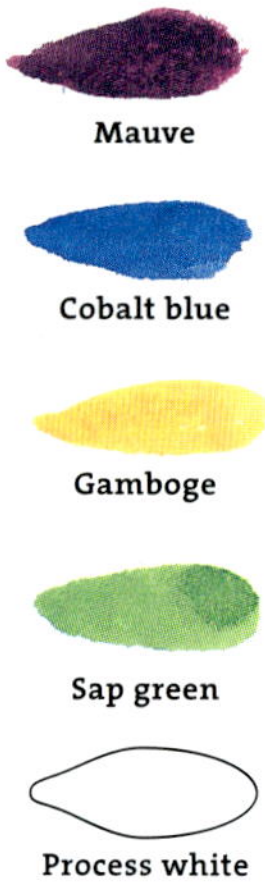

Technical information: Each flower is made up of fan brushstrokes, long dots and dots. Buds are painted with small short brushstrokes or dots.

Brushes to use: B2, B3, B4

Step 1 Mix two parts of mauve with one part of cobalt blue to make a purple. Dip a little bit of this mixture into process white to make a light purple. Load **B2** with the light purple and dip the nib of the brush into purple. Paint a fan brushstroke with a small movement.

Step 2 Each flower has two bigger upper petals and two small lower petals. Paint two fan brushstrokes as described in step 1 for the two upper petals. Dip **B2** into purple and add the two lower petals with long dots. Dip **B3** into gamboge and add one dot to each of the upper petals.

Step 3 Each flower is connected to a centre stalk with short stalks. To paint the stalks, use **B3** and sap green. Start with the centre stalk. Then add short side stalks.

Step 4 To paint a young flower head only with buds, use **B3** and sap green to start painting a centre stalk. Add short stalks along the centre stalk. Dip **B3** into purple and add a bud to each short stalk. The buds along the upper part of the stalk are bigger and decrease in size as they move downwards. Use small short brushstrokes for bigger buds and dots for smaller buds.

Step 5 To paint a flower head, start with the flowers at the front. Then add more flowers at the back. Add sections of the centre stalk and the short stalks connecting each flower to the centre stalk where they are visible. Add some buds to the lower end of the centre stalk.

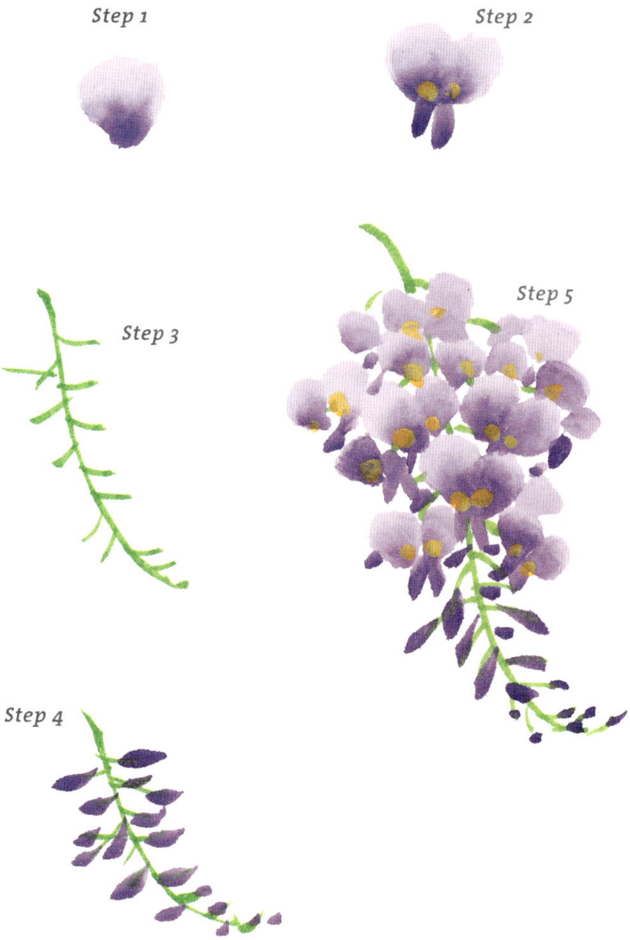

HIBISCUS FLOWERS

See also

leaves p80
finished painting p138

Technical information: The petals of a hibiscus flower are big. Use **B1** and two fan brushstrokes for each petal. Hold the brush at a low angle to the paper to paint wider brushstrokes.

Colour Palette

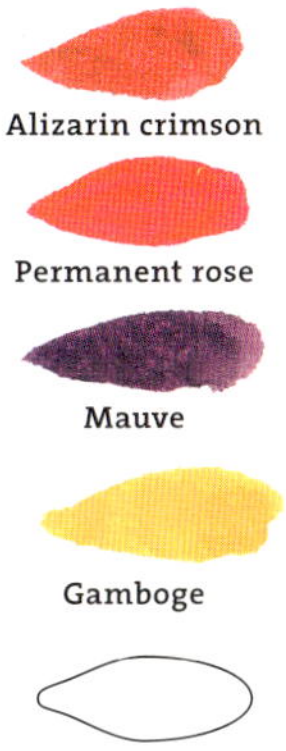

Brushes to use: B1, B3, B4

Step 1 Mix one part of alizarin crimson with one part of permanent rose. Load **B1** with this mixture. Hold the brush at a low angle and paint a fan brushstroke.

Step 2 Use two fan brushstrokes to make up a petal. Each petal has a dark patch at the base. Dip **B3** into mauve and add the patch as illustrated. Dip **B4** into mauve and add the veins as shown.

Step 3 Some petals curl and show their backs. Dilute the mixture described in step 1 to paint the back of the petal. Load **B1** with the diluted colour to paint a short brushstroke for the curling part of the petal. Dip **B1** into the undiluted mixture and complete the petal with fan brushstrokes.

Step 4 Dip **B3** into process white and paint a long stalk for the centre and add five little stalks to the top. Add short side stalks to the upper part. Mix one part of gamboge with one part of process white. Dip **B3** into this mixture and add dots to each short stalk.

Step 5 Paint five petals to make up a flower. The lower petal is painted with the brush held at a higher angle to the paper so that the fan brushstrokes are shorter. Use **B3** to add the centre as described in step 3. Clean **B3**, dip it into mauve and add the dark patch at the base of each petal. Use **B4** and mauve to add veins to each petal.

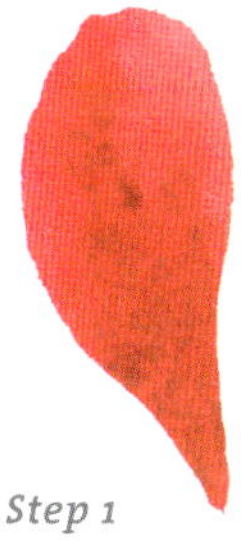

Step 1

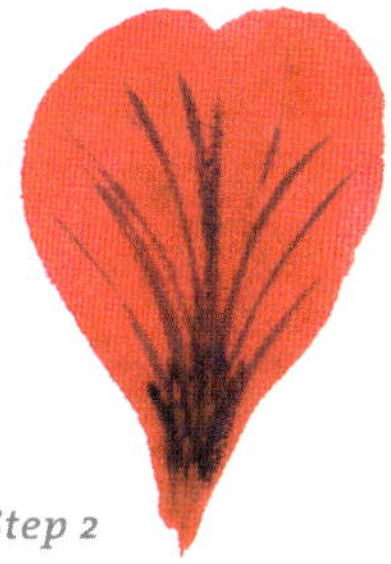

Step 2

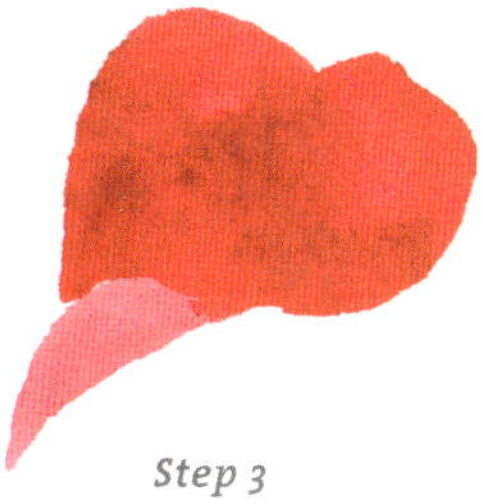

Step 3

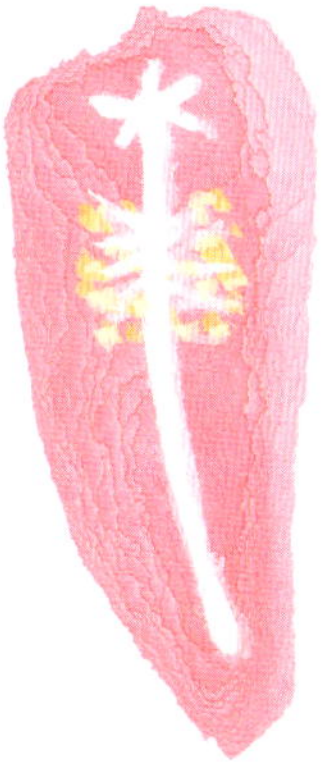

Step 4

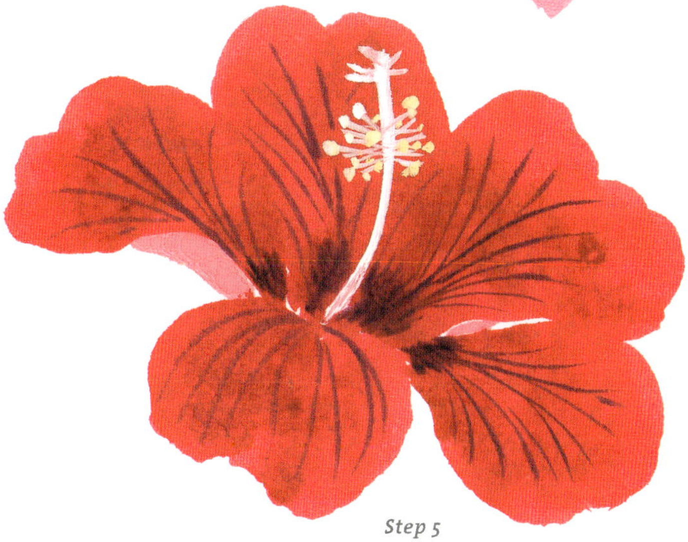

Step 5

See also
flowers p103
finished painting p132

GERANIUMS LEAVES

Colour Palette

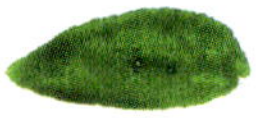

Sap green

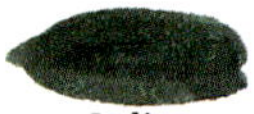

Indigo

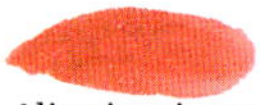

Alizarin crimson

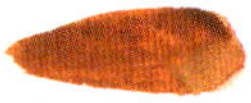

Burnt sienna

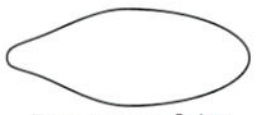

Process white

Technical information: Geraniums leaves are round. You will need six to eight fan brushstrokes to make up a leaf.

Step 1

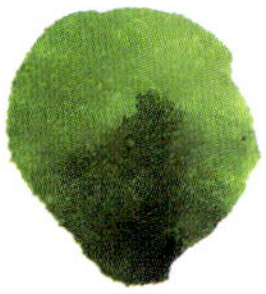

Step 2

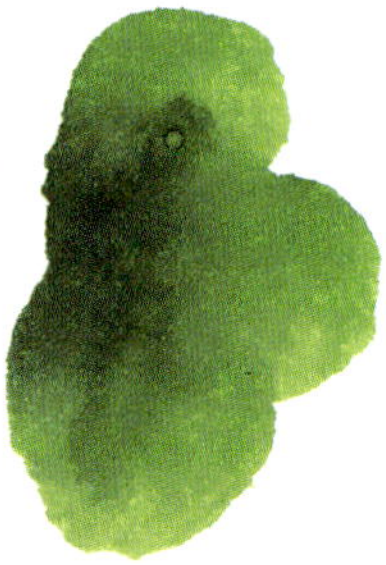

Step 3

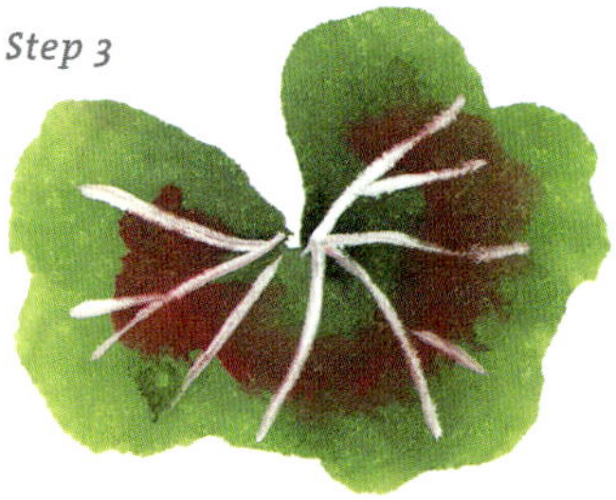

Step 4

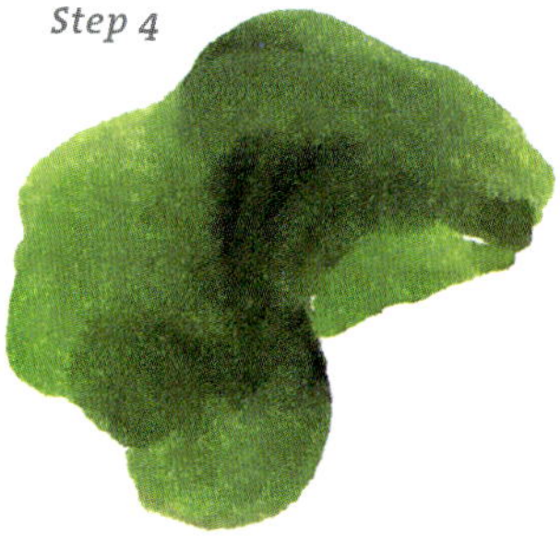

Step 5

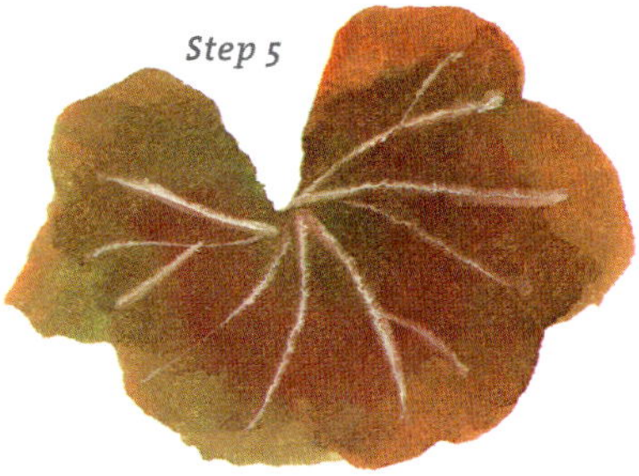

Step 6

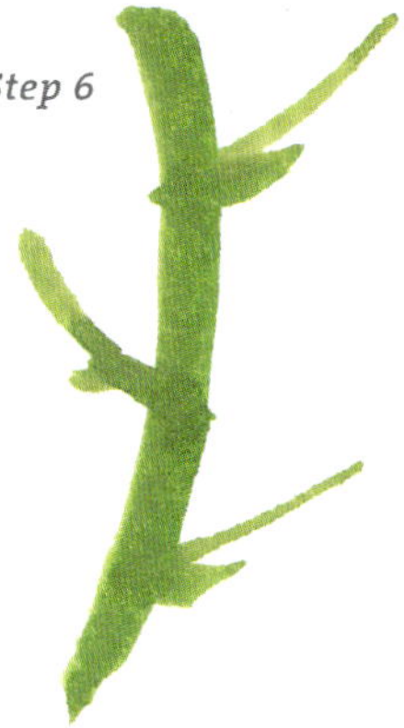

Brushes to use: B1, B3, B4

Step 1 Load **B1** with sap green and dip the nib of the brush into indigo. Hold the brush at a low angle to the paper and paint a wide fan brush-stroke.

Step 2 Each leaf has an opening. Start to paint a leaf from the opening. Load **B1** as described in step 1. Paint a few fan brushstrokes close together to form one half of a leaf. Remember to maintain the round shape.

Step 3 Reload the brush as described in step 1 and start from the other side of the opening to finish painting the leaf with more fan brush-strokes. Some leaves have red rings. Dip **B2** into alizarin crimson and add the red ring to the leaf while it is still wet. Dip **B4** into process white and add veins to the leaf.

Step 4 Use sap green for the under-sides of leaves. Paint a curling leaf, showing the underside of the leaf.

Step 5 Load **B1** with burnt sienna and dip the nib of the brush into sap green. Use this colour combination to paint an old leaf.

Step 6 Load **B2** with sap green. Hold the brush at a high angle to the paper and paint a long side brushstroke with regular stops to represent a stalk. Add a bract at each stop. A leaf stalk appears at the spot where there is a bract.

See also

flowers	p62
project 6	p116
water line	p155
greens	p155

CHRYSANTHEMUM LEAVES

Technical information: Chrysanthemum leaves have the most irregular arrangement. A leaf stalk can carry any number of leaves and the leaves differ in shape from each other.

Using the fan brushstroke is one way to paint chrysanthemum leaves. In fact, because of the irregular shapes and irregular amount of leaves in a stalk, the traditional way to paint them is to use all available brushstrokes. There is more about the painting of chrysanthemum leaves in project 6 and page 115. For the time being, I will show you how to paint chrysanthemum leaves with the fan brushstroke.

Colour Palette

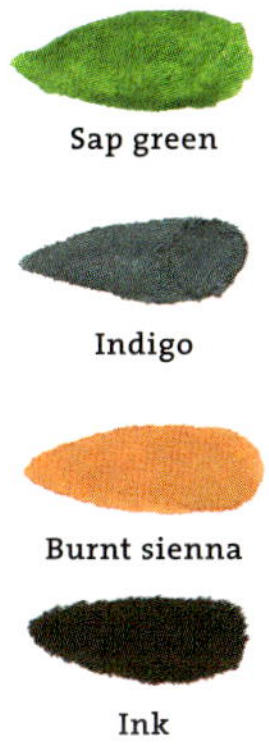

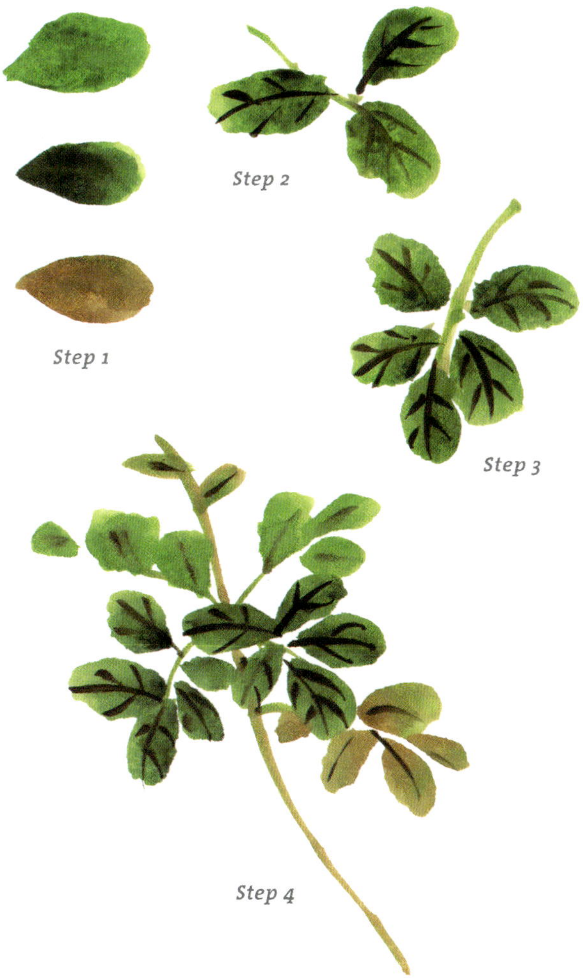

Brushes to use: B1, B2, B3, B4

Step 1 Load **B1** with sap green. Hold the brush at an angle to the paper and paint a fan brushstroke. Use sap green for young leaves, dark green for mature leaves and olive green for older leaves.

Step 2 Use **B1** and sap green to paint three leaves in the arrangement, as illustrated. Dip **B3** into sap green and paint a main leaf stalk and short stalks to connect the leaves to the main stalk. This is a leaf stalk with three leaves. Dip **B4** into ink and draw the veins on the leaves.

Step 3 Some leaf stalks have more than three leaves. I have used dark green for the leaves of this leaf stalk. Follow the instructions as in step 2.

Step 4 Use a clean and damp **B3** to draw a water line to represent the flower stalk of a chrysanthemum. Load **B1** with dark green and paint some groups of leaves in the lower middle part of the stalk. Mature leaves are usually at the front and middle of the stalk. Clean **B1** and reload with sap green. Add some younger leaves to the upper part of the stalk. Younger leaves are usually at the upper part of the stalk. Load **B2** with burnt sienna and dip the nib of the brush into sap green. Starting from the top, paint sections of the stalk where it is visible. Use **B3** and sap green to add leaf stalks. Dip **B4** into ink. Add veins to some of the leaves at the front. Load **B1** with olive green and add a few older leaves at the back.

See also

branches p95
flowers p102

Colour Palette

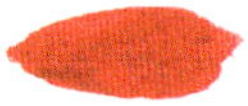

Alizarin crimson

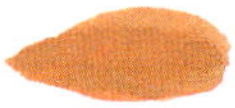

Burnt sienna

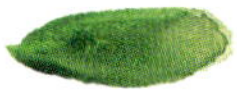

Sap green

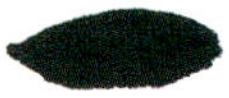

Ink

PROJECT 5 PAINTING PLUM BLOSSOM

Technical information: Plum blossom was the national flower of China until recently. China has now adopted the peony as the official national flower. Plum blossom remains the national flower of Taiwan.

The plum blossom flowers towards the very end of winter when the weather can still be severe. When you see plum blossoms blooming, you know that spring will not be far away. Plum blossom is able to withstand the cold and brave the winter, full of charm and beauty. Although the flowers are small and short lived, they demonstrate outstanding perseverance. The tree may look like a dead branch in the heart of winter but when it blossoms, the huge numbers of flowers fully load the tree, bringing hope of the coming spring and brightening the still and lifeless surroundings. For this reason, plum blossom symbolizes perseverance and hope. The Chinese adore such character.

When the blossom flowers, there will be no leaves yet. Leaves appear when the petals start to fall. The plum blossom painted by artists is

Brushes to use: B1, B2, B3, B4

Step 1 Wipe **B1** dry and load the dry **B1** with burnt sienna. Dip the nib of the brush into ink. Wipe off excess moisture from the brush at the side of the mixing dish. Hold the brush at a low angle to the paper and paint an old rugged trunk. Again load **B1** with burnt sienna and dip the nib of the brush into ink. Hold the brush at a high angle and add young shoots to the trunk, leaving gaps for flowers later on.

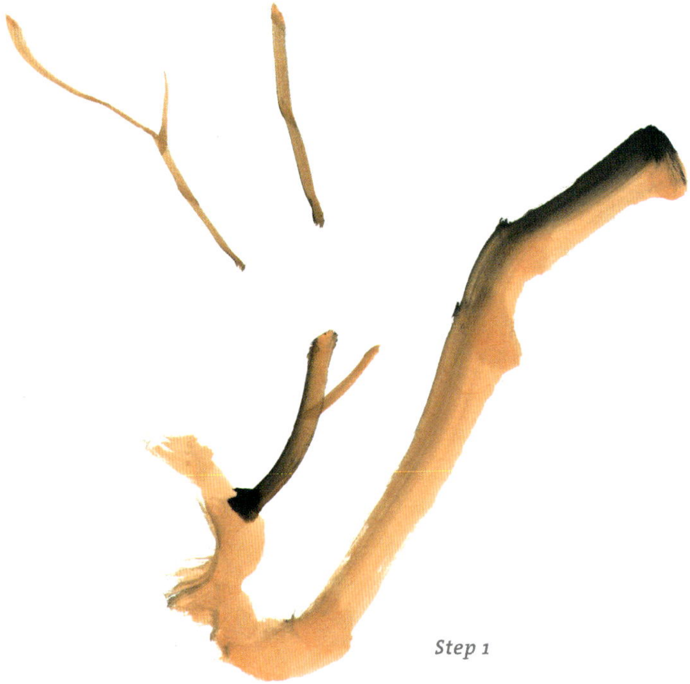

Step 1

the ornamental type. There are white ones, pink ones and crimson ones but the most popular is the pink variety.

Chinese paintings of plum blossom emphasize the composition and strength of the tree trunks and branches. In order to do that, one always begins by painting the trunks and branches, leaving gaps for the flowers to fill up later on. Artists feel that if the flowers are painted first, it will be difficult to connect them with the branches using sweeping movements, so the whole painting will be lacking in strength.

The most popular composition of plum blossom in painting shows the old rugged trunks contrasting with a vigorous young branch. It is a symbol of old China which will never die but live on, bursting with new life. No wonder plum blossom is a symbol of hope.

This project follows the tradition of painting the trunk and the main branches first, leaving gaps for the flowers to fill in later. The trunk is very old with young shoots loaded with flowers.

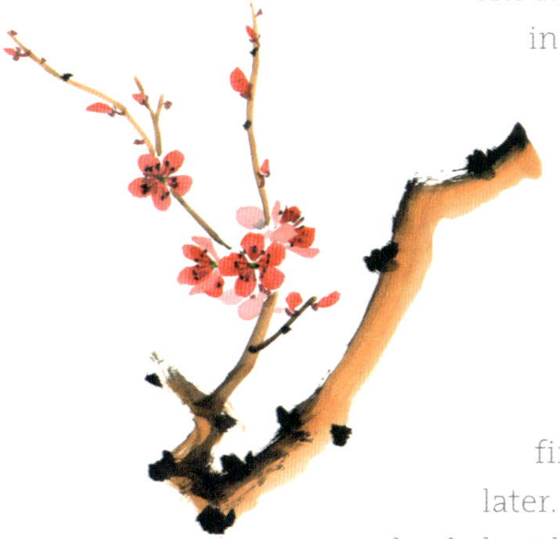

Step 2

Step 2 Use **B2** and alizarin crimson to paint flowers. First fill the gaps and then paint some more flowers behind branches. Use **B3** with sap green to add dots where the centres of the flowers are visible. Mix alizarin crimson with a tiny bit of ink to make a dark red. Use **B4** with this dark red to add centres to each flower. Use **B3** and burnt sienna to add extra short branches. Dip **B4** into dark red to add short stalks connecting flowers to the branches.

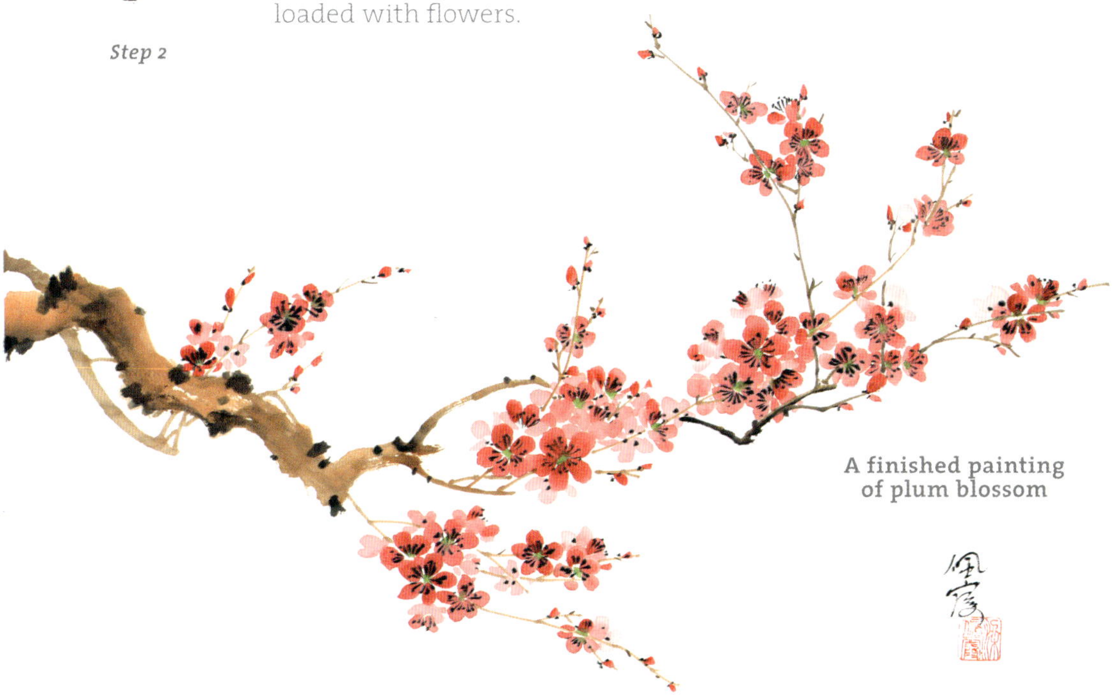

A finished painting of plum blossom

See also
fan brushstroke p100
wrist movement p32

BRUSHSTROKE 7
REVERSE FAN BRUSHSTROKE

When using the two-colour effect, it is more convenient to load the darker colour at the nib of the brush. Using the fan brushstroke to paint flowers with the two-colour loading will produce flowers with darker centres. To paint flowers with darker edges, use the reverse fan brushstroke.

The wrist movement is again used to paint the reverse fan brushstroke, but instead of moving the neck of the brush, the nib of the brush is moved where the darker colour is loaded while keeping the neck of the brush still.

I shall demonstrate how to make use of the reverse fan brushstroke to paint Shirley poppies, roses and morning glory.

You have seen how to use fan brushstrokes to paint chrysanthemum leaves. This section shows you how to paint them with the reverse fan brushstroke. There are many ways to paint chrysanthemum leaves, but reverse fan brushstroke is my favourite.

Fig. 1 Fully load **B2** with ink or colour. Hold the brush at an angle to the paper in a position as shown. Move the brush with the wrist movement. Move the nib of the brush, only keeping the neck of the brush still. The resulting brushwork is fan shaped. I start the reverse fan brushstroke from the left, but you can also start from the right and move to the left. The result will be the same.

Fig. 2 A reverse fan brushstroke painted with **B2**.

Fig. 3 A smaller movement produces a narrower brushstroke.

Fig. 4 A bigger movement produces a wider brushstroke.

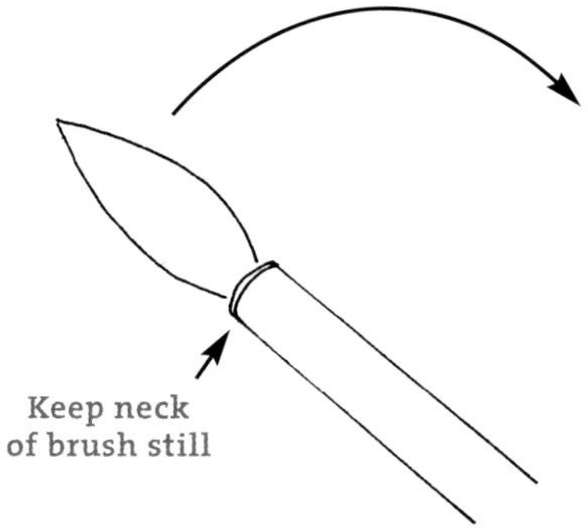

Fig. 1

Fig. 2

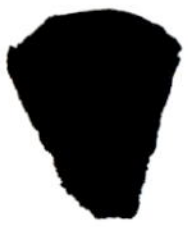

Fig. 3

Fig. 4

PRACTISING REVERSE FAN BRUSHSTROKE

The size of a reverse fan brushstroke varies according to the angle of the brush to the paper – the lower the angle, the bigger the brushstroke. However, it is more effective to use different brushes to create different sizes of brushstroke.

Fig. 1

Fig. 2

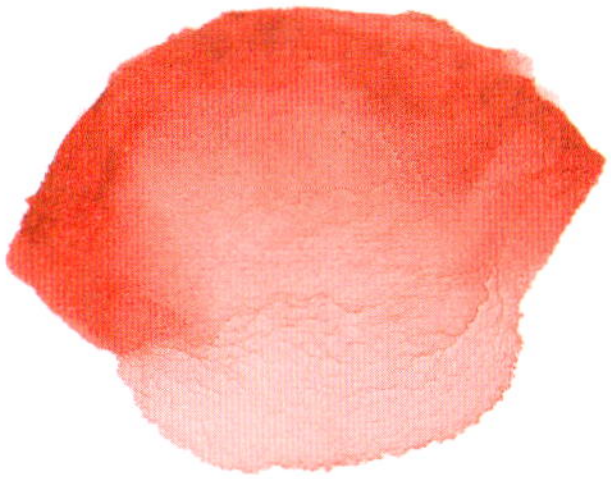

Fig. 3

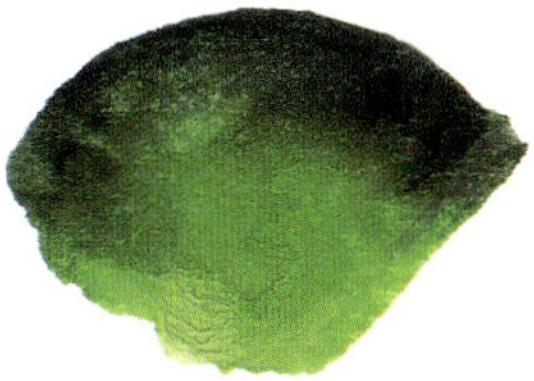

Fig. 4

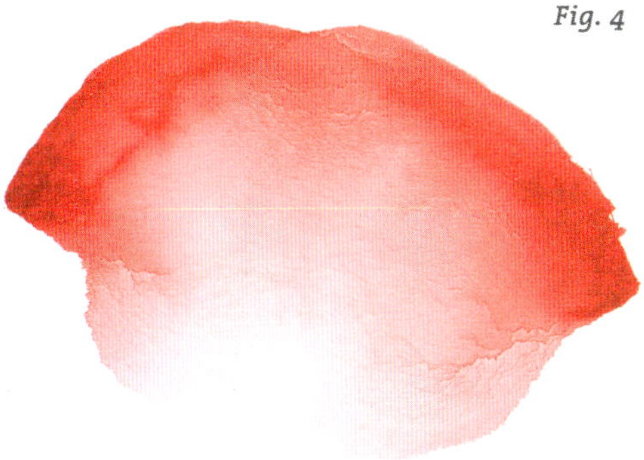

Fig. 5

Fig. 1 Paint a reverse fan brushstroke with **B3** and ink. **B3** is a small brush so the brushstroke is smaller.

Fig. 2 Use **B1** and ink to paint a reverse fan brushstroke. **B1** is a bigger brush so the resulting brushstroke is bigger.

Fig. 3 Load **B2** with two tones of alizarin crimson. Paint a reverse fan brushstroke.

Fig. 4 Load **B2** with sap green and dip the nib of the brush into indigo. Paint a reverse fan brushstroke with the two colours.

Fig. 5 Load **B2** with two tones of alizarin crimson. Paint two reverse fan brushstrokes side by side to make a wider brushstroke. Flowers such as Shirley poppies have very wide petals. You will need two or three reverse fan brushstrokes to paint each petal.

See also

leaves p82
stalks p96
finished painting p139

SHIRLEY POPPY FLOWERS

Technical information: Shirley poppy flowers have very large, wide petals. Use two or three reverse fan brushstrokes to make up a petal.

Colour Palette

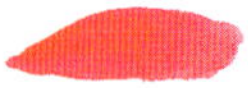

Permanent rose

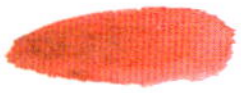

Alizarin crimson

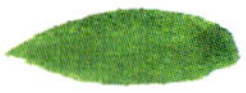

Sap green

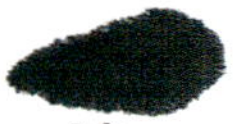

Ink

Step 1

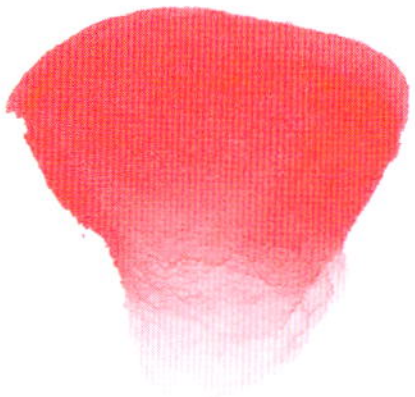

Step 2

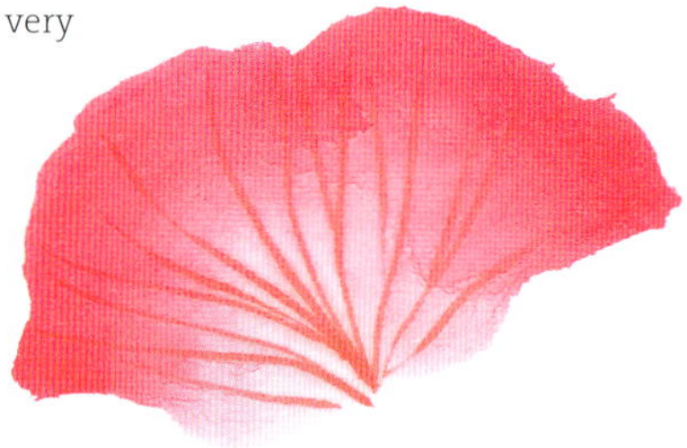

Step 3

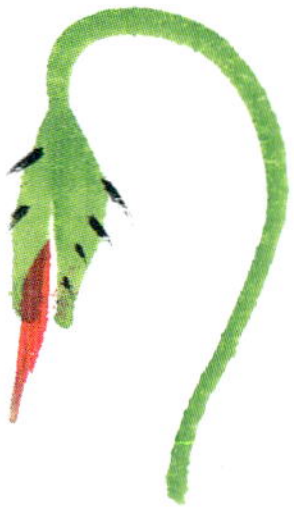

Step 4

Step 5

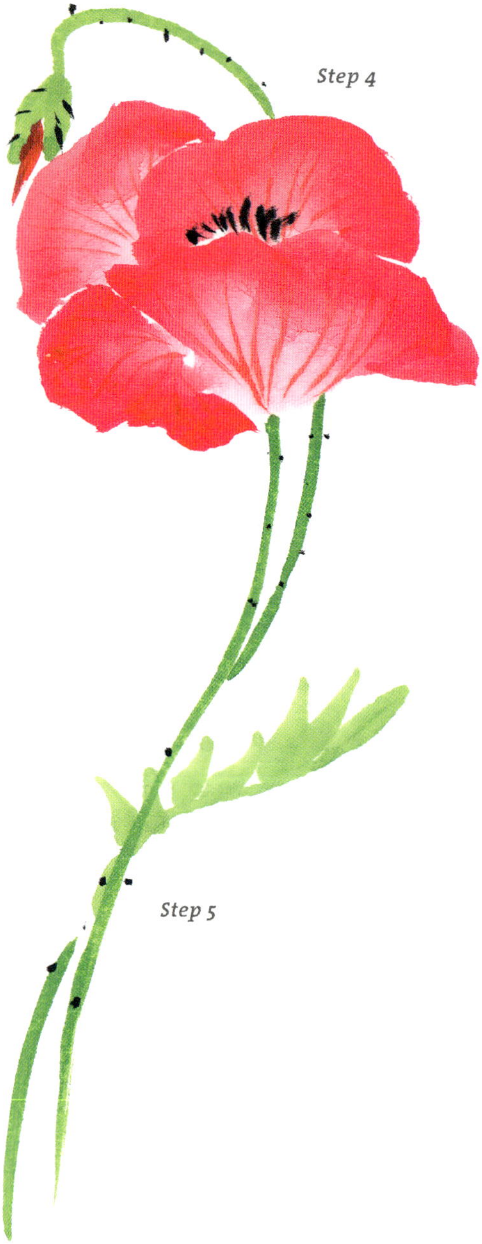

Brushes to use: B1, B2, B3, B4

Step 1 The petals of a Shirley poppy are very delicate and thin, like tissue paper. In order to capture the features, we will not use too heavy a colouring. Use a clean and wet **B1** and dip only the nib of the brush into permanent rose. Paint two or three reverse fan brushstrokes close together to make up a petal.

Step 2 When the petal is dry dip **B4** into alizarin crimson and paint the veins.

Step 3 Load **B2** with sap green. Paint two short brushstrokes and a stalk for a bud. Dip the nib of **B2** into permanent rose to add the tip of the bud. Dip **B4** into ink and add the hairs to the sepals.

Step 4 Each flower has four petals. Use **B1** to paint four petals following the instructions given in step 1 and step 2. Dip **B4** into ink. Use small short brushstrokes to add the centre to the flower.

Step 5 Load **B3** with sap green and paint the long stalk and a leaf. Add another long stalk. Use **B2** and sap green to add a bud at the tip of this stalk following the instructions given in step 3. Dip **B4** into ink and add the hair to the bud. Add tiny dots along the stalks to indicate hair.

ROSES

See also
leaves p75
finished painting p143

Technical information: A single rose has many petals of different sizes. The outside ones are bigger and those in the centre are smaller. Use a single reverse fan brushstroke for a small petal and multiple brushstrokes for a wider petal.

Colour Palette

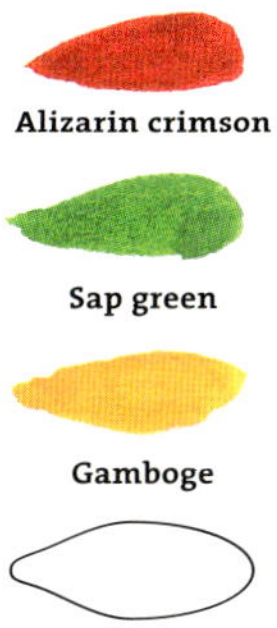

Alizarin crimson
Sap green
Gamboge
Process white

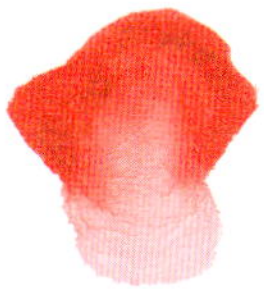

Step 1

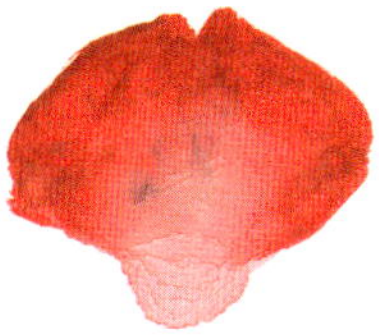

Step 2

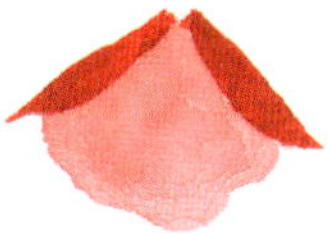

Step 3

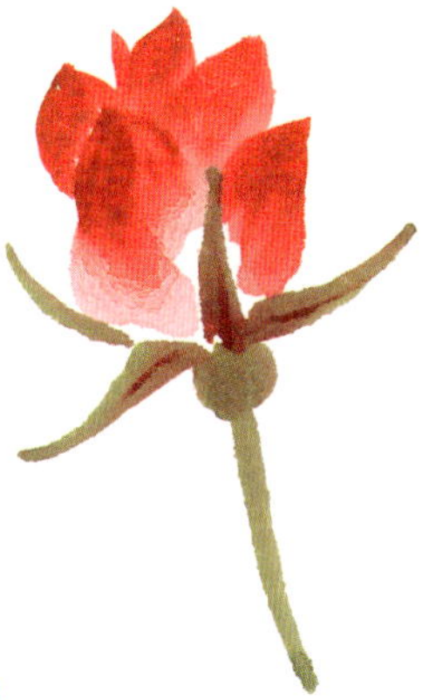

Step 5

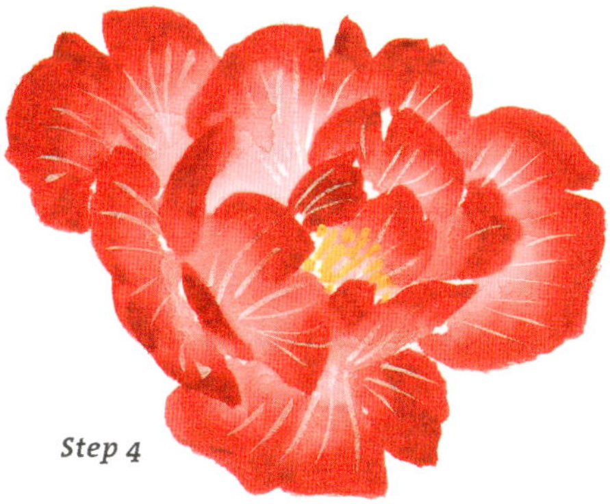

Step 4

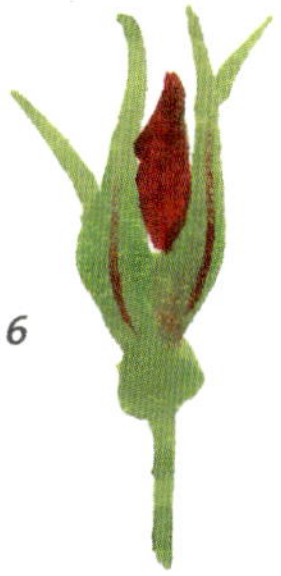

Step 6

Brushes to use: B2, B3, B4

Step 1 Dip the nib of a clean wet **B2** into alizarin crimson. Paint a reverse fan brushstroke. Use a single reverse fan brushstroke for a small petal.

Step 2 Use two reverse fan brushstrokes for a bigger petal. Sometimes the upper edge of a large petal splits.

Step 3 Sometimes a petal curls at the edge. Use **B2** and alizarin crimson to paint two small short brushstrokes for the curling edge. Finish painting the petal with diluted alizarin crimson.

Step 4 Start a rose with the petal at the front. Add petals towards the back. Maintain a cup shape. The petals in the centre are smaller, while those towards the outside are bigger. Follow the instructions in step 1, step 2, and step 3 to paint the petals. Dip **B4** into process white and add veins to some of the petals. Mix one part of gamboge with one part of process white. Dip **B4** into this mixture and use small short brushstrokes to paint the centre of the flower.

Step 5 Start to paint a half-opened bud with the sepals. Load **B3** with sap green and dip the nib of the brush into alizarin crimson. Use short brushstrokes to paint the sepals. Add a base to the sepals with a dot and then a stalk. Use **B4** and alizarin crimson to paint the veins on the sepals. Use **B2** to paint the petals according to the instructions in step 1.

Step 6 Load **B2** with sap green and dip the nib of the brush into alizarin crimson. Paint the sepals of a bud with short brushstrokes. Add the base of the bud with a dot.
Add the stalk. Dip **B2** into alizarin crimson and add a long dot to finish painting the bud. Dip **B4** into alizarin crimson and paint veins on the sepals.

See also

leaves p56
climbers p97
finished painting p151

MORNING GLORY FLOWERS

Technical information: Use reverse fan brushstrokes close together to paint the flower. Use short brushstrokes for buds. Refer to the section on painting climbers.

Colour Palette

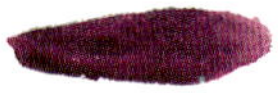

Mauve

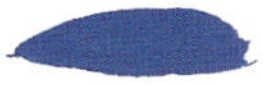

Cobalt blue

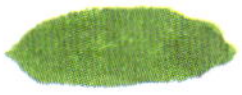

Sap green

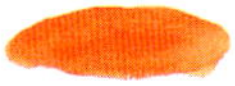

Cadmium orange

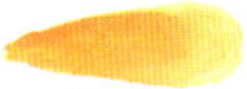

Gamboge

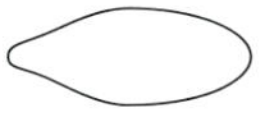

Process white

Brushes to use: B2, B3, B4

Step 1 Make a purple by mixing two parts of mauve with one part of cobalt blue. Dip the nib of a clean and wet **B2** into this purple. Paint a reverse fan brushstroke.

Step 2 Use five reverse fan brushstrokes close together to make up a round flower. Use **B3** and gamboge to add a dot in the centre. Dip **B3** into cadmium orange and paint a smaller dot on top. Dip **B4** into process white and add the petal veins.

Step 3 Dilute some purple. Dip the nib of a clean and wet **B2** into this diluted purple and use this to paint the petal back. Use three reverse fan brushstrokes for a flower viewed from the side. Use **B2** and diluted purple for the tube of the flower. Dip **B3** into sap green and paint two sepals on the flower. Add a stalk.

Step 4 Paint a short brushstroke with **B2** and purple for a bud. Add the sepals and a stalk with **B3** and sap green.

Step 5 Paint a few flowers. Load **B3** with sap green and paint the long stalk. Add another stalk to twine around it, and add sepals and flower stalks to connect the flowers to the long stalks. Add buds.

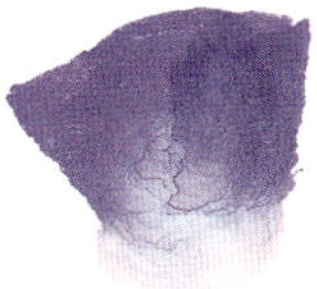

Step 1

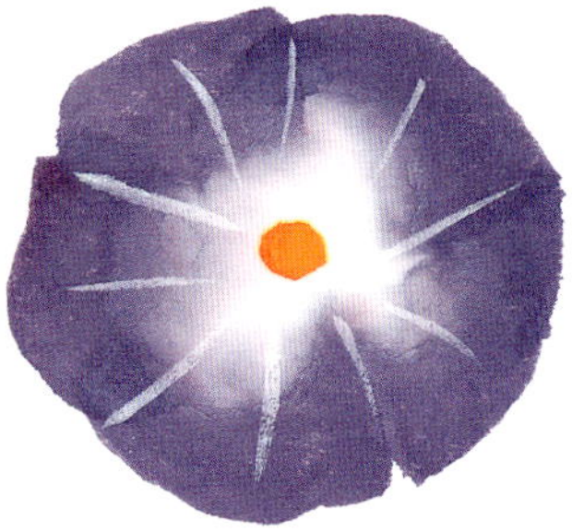

Step 2

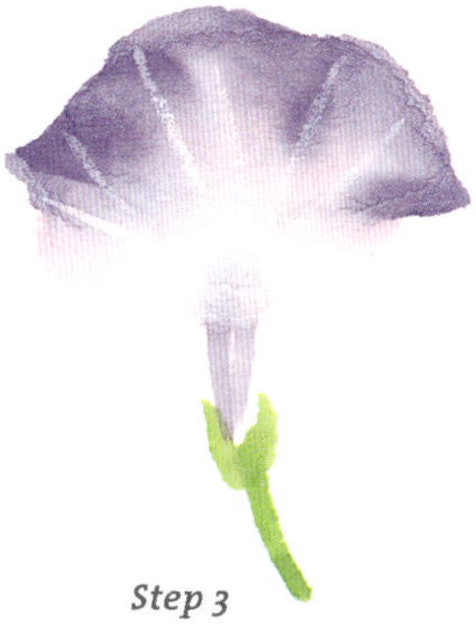

Step 3

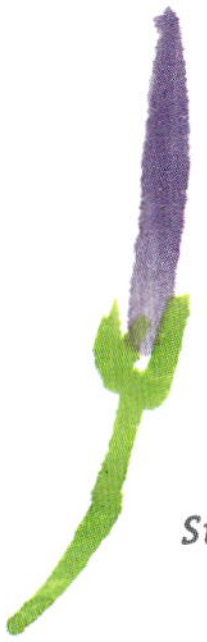

Step 4

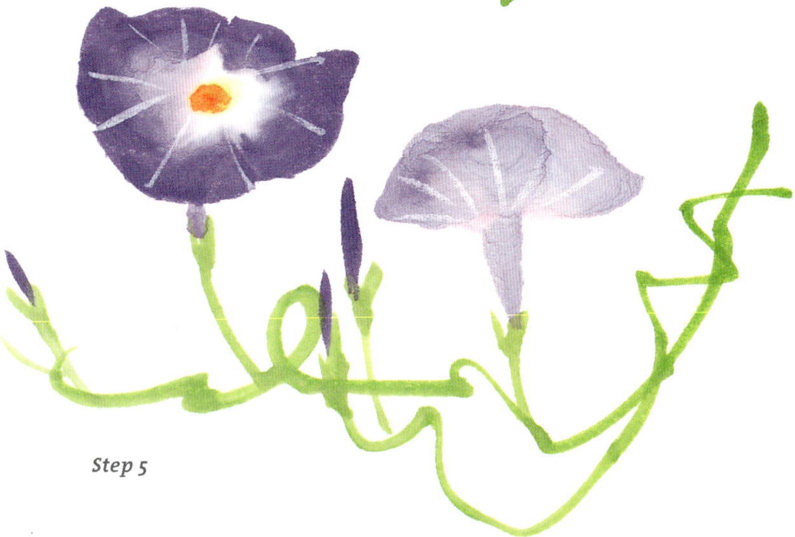

Step 5

CHRYSANTHEMUM LEAVES

See also

leaves	**p107**
flowers	**p62, p116**

Technical information:The reverse fan brushstroke is a more flexible brushstroke and is therefore a good one to use for representing the chrysanthemum leaves. The colour combinations, too, are better with the reverse fan brushstroke. The darker colours fall on the edges of the leaves.

Colour Palette

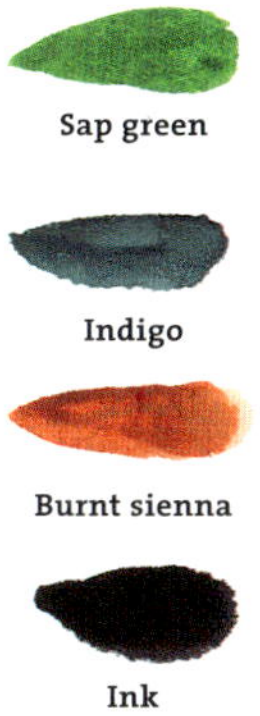

Step 1

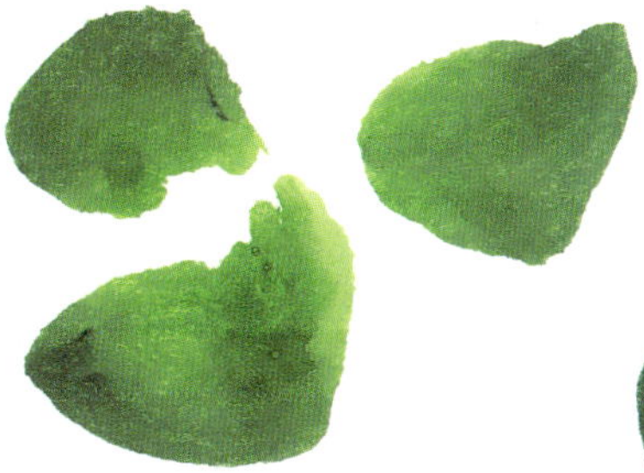

Step 2

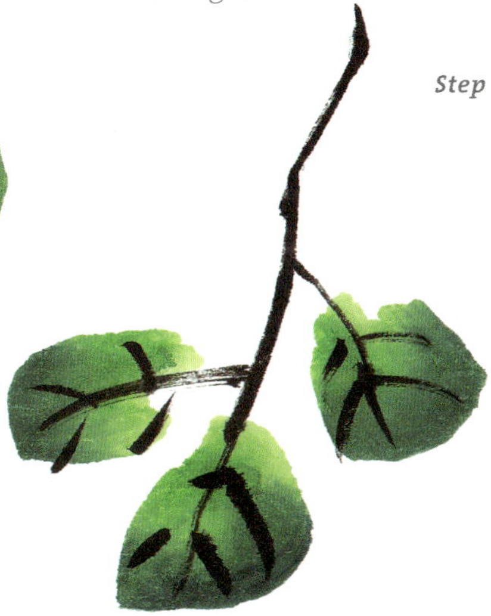

Step 3

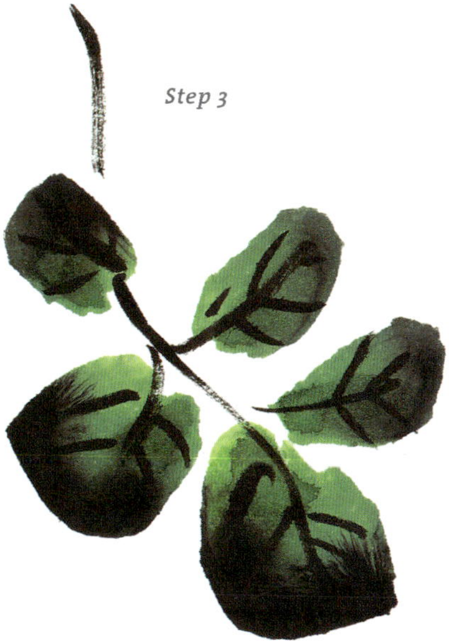

Step 4

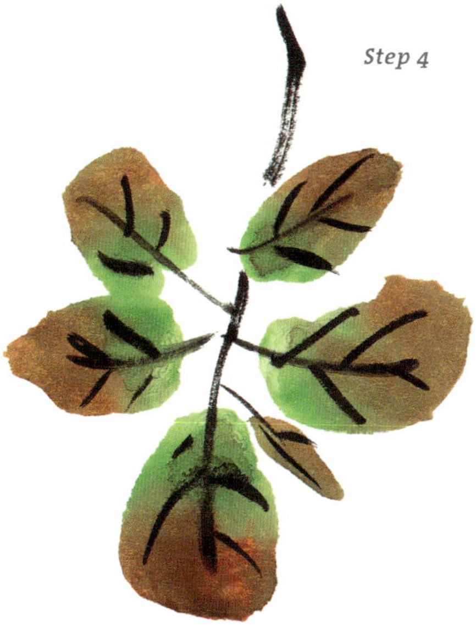

Brushes to use: B1, B3, B4

Step 1 Load **B1** with sap green. Dip the nib of the brush into indigo. Paint three reverse fan brushstrokes to represent the leaves along a leaf stalk.

Step 2 Dip **B3** into ink and add the leaf stalk. Use **B4** and ink to paint the veins on the leaves. Sometimes a leaf stalk carries three leaves.

Step 3 Sometimes a leaf stalk carries five leaves. Load **B1** with dark green and dip the nib of the brush into ink. Paint five leaves. Use **B3** and ink to add the leaf stalk. Use **B4** and ink to add the veins.

Step 4 There are often one or two small leaflets among the bigger ones. Load **B1** with sap green and dip the nib of the brush into burnt sienna. Paint some big leaves and one or two leaflets. Use **B3** and ink to add the leaf stalk. Use **B4** and ink to add the veins.

See also

leaves p107, p115
flowers p62

PROJECT 6
PAINTING CHRYSANTHEMUM

Colour Palette

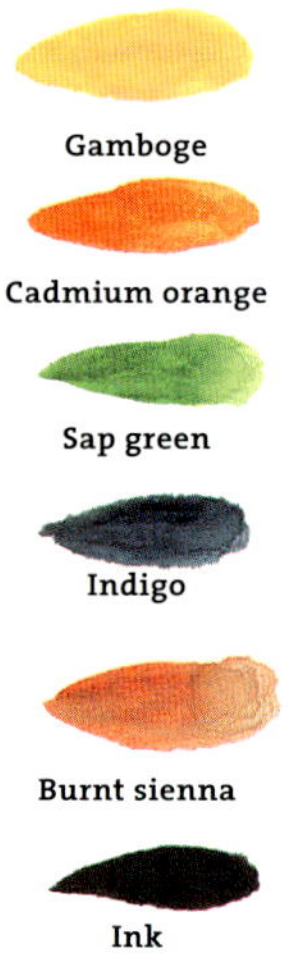

The most popular way of painting chrysanthemums is to paint the flowers in outline and then fill the petals informally with colours. Leaves painted are non-outline style brushstrokes. The emphasis in a chrysanthemum painting is on the graceful postures of the plants. In order to achieve this, stalks are painted first with sweeping brushstrokes before flowers and leaves are added.

Painting chrysanthemum leaves is considered to be a challenge to artists because of their diversity in shape, colour and posture, even in a single plant. Using a

Brushes to use: B1, B2, B3, B4

Step 1 Dip **B3** into ink and practise painting some petals. Each petal is made up of two lines. Draw petals in different postures.

Step 2 Start a flower from the centre with small petals. Add larger petals as you move outwards. Load **B3** with gamboge and dip the nib of the brush into cadmium orange. Dab the colours informally onto the petals, starting at the centre and moving outwards. Reload the brush if colours run out.

Step 3 Load **B3** with sap green and paint five dots as sepals. Add a stalk. Dip **B3** into ink and add the petals. Colour the petals as in step 2. This is a flower from the back.

Step 4 Use **B3** and sap green to paint a few sepals for a bud. Add a few petals and colour them as in step 3.

Painting chrysanthemum flowers

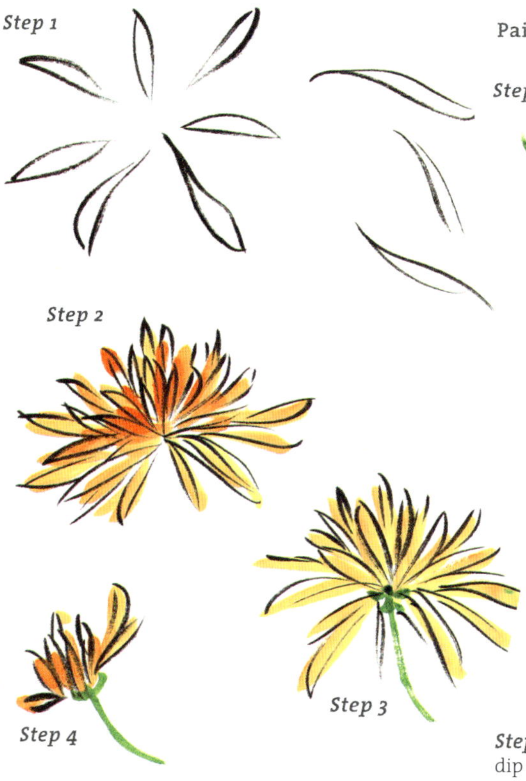

Painting chrysanthemum stalks

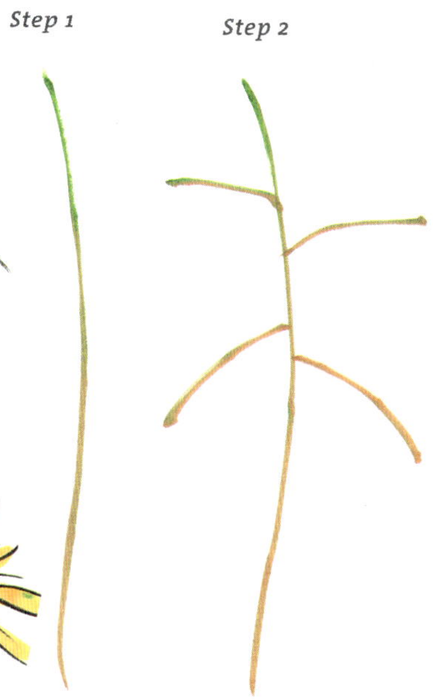

Step 1 Load **B2** with burnt sienna and dip the nib of the brush into sap green. Paint a stalk with regular stops.

Step 2 Reload **B2** with burnt sienna and dip the nib of the brush into sap green. Paint a framework of stalks and side stalks. Reload the brush if colours run out.

variety of brushstrokes, dots, short brushstrokes, fan brushstrokes and reverse fan brushstrokes will meet this challenge and all can be used to create even a single stalk of leaves.

Painting a stalk of leaves

Step 1 Load **B2** with burnt sienna and dip the nib of the brush into sap green. Paint a long stalk with regular stops.

Step 2 Load **B1** with sap green and dip the nib into indigo. Paint mature leaves at the front along the middle of the stalk. Use a mixture of dots, short brushstrokes, fan brushstrokes and reverse fan brushstrokes for each stalk of leaves.

Step 3 Load **B1** with sap green and paint young leaves along the upper part of the stalk, again with a mixture of brushstrokes.

Step 4 Load **B1** with sap green and dip the nib of the brush into burnt sienna. Paint older leaves along the lower part of the stalk and behind the mature leaves using a variety of brushstrokes.

Step 5 Load **B2** with burnt sienna and dip the nib of the brush into sap green. Add short stalks connecting all the leaves with the main stalk. Use **B4** and ink to add veins to some of the leaves in the front.

Step 6 Load **B2** with light green and add sprouting leaves with short brushstrokes along the upper part of the stalk and at the joints of the leaf stalks with the main stalk.

Painting a stalk of leaves

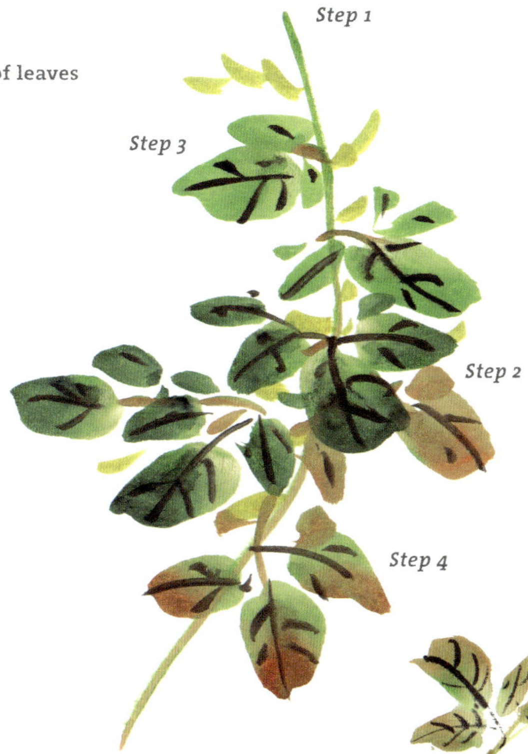

A painting of chrysanthemum

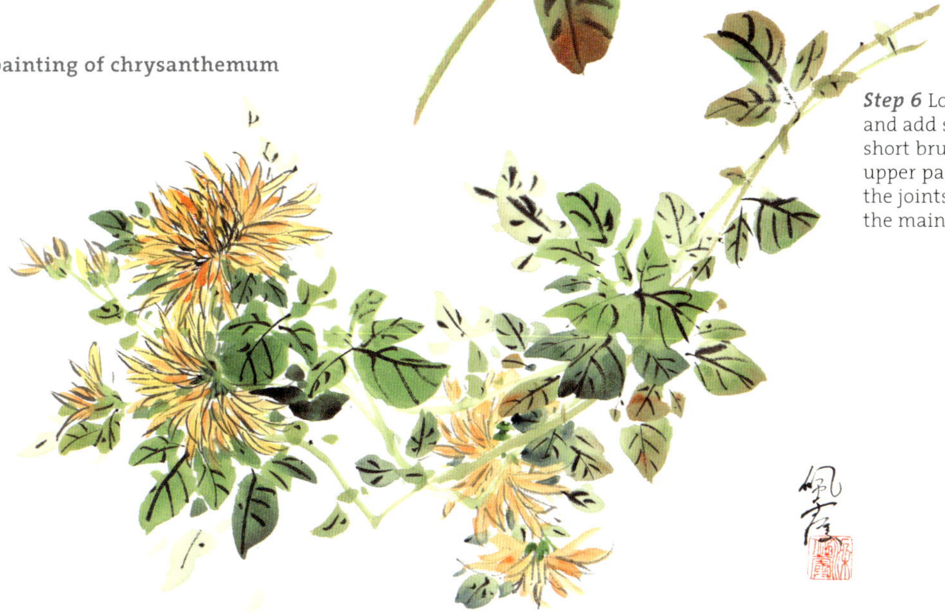

CHAPTER 4

COMBINING BRUSHSTROKES

Some flowers and leaves require more than one type of brushstroke to paint them. Petals like those of iris and peony and leaves like those of lotus have unusual shapes and more complicated colour combinations. In this section I will show you how to combine different basic brushstrokes when painting these shapes. I have chosen only a limited number of flowers and leaves, but the techniques cover a wide variety of complicated shapes. I hope that by the time you have finished practising all the flowers in this section and become used to combining basic brushstrokes, you will learn to tackle any other shapes by creating your own combinations of brushstrokes.

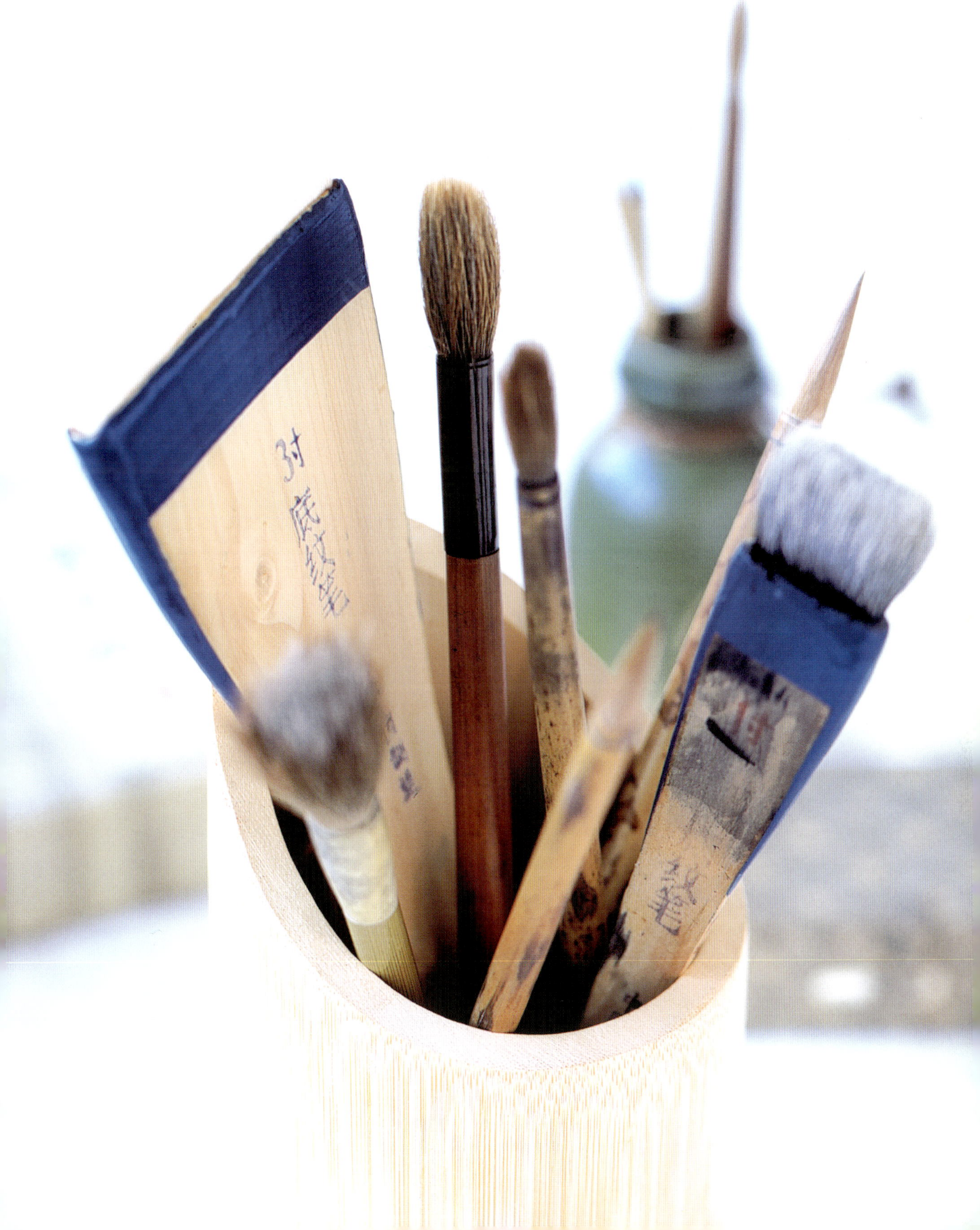

See also

leaves p78
short brushstroke p60
reverse fan brushstroke p110
finished painting p133

CLEMATIS FLOWERS

Colour Palette

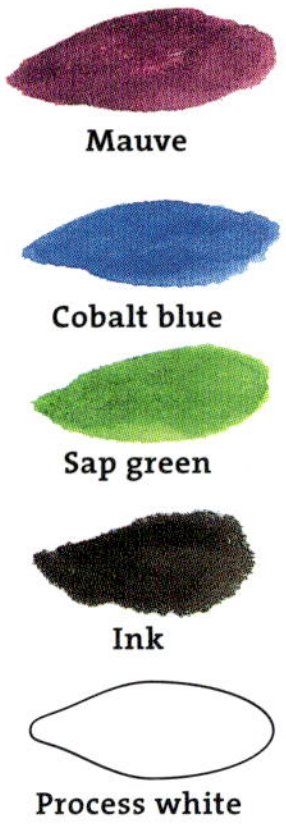

Technical information: There are many varieties of clematis with a wide range of shapes and colours. The more common types are used for this demonstration. Clematis flowers are painted with short brushstrokes and reverse fan brushstrokes.

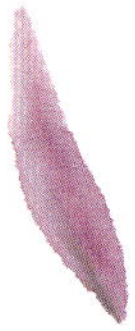

Step 1

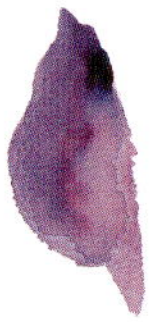

Step 2

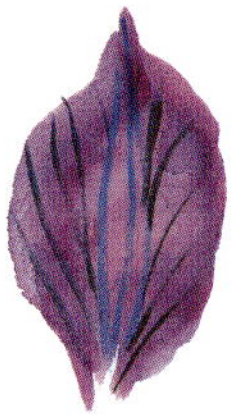

Step 3

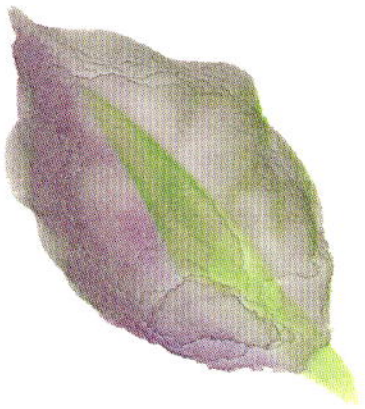

Step 4

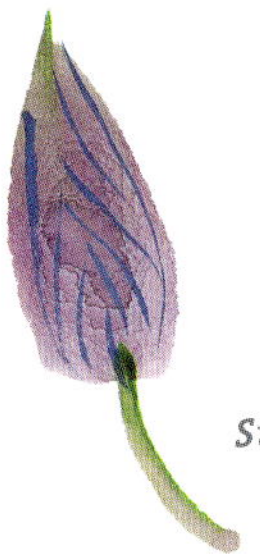

Step 5

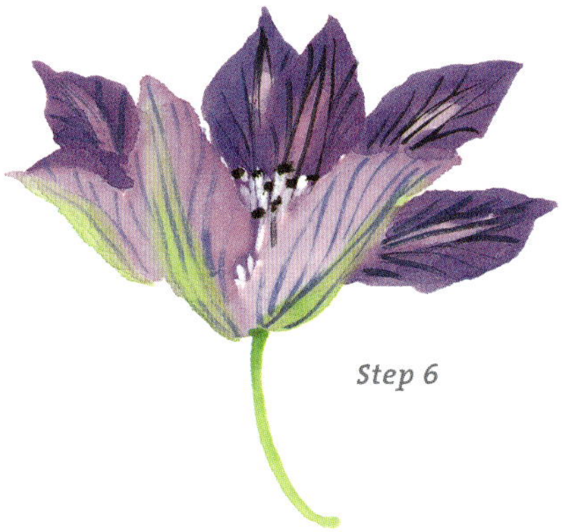

Step 6

Brushes to use: B1, B3, B4

Step 1 Make a purple by mixing two parts of mauve with one part of cobalt blue. Dilute a small amount of this purple. Load **B1** with the diluted purple and paint a short brushstroke.

Step 2 Load **B1** with diluted purple and dip the nib of the brush into undiluted purple. Paint a reverse fan brushstroke along one side of the short brushstroke. Slide the brush when you are painting the brushstroke until the reverse fan brushstroke covers one side of the short brushstroke.

Step 3 Repeat the same technique with the other side of the short brushstroke. This is a petal with the front facing. Mix a little bit of ink into a small amount of purple to make it darker. Dip **B4** into this mixture and paint the veins as shown in the illustration.

Step 4 To paint the back of a petal, use **B1** with diluted sap green to paint the short brushstroke. Then dip the nib of the brush into diluted purple to paint the reverse fan brushstrokes along the two sides of the short brushstrokes.

Step 5 To paint a bud, load **B1** with diluted purple and dip the tip of the brush into diluted sap green. Paint two long dots side by side for a bud. Use **B4** and the mixture described in step 3 to add the veins. Paint a short stalk with **B3** and sap green.

Step 6 To paint a flower, start with the petals at the front. Add more petals towards the back to finish the flower. A flower of the common type of clematis usually has six to eight petals. Add the veins. Dip **B4** into process white and paint small short brushstrokes for the centre of the flower. Add a dot on the tip of each short brushstroke with **B4** and ink. Dip **B3** into sap green and add a stalk.

CAMELLIA FLOWERS

See also

leaves **p74**
fan brushstroke **p100**
finished painting **p140**

Use fan brushstrokes to paint the petals. The petals are not very big so use **B2** to paint the flower.

Colour Palette

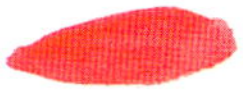

Permanent rose

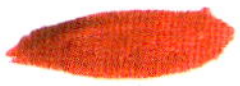

Alizarin crimson

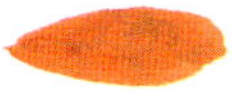

Burnt sienna

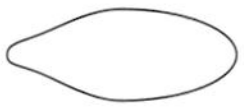

Process white

Step 1

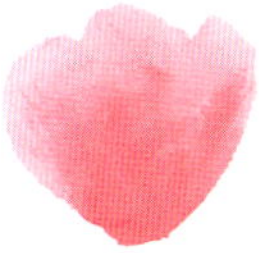

Step 2

Step 3

Step 4

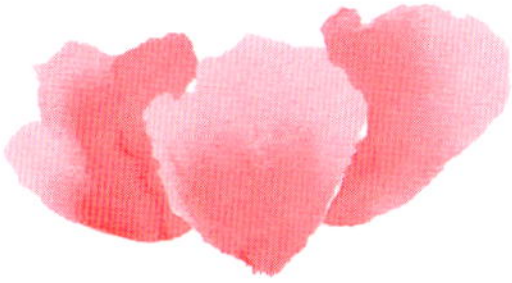

Step 5

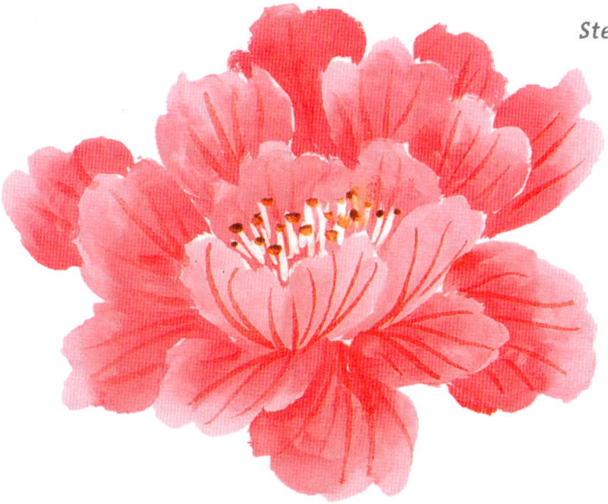

Brushes to use: B2, B4

Step 1 Make a pink colour by mixing a little bit of permanent rose into process white. Load **B2** with the pink and dip the nib of the brush into permanent rose. Paint a fan brushstroke. Some petals have uneven edges. You can achieve this by pressing and lifting the neck of the brush from time to time during painting the fan brushstrokes.

Step 2 A bigger petal requires a wider fan brushstroke. You can make bigger movements when you paint the fan brushstrokes, or, you can use two fan brushstrokes to paint each wide petal. Use **B4** and alizarin crimson to paint the veins of the petal.

Step 3 Use only pink to paint the back of a petal.

Step 4 The petals are very close to each other. The two-tone loading of the brush allows two adjacent petals to be separated instead of merging into one shape. A petal will have a darker base and a paler edge because of the two tones in the brush. The petal next to it will have the darker base attached to the paler edge of the previous petal, making the two petals separate from each other. You can use the same technique to paint flowers with many petals close together. Some examples are roses, begonias and tree peonies.

Step 5 Start painting a flower with the petals at the centre and in the front. Remember to use only pink for the back of petals. Build up the flower by adding petals outwards and towards the back. Bear in mind the technique described in step 4. Add the veins with **B4** and alizarin crimson. Dip **B4** into process white and paint small short brushstrokes for the centre. Dip **B4** into burnt sienna and add a dot to the top of each short brushstroke.

See also

leaves p88
short brushstroke p60
fan brushstroke p100
reverse fan brushstroke p110
finished painting p135

IRIS FLOWERS

Technical information: An iris flower has three upper petals and three lower petals. Use reverse fan brushstrokes to paint the upper petals. Use fan brushstrokes to paint the lower petals.

Colour Palette

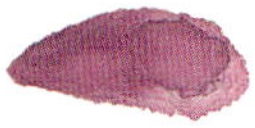

Mauve

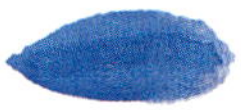

Cobalt blue

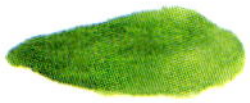

Sap green

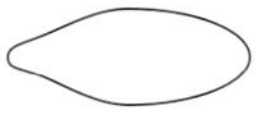

Process white

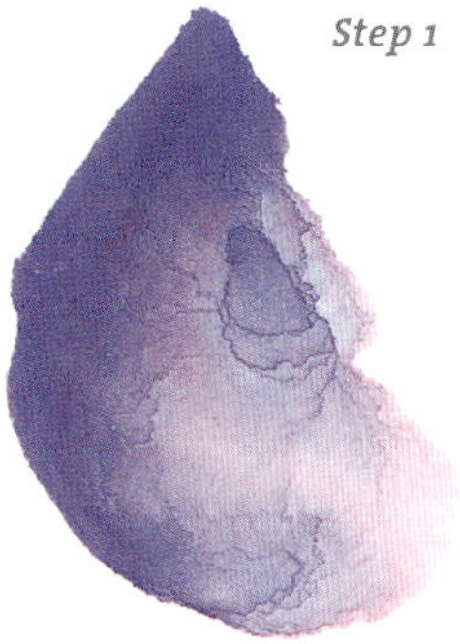

Step 1

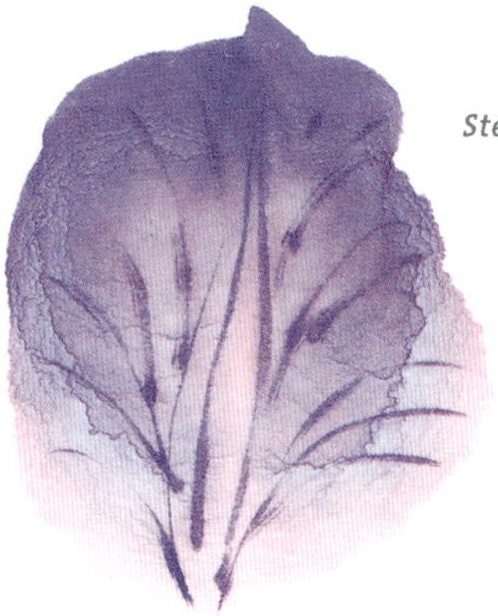

Step 2

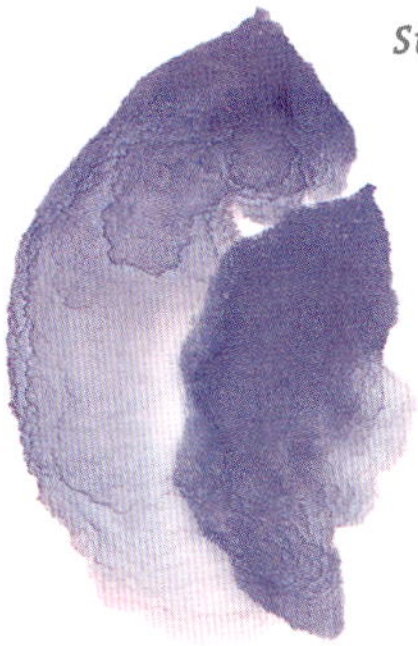

Step 3

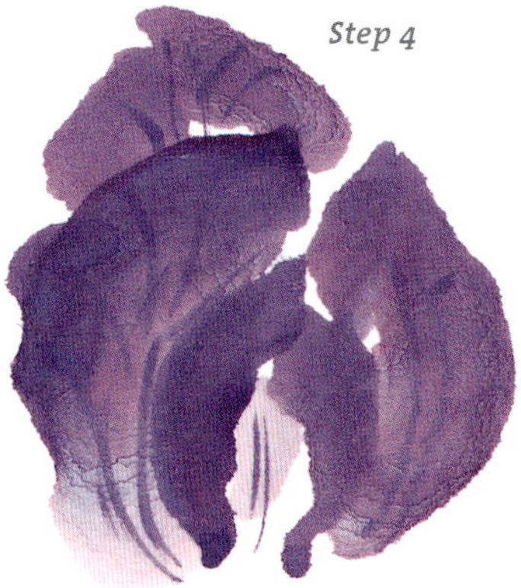

Step 4

Brushes to use: B1, B2, B3, B4

Step 1 Mix two parts of mauve with one part of cobalt blue to make a purple. Dip the nib of a clean wet **B1** into purple and paint a reverse fan brushstroke, sliding the brush as you paint to lengthen the brushstroke. Keep the nib of the brush to the left.

Step 2 Use the technique described in step 1 to paint a second reverse fan brushstroke next to the first one, but this time keep the nib of the brush to the right. These two reverse fan brushstrokes form an upper petal. Dip **B4** into purple and add the veins as illustrated.

Step 3 Some petals curl at the edges. Paint the curling edge with a smaller reverse fan brushstroke by holding the brush at a higher angle. Then add another reverse fan brushstroke at the lower angle to finish painting the petal.

Step 4 The three upper petals are evenly spaced. Paint the one at the front first before adding the others.

Step 5

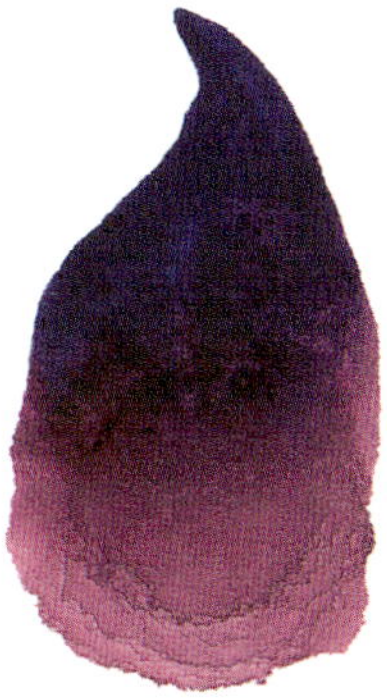

Step 6

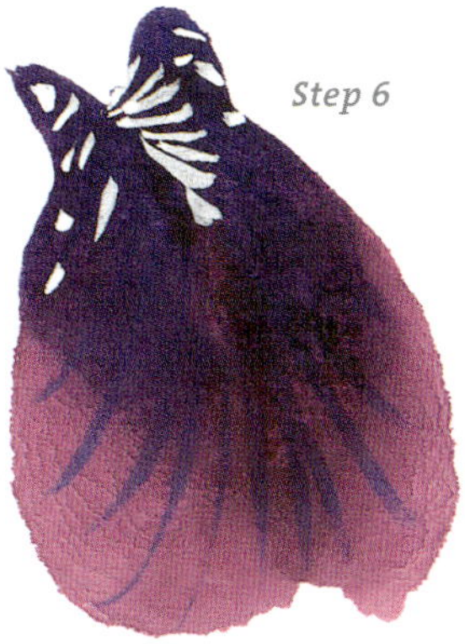

Step 7

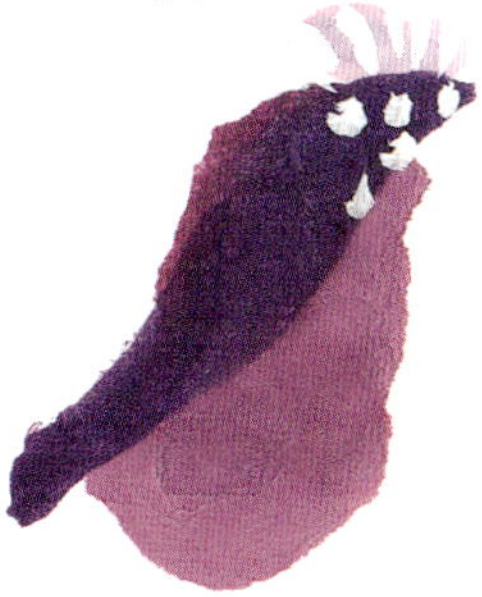

Step 8

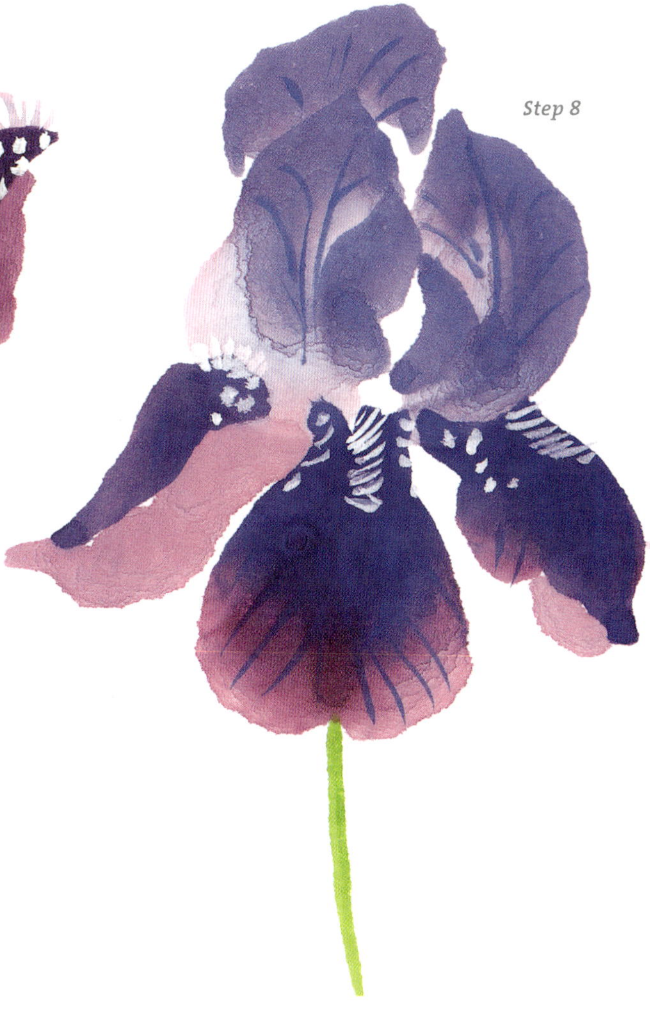

Step 5 To paint a lower petal, load **B1** with mauve and dip the nib of the brush into purple. Start painting half a petal by pressing the brush onto the paper and then slide downwards with a fan brushstroke. Keep the nib of the brush at the centre of the petal and the neck of the brush to the right.

Step 6 Paint a second fan brushstroke using the technique described in step 5 but this time with the neck of the brush to the left. The two fan brushstrokes make a lower petal. Use **B4** and purple to add the veins. Each lower petal has white markings and a beard at the upper part. Dip **B3** into process white to paint small short brushstrokes for the markings and the beard.

Step 7 The lower petals usually curl inwards. Paint a petal viewed from the side. Start with the upper part of the petals using the technique described in step 5. Then use diluted mauve to paint the under part. Add the veins, markings and beard.

Step 8 Paint three upper petals. Then paint three lower petals. Use **B4** and purple to add the veins to each petal. Dip **B3** into process white to add the markings and beards to the lower petals. Load **B2** with sap green and add a stalk.

See also

leaves p87
short brushstroke p60
reverse fan brushstroke p110
stalks p96
finished painting p142

TULIPS

Colour Palette

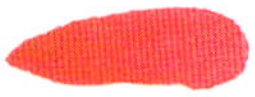

Permanent rose

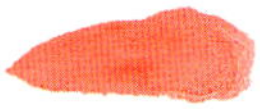

Cadmium red

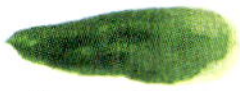

Sap green

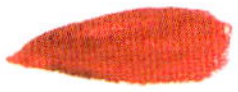

Alizarin crimson

Technical information: Use reverse fan brushstrokes to paint the petals. Slide the brush when you paint the brushstrokes to make them longer.

Step 1

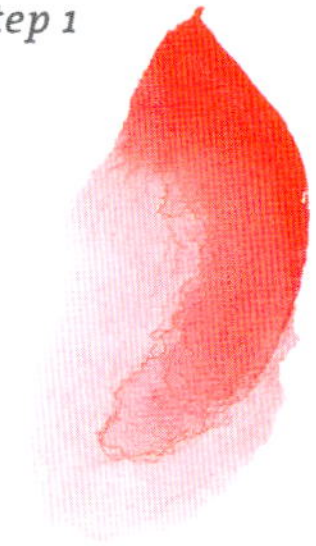

Step 2

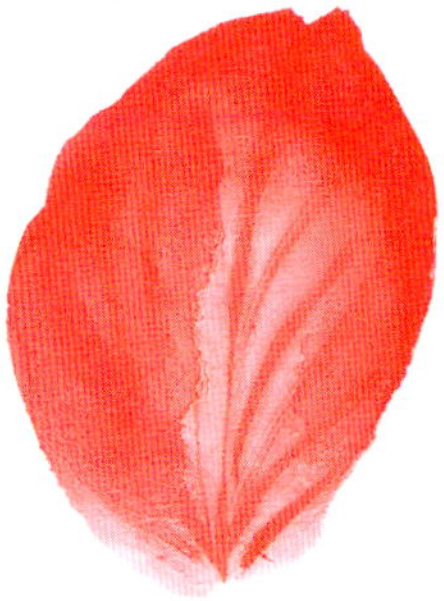

Step 3

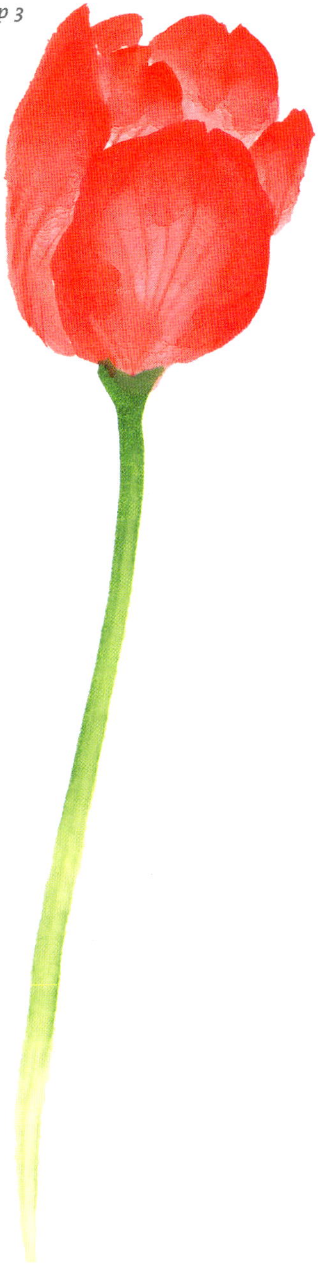

Brushes to use: B1, B2, B4

Step 1 Mix one part of permanent rose with one part of cadmium red. Load **B1** with diluted permanent rose and dip the nib of the brush into this mixture. Paint a reverse fan brushstroke, sliding the brush downwards when you paint the brushstroke so that the resulting shape is longer. Keep the nib of the brush to the left.

Step 2 Paint another reverse fan brushstroke in the same way next to the first one but keep the nib of the brush to the right. The two reverse fan brushstrokes painted in this way make a petal. Use **B4** and alizarin crimson to add veins to the petal as illustrated.

Step 3 Start to paint a flower with the petals at the front. Build up the flower by adding more petals towards the back. Paint the veins as described in step 2. Load **B2** with sap green and add a stalk.

See also

leaves p89
short brushstroke p60
fan brushstroke p100
reverse fan brushstroke p110
finished painting p147

PEONY FLOWERS

Technical information: The peony used here for demonstration is the perennial type. A peony flower has many petals of different shapes and sizes. The lower petals are larger and can be painted with reverse fan brushstrokes. The upper petals are very irregular in shape. They can be painted with short brushstrokes and fan brushstrokes.

Colour Palette

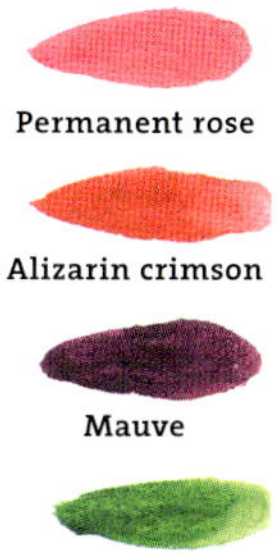

Permanent rose

Alizarin crimson

Mauve

Sap green

Step 1

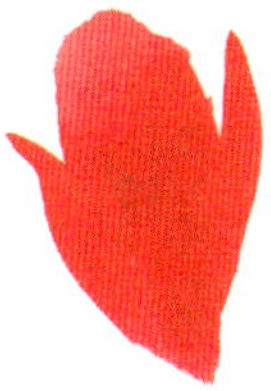

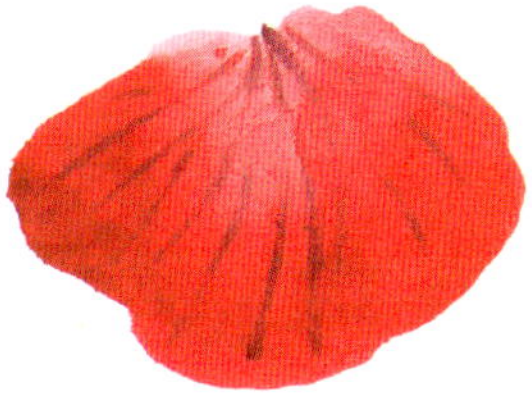

Step 5

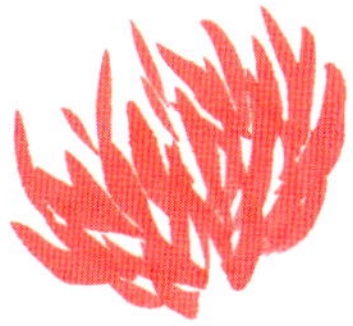

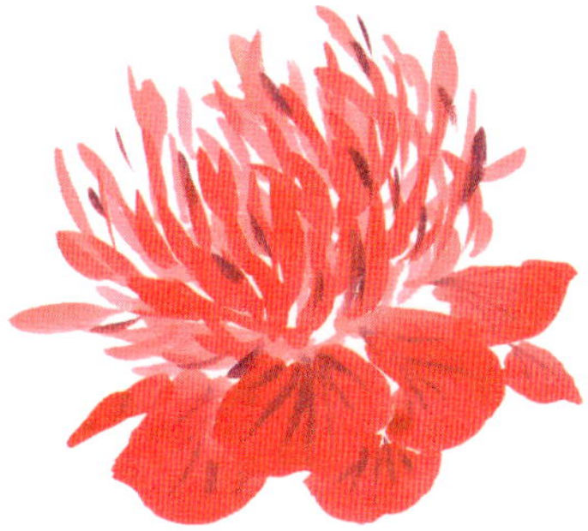

Step 2

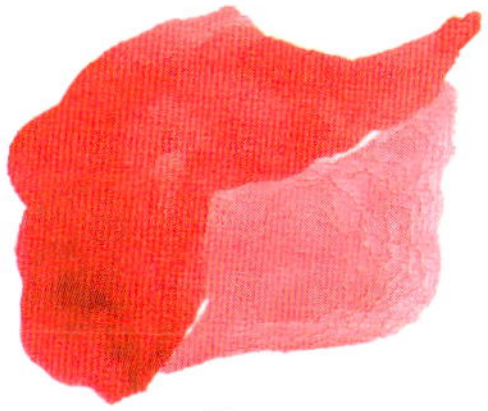

Step 3

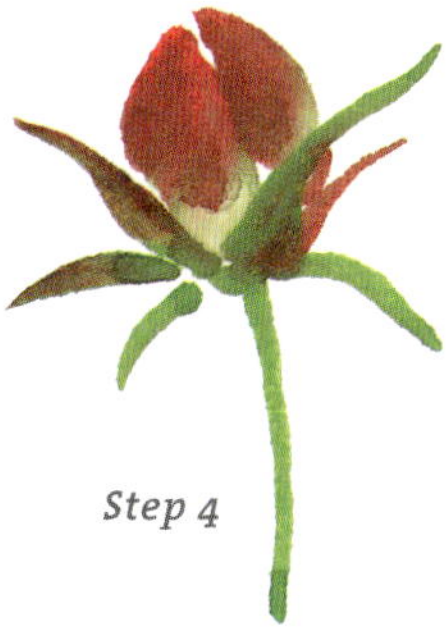

Step 4

Brushes to use: B1, B2, B4

Step 1 Mix one part of permanent rose with one part of alizarin crimson. Load **B1** with this mixture to paint the upper petals. Use a single short brushstroke to paint a small one and two or three short brushstrokes to paint the slightly bigger ones. An even bigger one is made up of two short brushstrokes, one on each side of a fan brushstroke.

Step 2 The lower petals are larger. Load **B1** with permanent rose and dip the nib of the brush into the mixture described in step 1. Paint a reverse fan brushstroke for each petal. Use **B4** and alizarin crimson to add the veins.

Step 3 Some lower petals curl. Use diluted permanent rose for the underside of a petal. Start with the underside then finish the petal with the same loading of colours described in step 2.

Step 4 To paint a bud, load **B2** with sap green and the nib of the brush with permanent rose. Paint the sepals with short brushstrokes and add a stalk. Dip **B2** into the mixture described in Step 1 and add the bud with two or three long dots.

Step 5 Start with the upper part of the flower with a variety of small petals as described in step 1. Load **B1** with diluted permanent rose to add more petals. Then dip **B1** into mauve to add a few small petals to highlight. Add the lower petals, starting with the top ones, then add the lower ones. Use **B4** and alizarin crimson to add veins.

See also

leaves	p81
fan brushstroke	p100
short brushstroke	p60
finished painting	p145

PANSY FLOWERS

Colour Palette

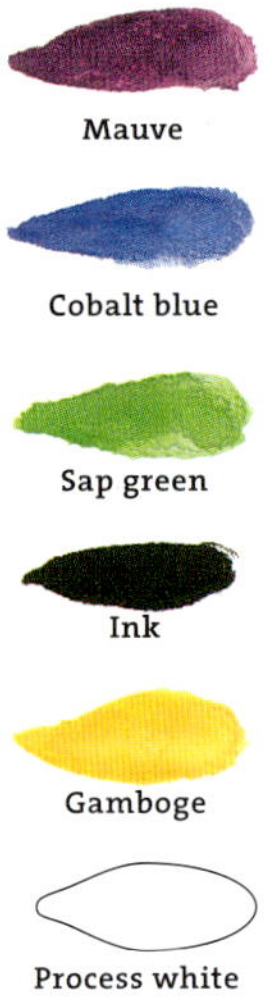

Technical information: All the petals of a pansy flower can be painted with fan brushstrokes. Use a short brushstroke to paint a bud.

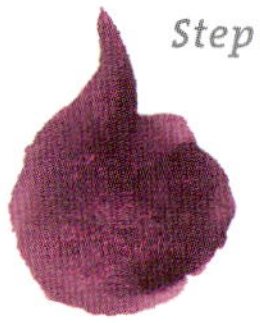

Step 1

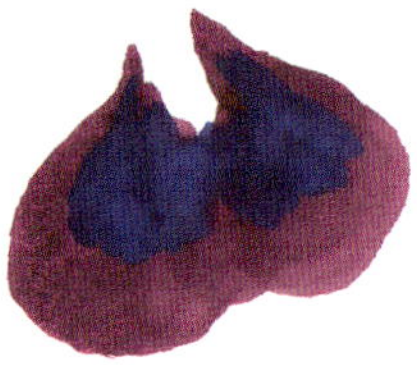

Step 2

Step 3

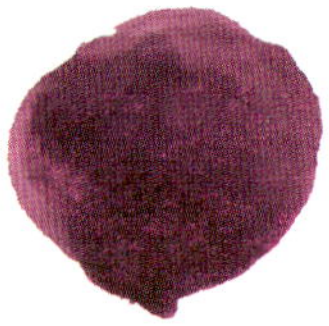

Step 4

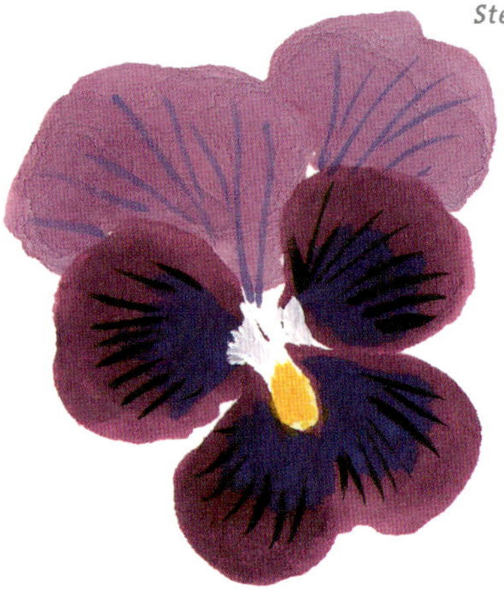

Step 5

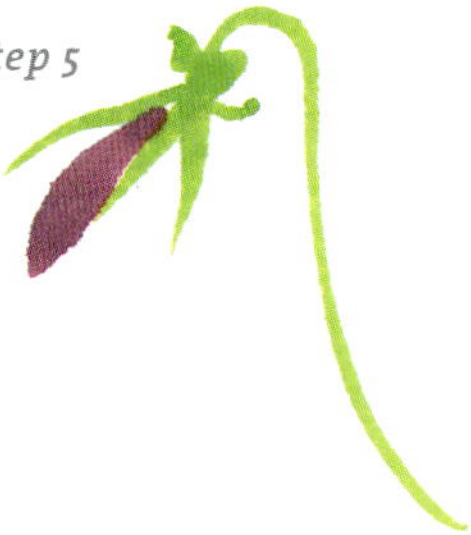

Brushes to use: B1, B2, B3, B4

Step 1 A pansy flower has a very wide lower petal. Load **B1** with mauve. Hold the brush at a low angle and paint a fan brushstroke.

Step 2 Use two fan brushstrokes to paint a lower petal as illustrated. Leave a space in the upper middle for the centre. Some petals have dark patches. Make a purple by mixing two parts of mauve with one part of cobalt blue. Dip **B2** into the purple and paint a dark patch on the lower petal.

Step 3 There are two middle petals and two upper petals. Paint a wide fan brushstroke for each. In this illustration mauve has been used for the middle petals and diluted mauve for the upper petals.

Step 4 Load **B1** with mauve. Start a flower with the lower petal. Use the same brush and same loading of colours. Add the two middle petals just above the lower one. Paint each petal with a wide fan brushstroke. Clean **B1** and load with diluted mauve. Paint the two uppermost petals. Load **B2** with purple to paint the dark patches on the lower petal and the two middle petals. Use **B4** and purple to paint the veins of the uppermost petals. Use **B4** and ink to paint the veins of the three lower petals. Dip **B3** into process white and add a dot at the base of each of the middle petals. Dip **B4** into gamboge and add the centre to the lower petal.

Step 5 Load **B3** with sap green and paint the sepals of a bud, as illustrated. Add a stalk. Use **B2** and purple to paint a short brushstroke for the bud.

See also

flowers p66
fan brushstroke p100
finished painting p150
greens p155

LOTUS LEAVES

Technical information: Lotus leaves are very big and each one needs many fan brushstrokes.

Colour Palette

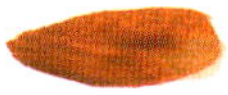

Burnt sienna

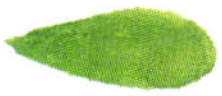

Sap green

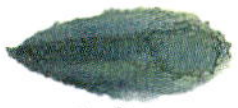

Indigo

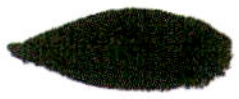

Ink

Step 1

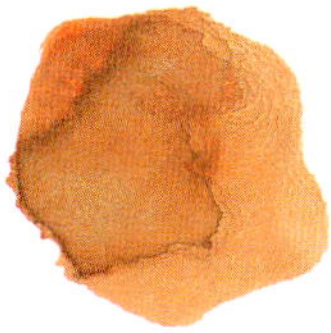

Step 2

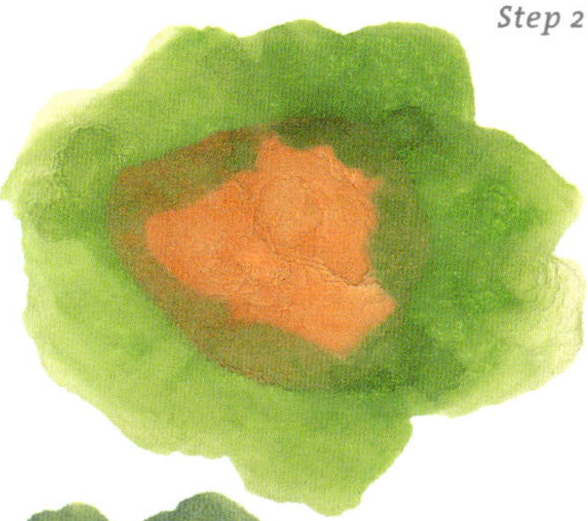

Step 3

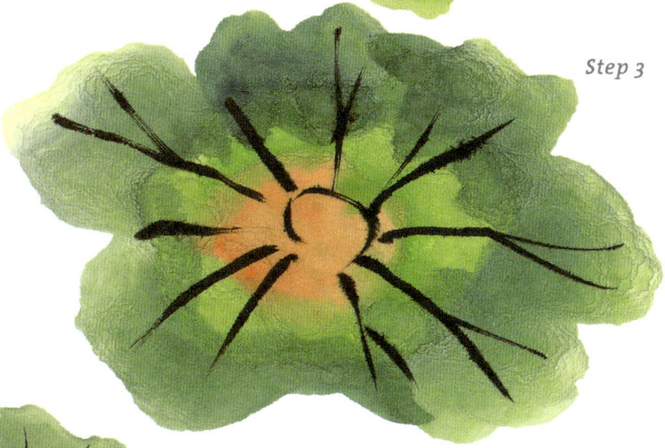

Step 4

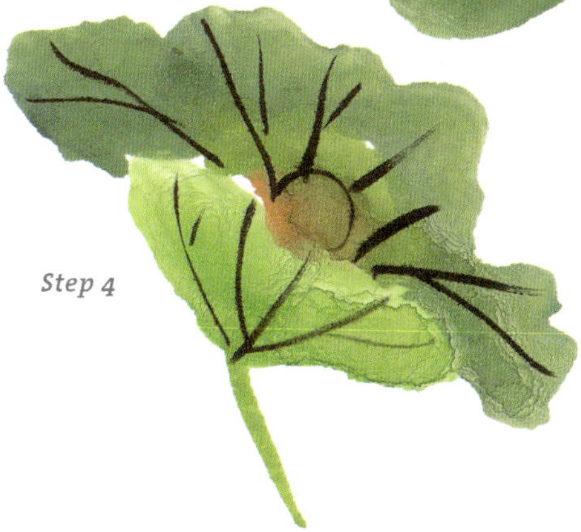

Step 5

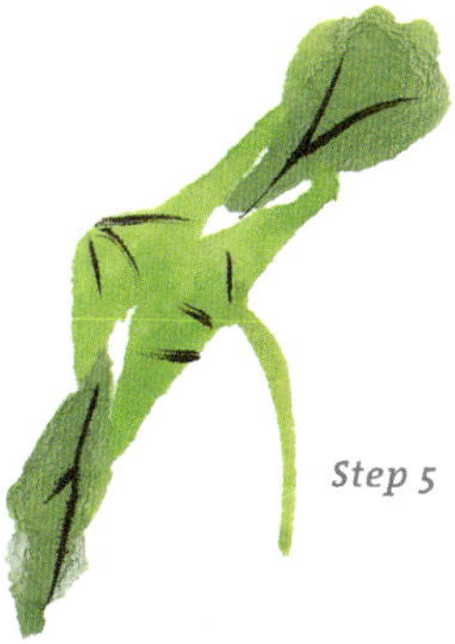

Brushes to use: B1, B2, B3, B4

Step 1 Load **B1** with burnt sienna. Start painting a central patch for the leaf.

Step 2 Dip **B1** generously into sap green and add fan brushstrokes around the burnt sienna patch while the patch is still wet, so that the two colours merge at their edges.

Step 3 Load **B1** with dark green. Add dark green fan brushstrokes around the outside edges of the sap green fan brushstrokes while they are still wet. Dip **B4** into ink and add the veins, as illustrated.

Step 4 Paint a leaf with a curling edge. Load **B1** with sap green and start painting the curling edge using a fan brushstroke. Finish the leaf as described in steps 1 to 3. Dip **B3** into sap green and add a stalk.

Step 5 Load **B2** with sap green and paint two short brushstrokes to represent the curling edge of an unopened leaf. Dip **B2** into dark green to add the final parts of the leaf. Use **B4** and ink to add veins. Dip **B3** into sap green and add a stalk.

See also

leaves	p82
reverse fan brushstroke	p110
long dot	p50
finished painting	p146

POPPY FLOWERS

Colour Palette

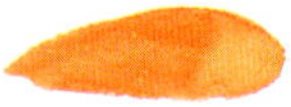

Cadmium orange

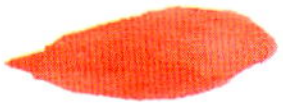

Cadmium red

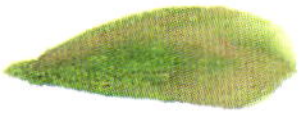

Sap green

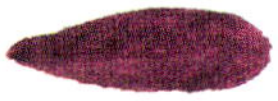

Mauve

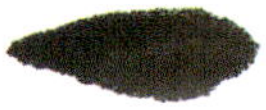

Ink

Technical information: Poppy petals are very wide and large. Use multiple reverse fan brushstrokes for each petal. Hold the brush at a very low angle to the paper.

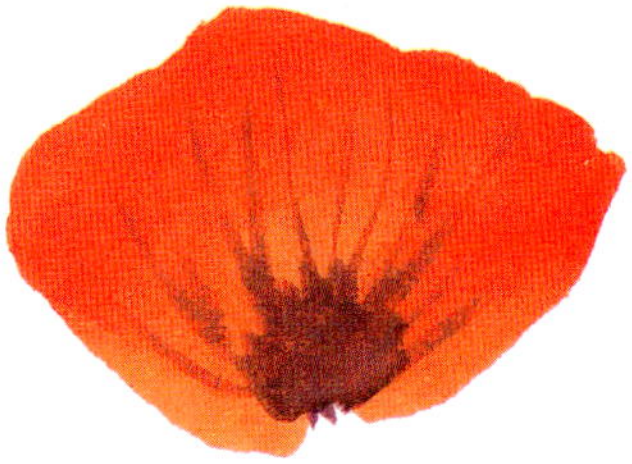

Step 1

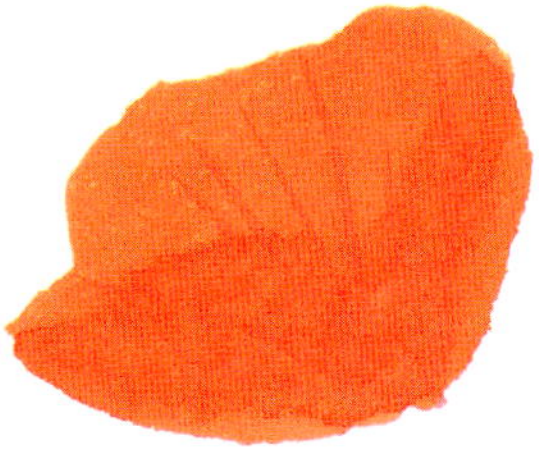

Step 2

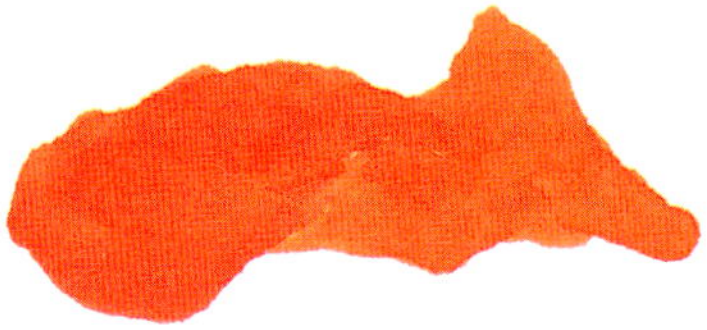

Step 3

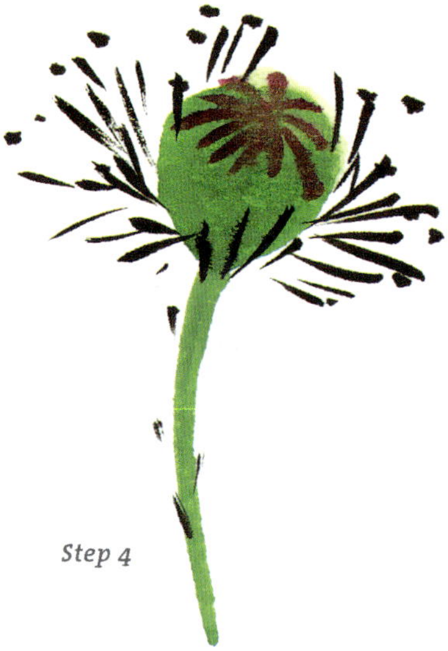

Step 4

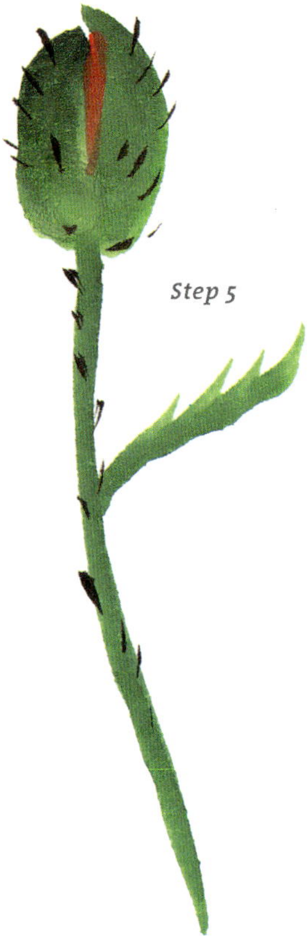

Step 5

Brushes to use: B1, B2, B3, B4

Step 1 Load **B1** with cadmium orange and dip the nib of the brush into cadmium red. Paint two or three reverse fan brushstrokes to make up a petal. Each petal has a dark patch at the base. Use **B3** and mauve to paint the dark patch. Use **B4** and mauve to paint the veins.

Step 2 Load **B1** and cadmium orange to paint the back of a petal. Use diluted mauve for the patch and the veins.

Step 3 Paint a petal with a curling edge. Start at the curling edge with cadmium orange. Add the front of the petal with the colour loading described in step 1.

Step 4 At the centre of the flower is a seed head. Use **B1** and sap green to paint a fan brushstroke with the brush held at a high angle to the paper. Load **B2** with mauve and add the dark markings at the top of the seed head. Dip **B3** into ink and add the stamens. Add a dot on top of each stamen.

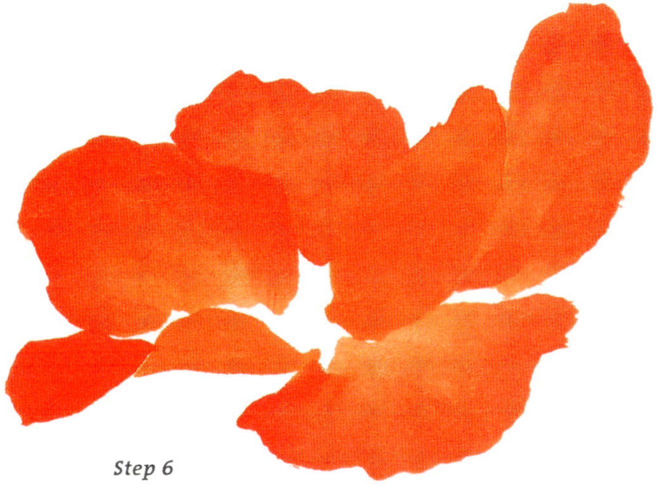

Step 6

Step 5 Load **B1** with sap green and dip the nib of the brush into indigo. Paint two sepals of the bud with long dots. Use **B2** and sap green to add a stalk and leaf. Dip **B4** into ink and add the hair on the sepals and along the stalk. Dip **B3** into cadmium red to fill the gap between the two sepals.

Step 6 The poppy flower in this illustration has six petals, three on the inside and three outside. Start with the petal on the front. Add more petals towards the back.

Step 7 Add the central seed head. Paint dark patches on each petal and the veins.

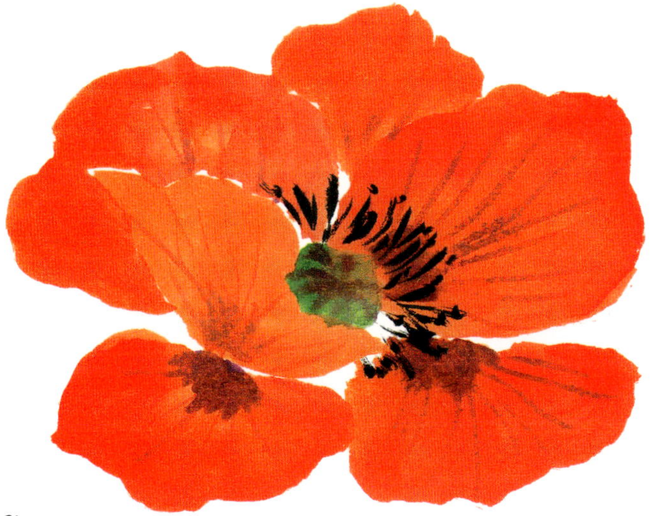

Step 7

CHAPTER 5

GALLERY

In this chapter, related flowers, leaves, stalks and branches are put together to form paintings.

The usual method to construct a flower painting is as follows:

Step 1 Start with the main group of flowers or leaves at the front.

Step 2 Add other groups of flowers or leaves towards the back.

Step 3 Paint the main branches or main stalks. Add other branches or stalks to connect the flowers and leaves to the main ones.

Step 4 Add more flowers and leaves in diluted tones to create depth.

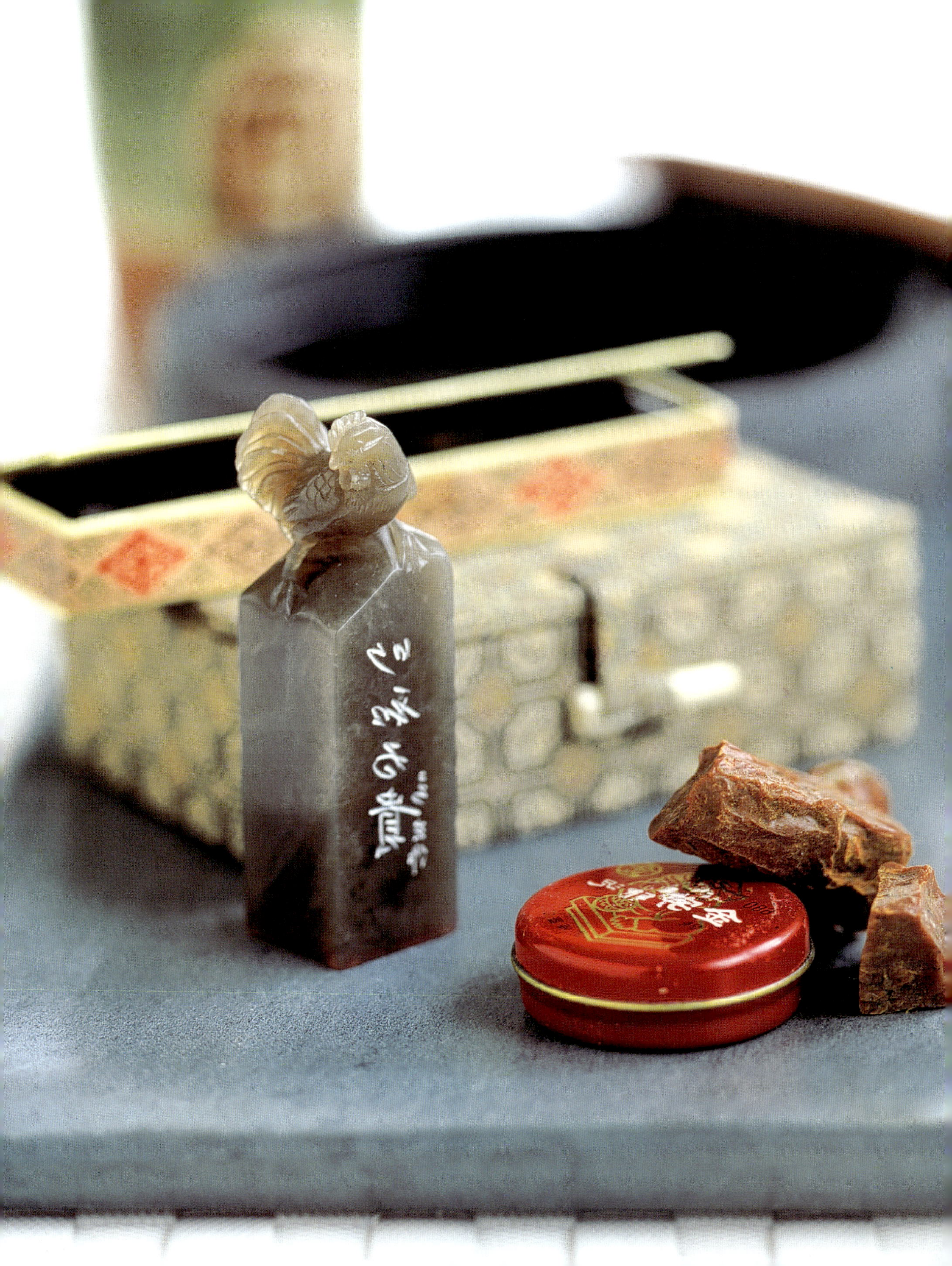

See also

leaves	**p106**
flowers	**p103**

GERANIUMS

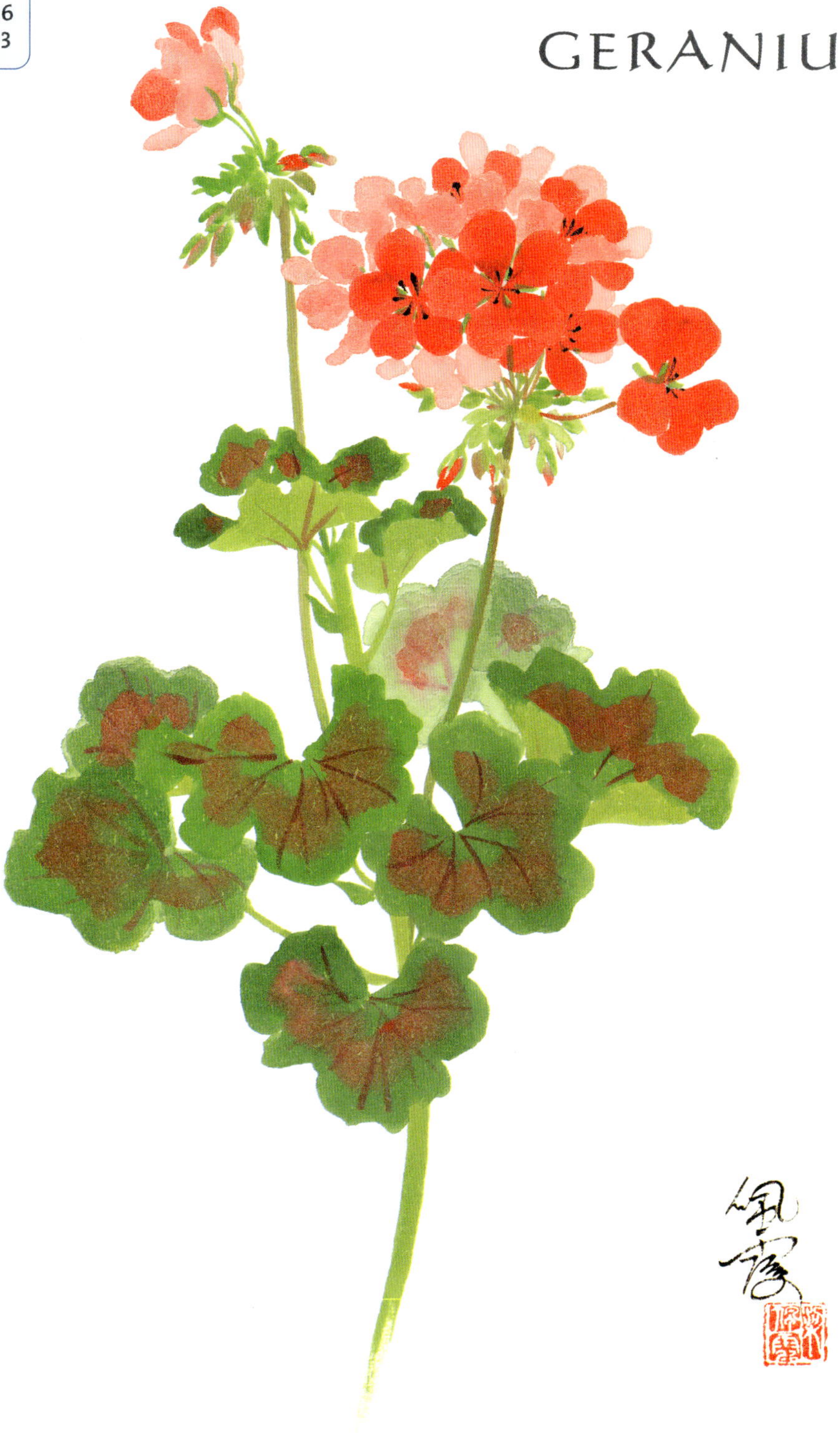

CLEMATIS

See also

leaves	**p78**
climbers	**p97**
flowers	**p120**

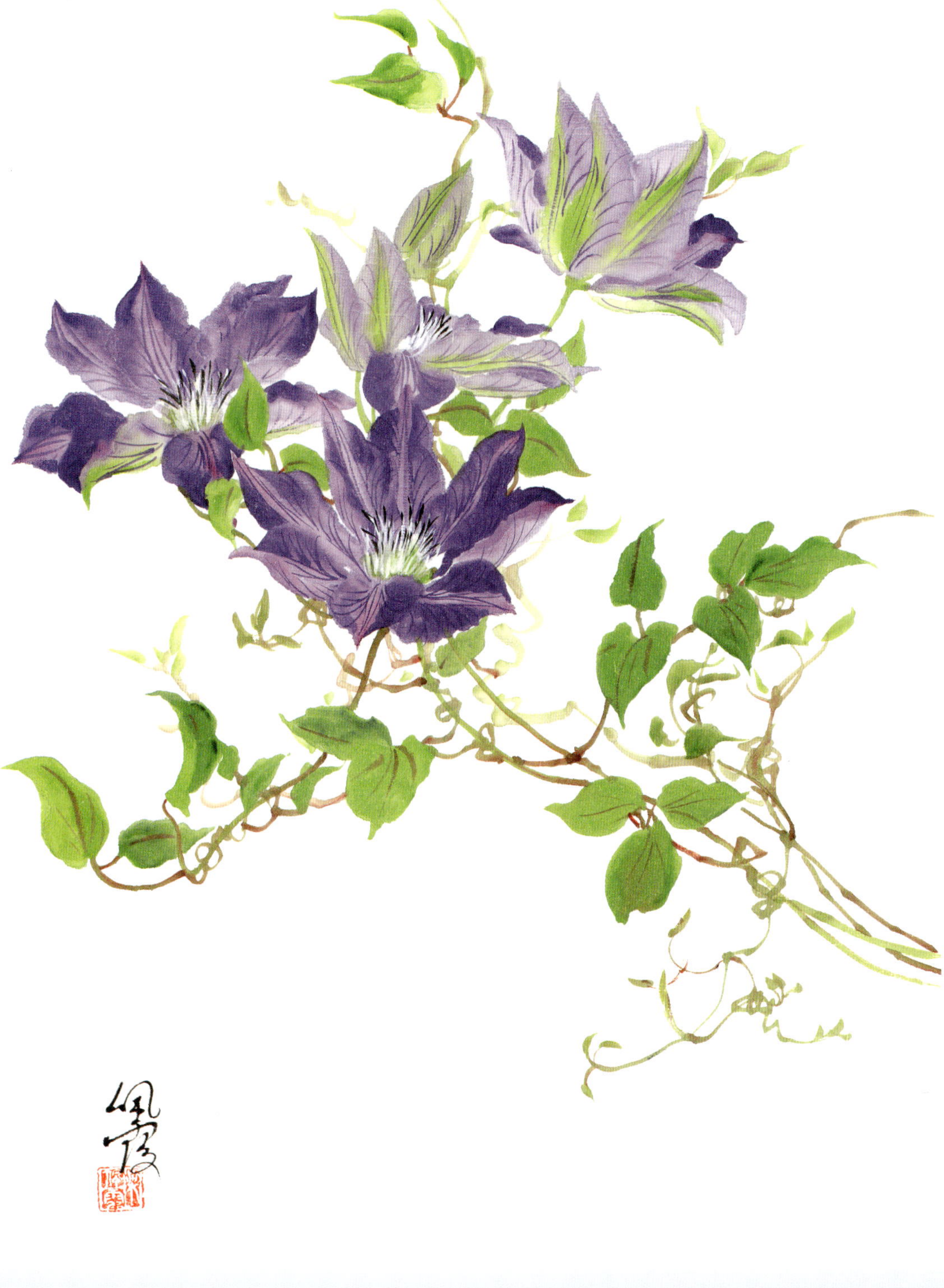

See also

leaves	p77
climbers	p97
flowers	p63

HONEYSUCKLE

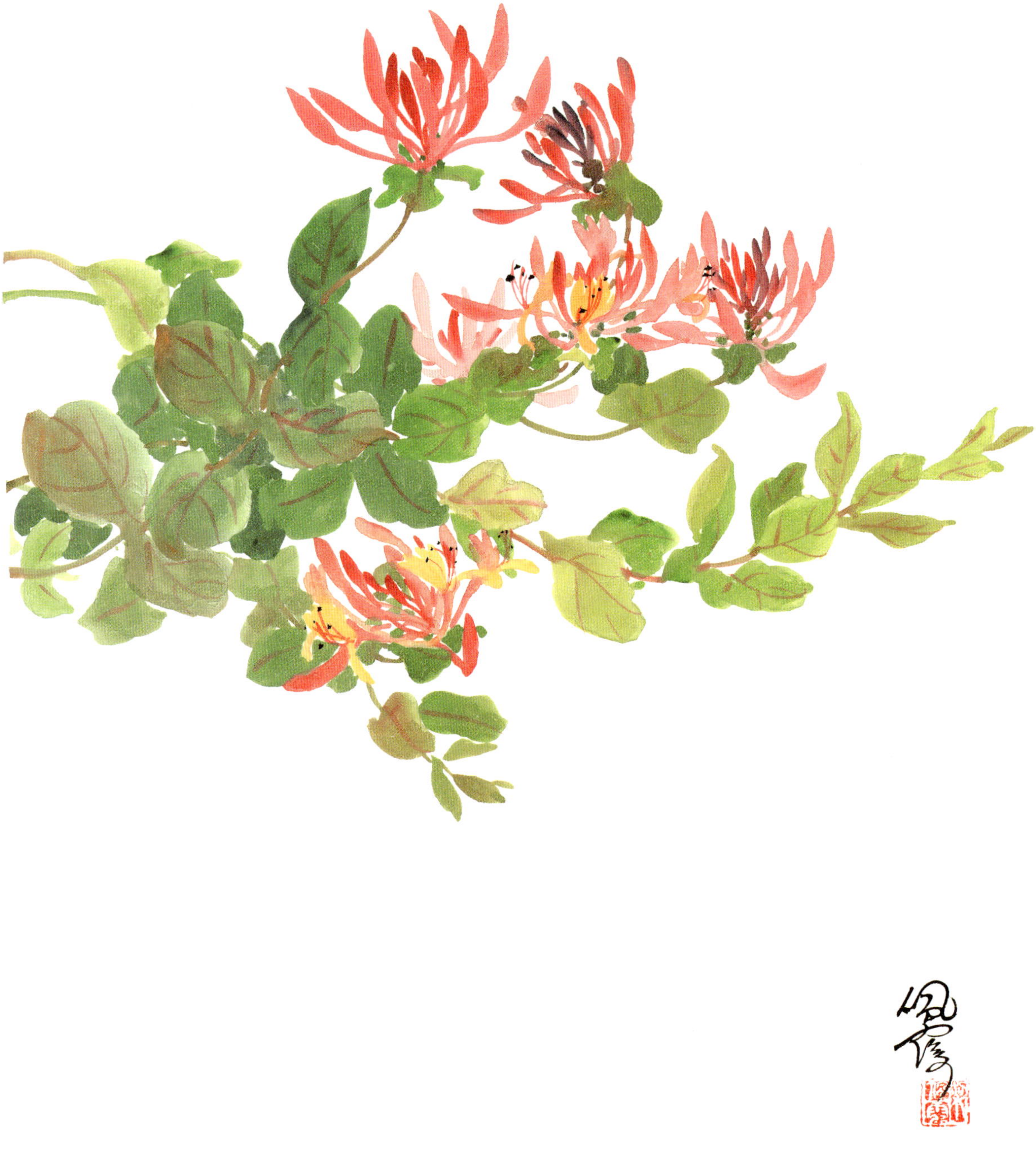

IRIS

See also

leaves **p88**
flowers **p59**

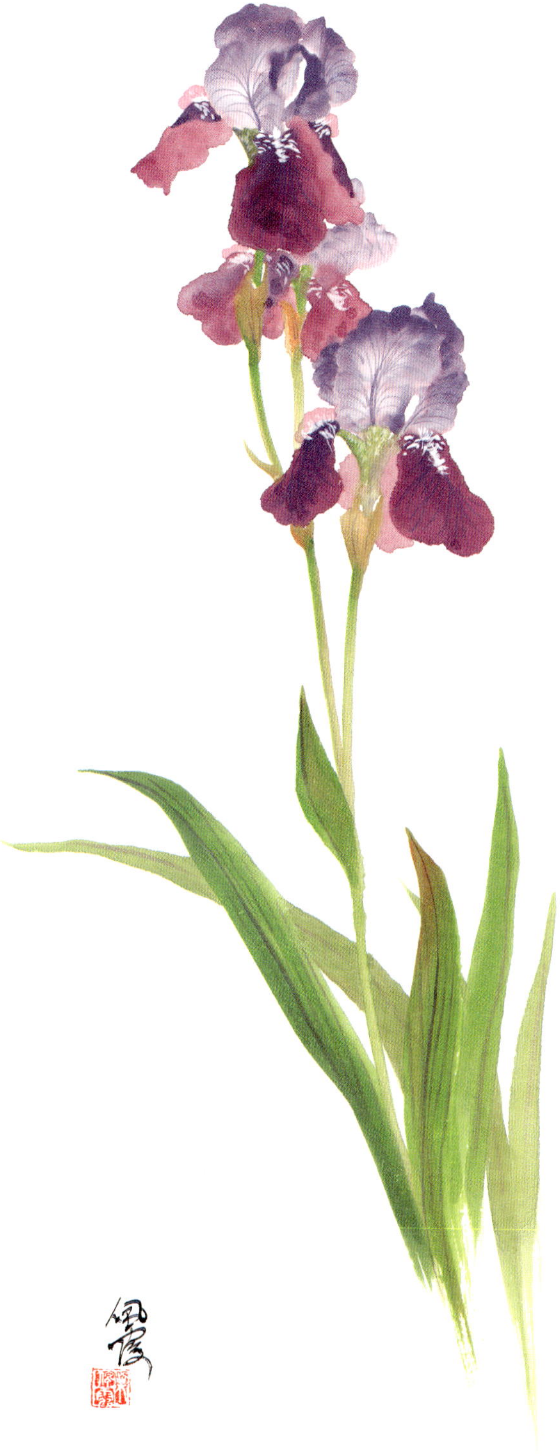

See also
leaves **p76**
flowers **p64**

LILY

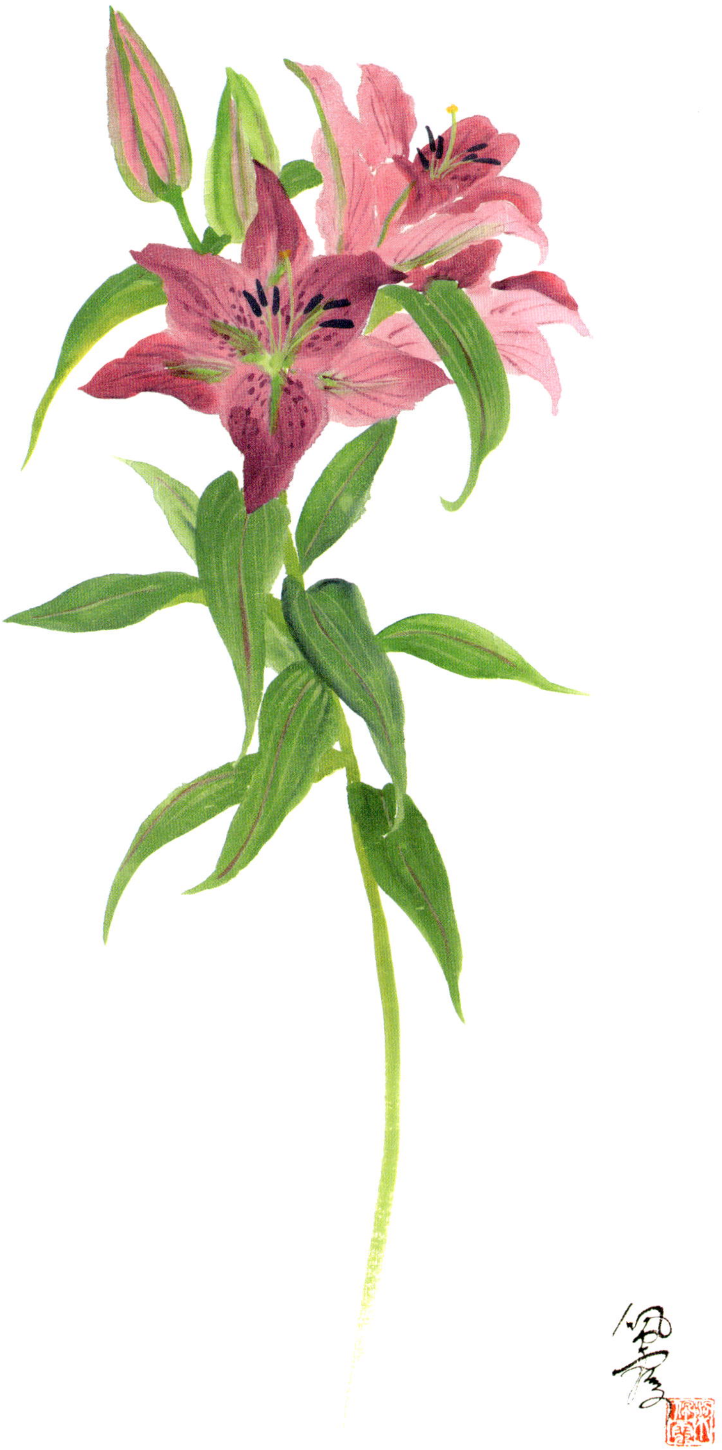

WISTERIA

See also

leaves p72
climbers p97
flowers p104

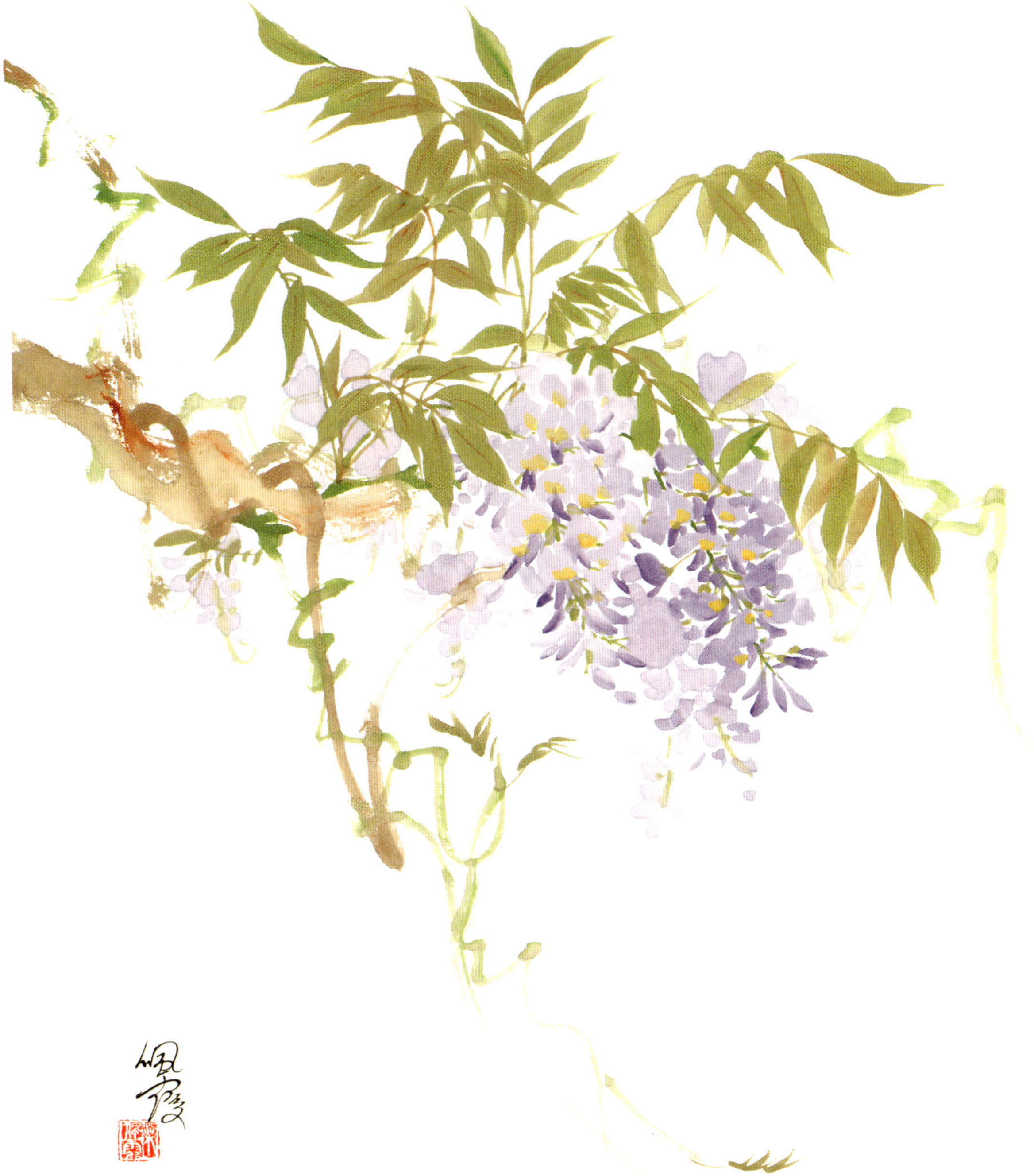

See also
leaves p80
flowers p105

HIBISCUS

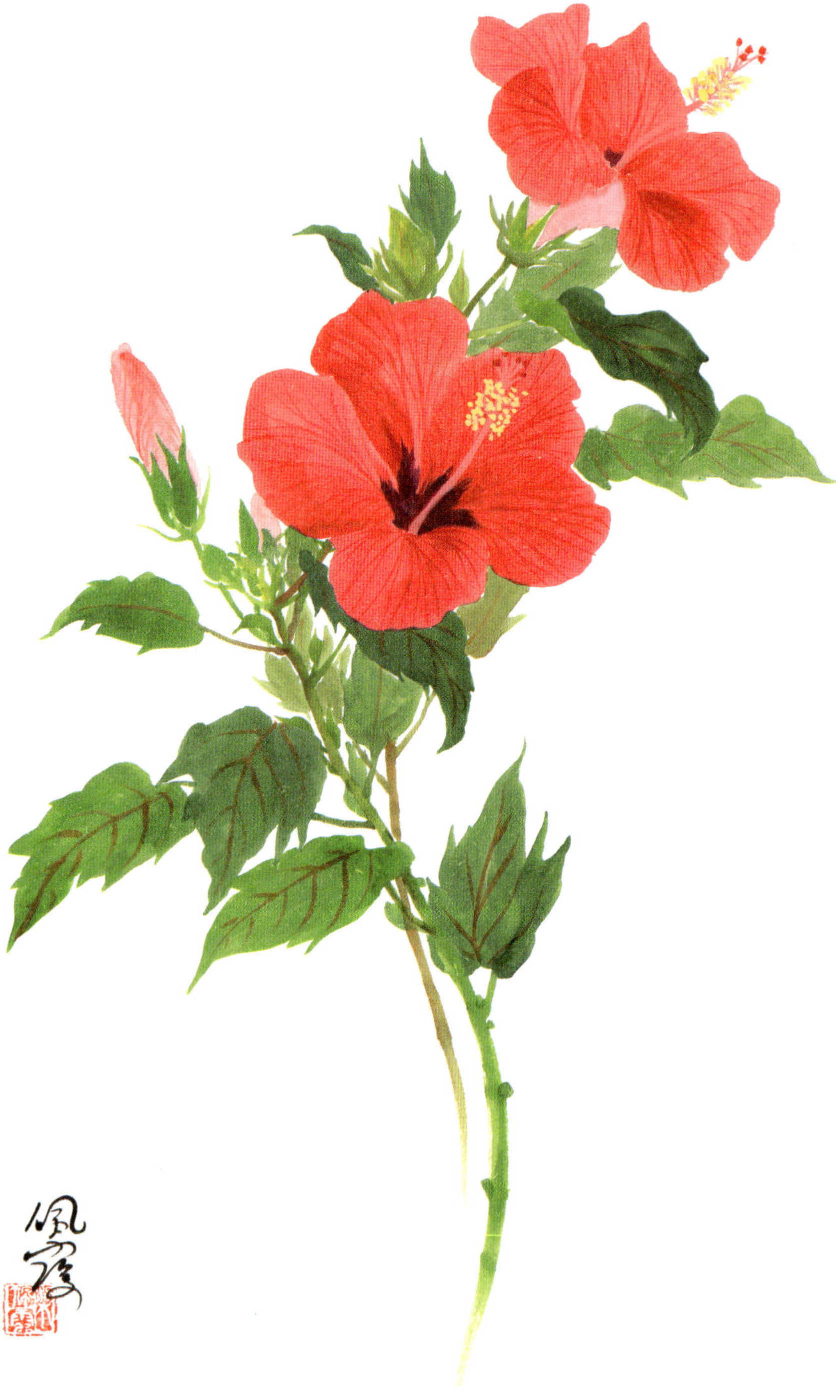

SHIRLEY POPPY

See also

leaves p82
flowers p112

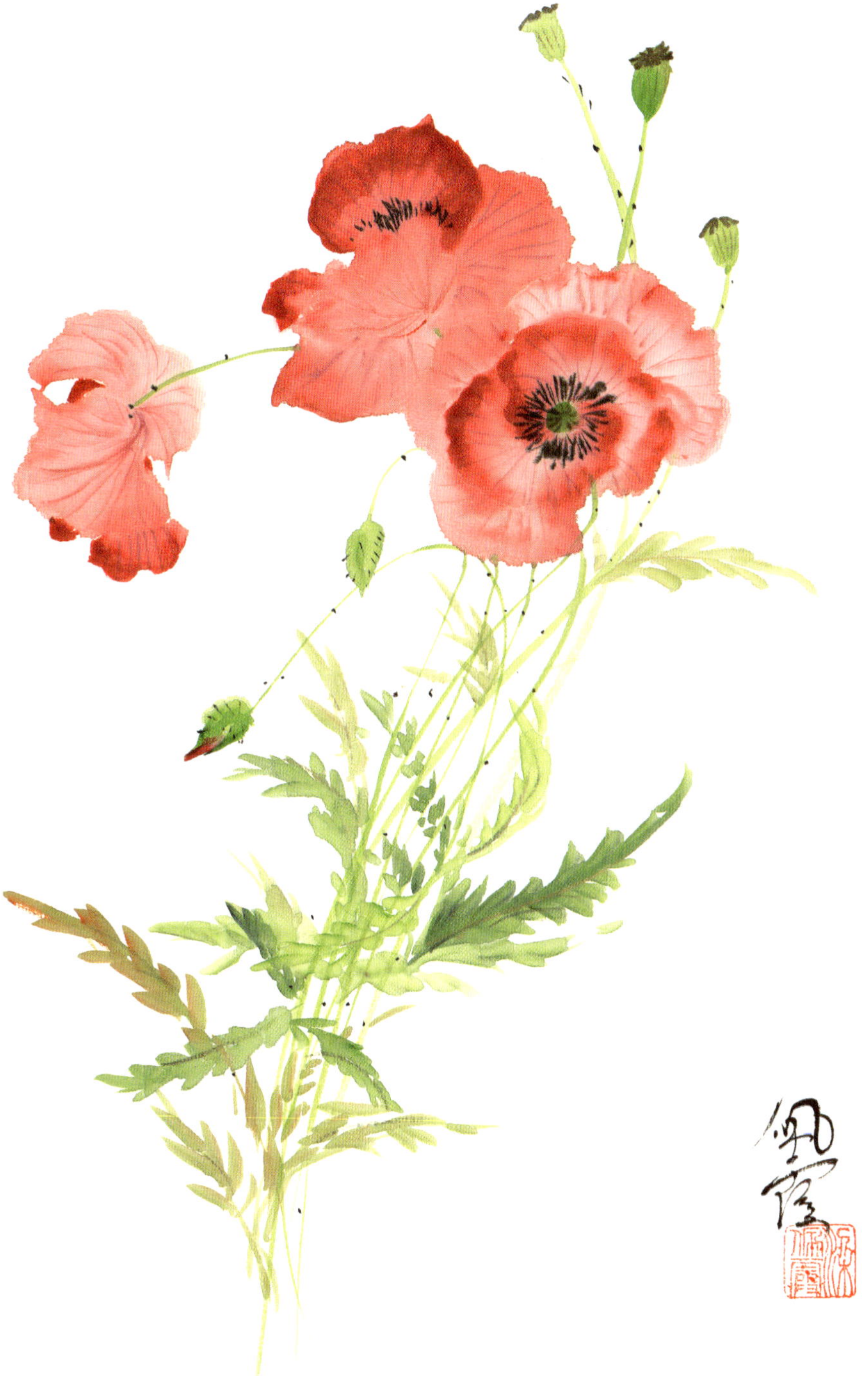

See also

leaves p74
flowers p121

CAMELLIA

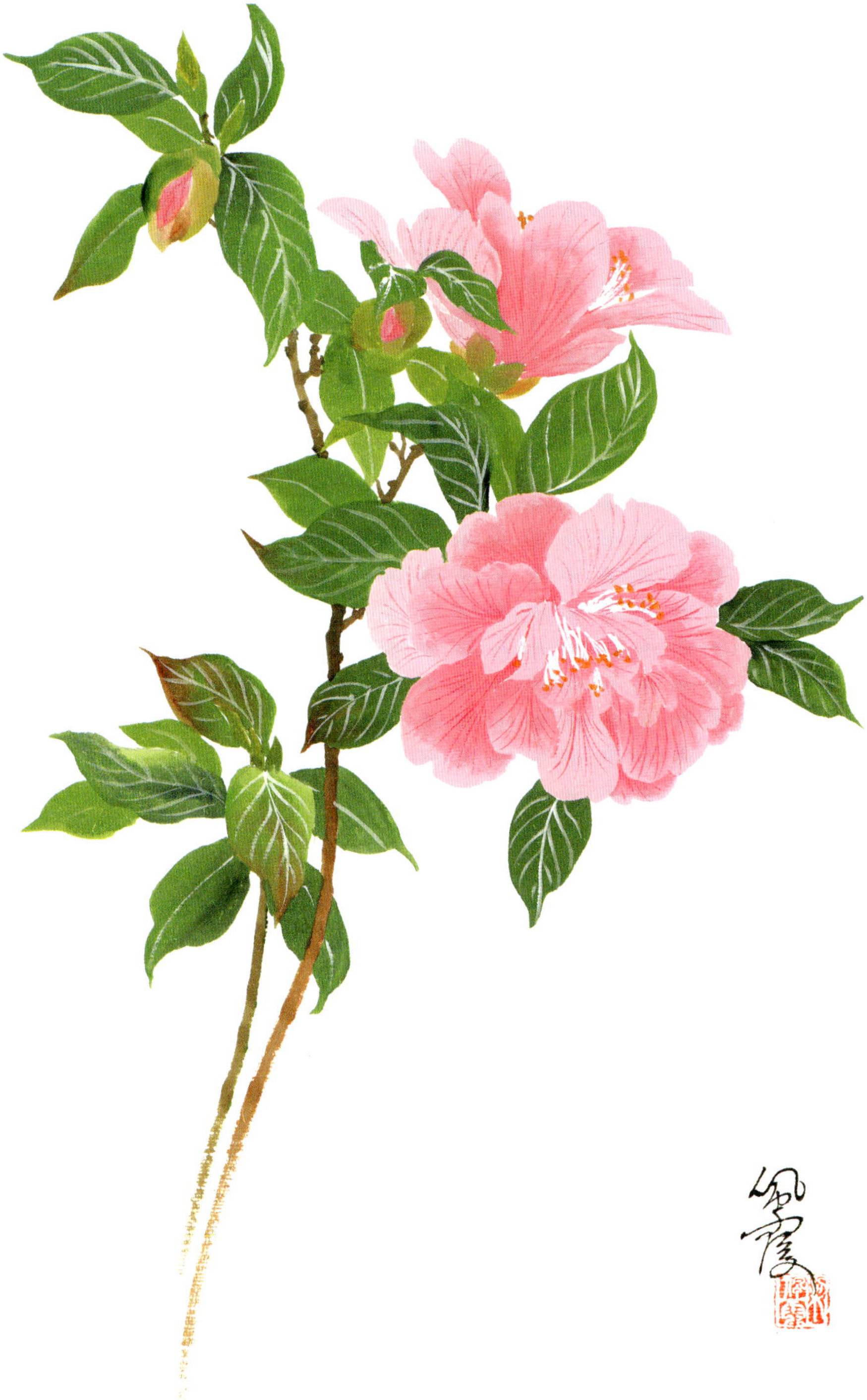

HYDRANGEA

See also
leaves **p79**
flowers **p53**

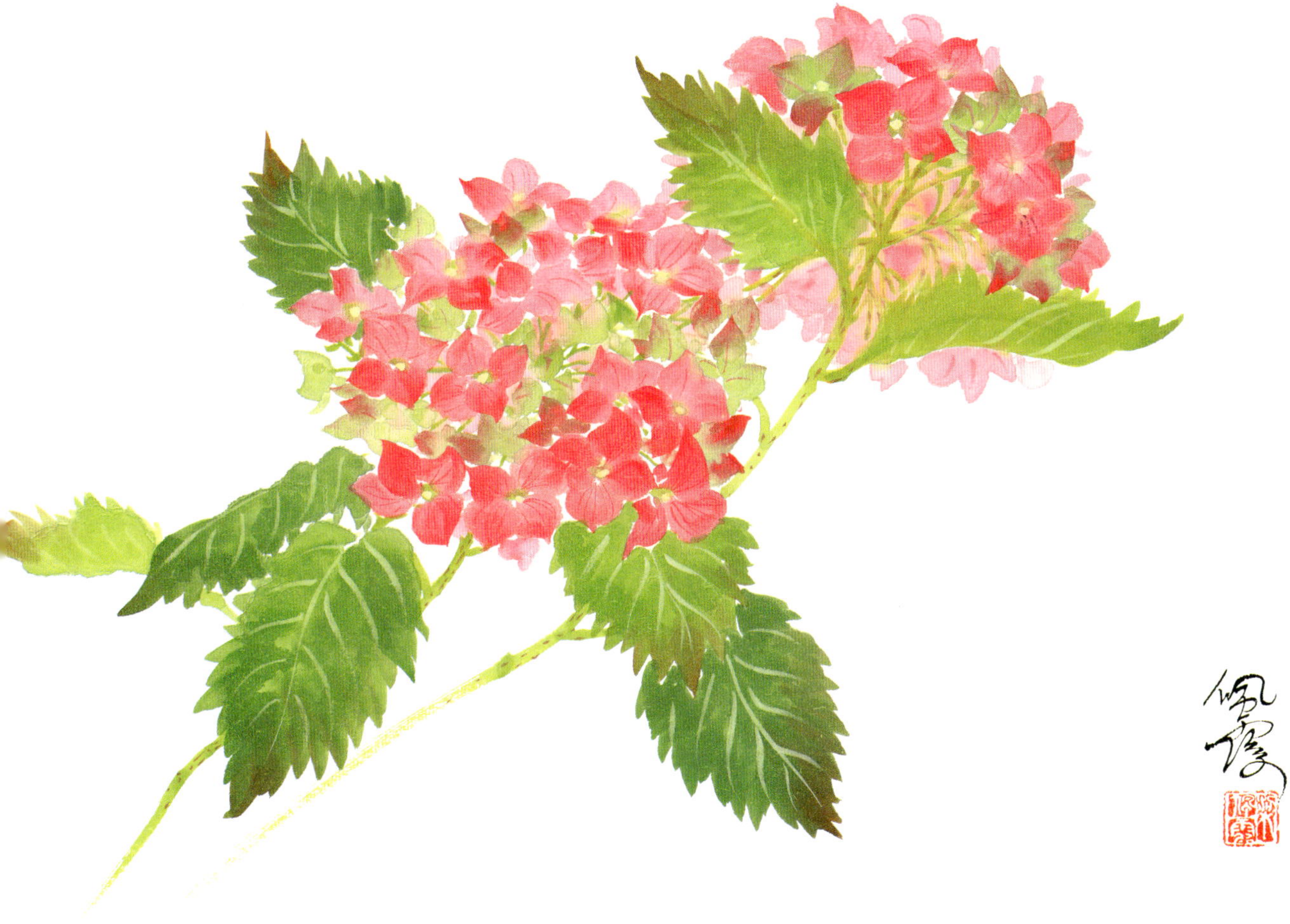

See also

leaves p87
flowers p124

TULIP

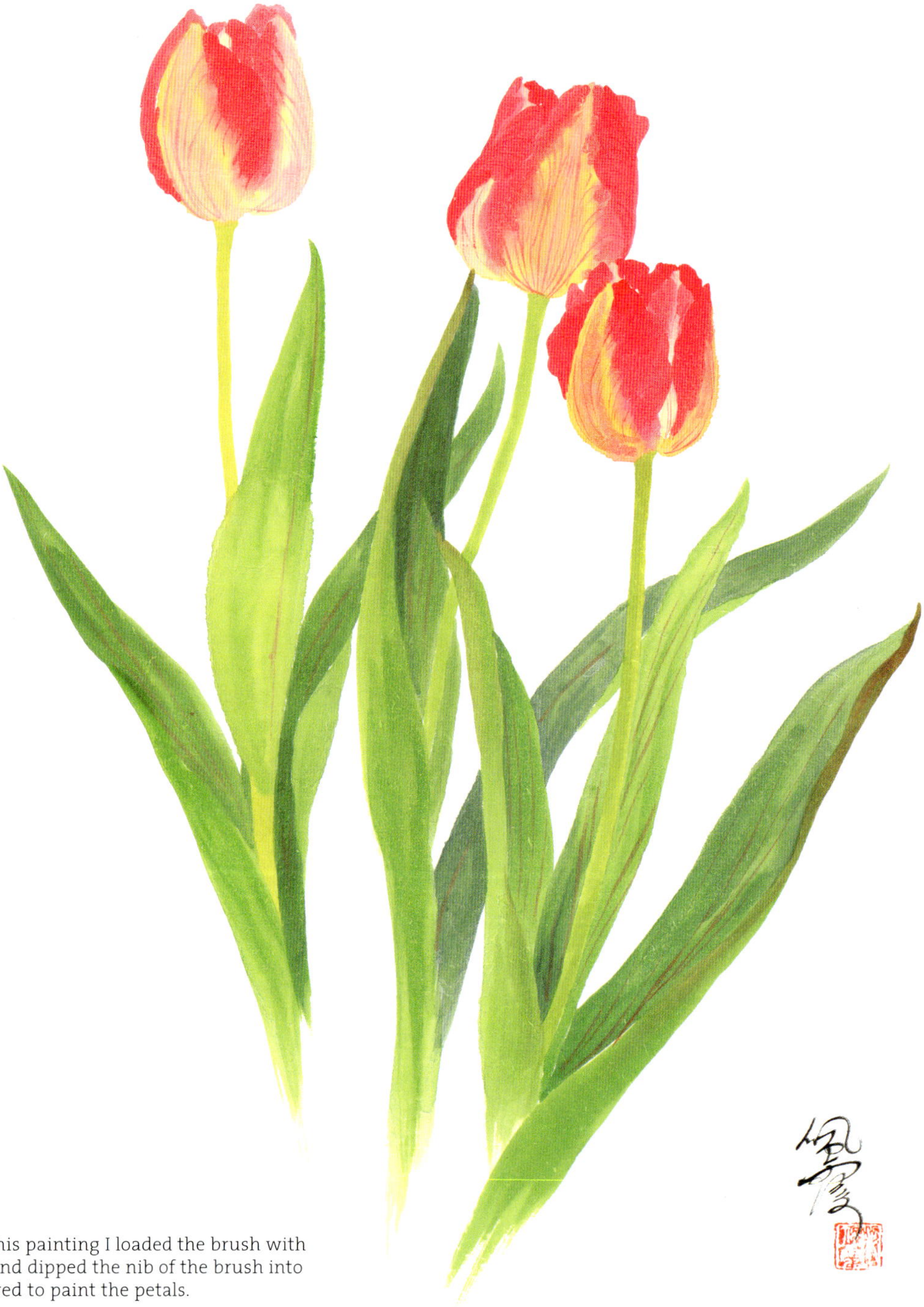

Note: For this painting I loaded the brush with gamboge and dipped the nib of the brush into Cadmium red to paint the petals.

See also

leaves p75
flowers p113

ROSE

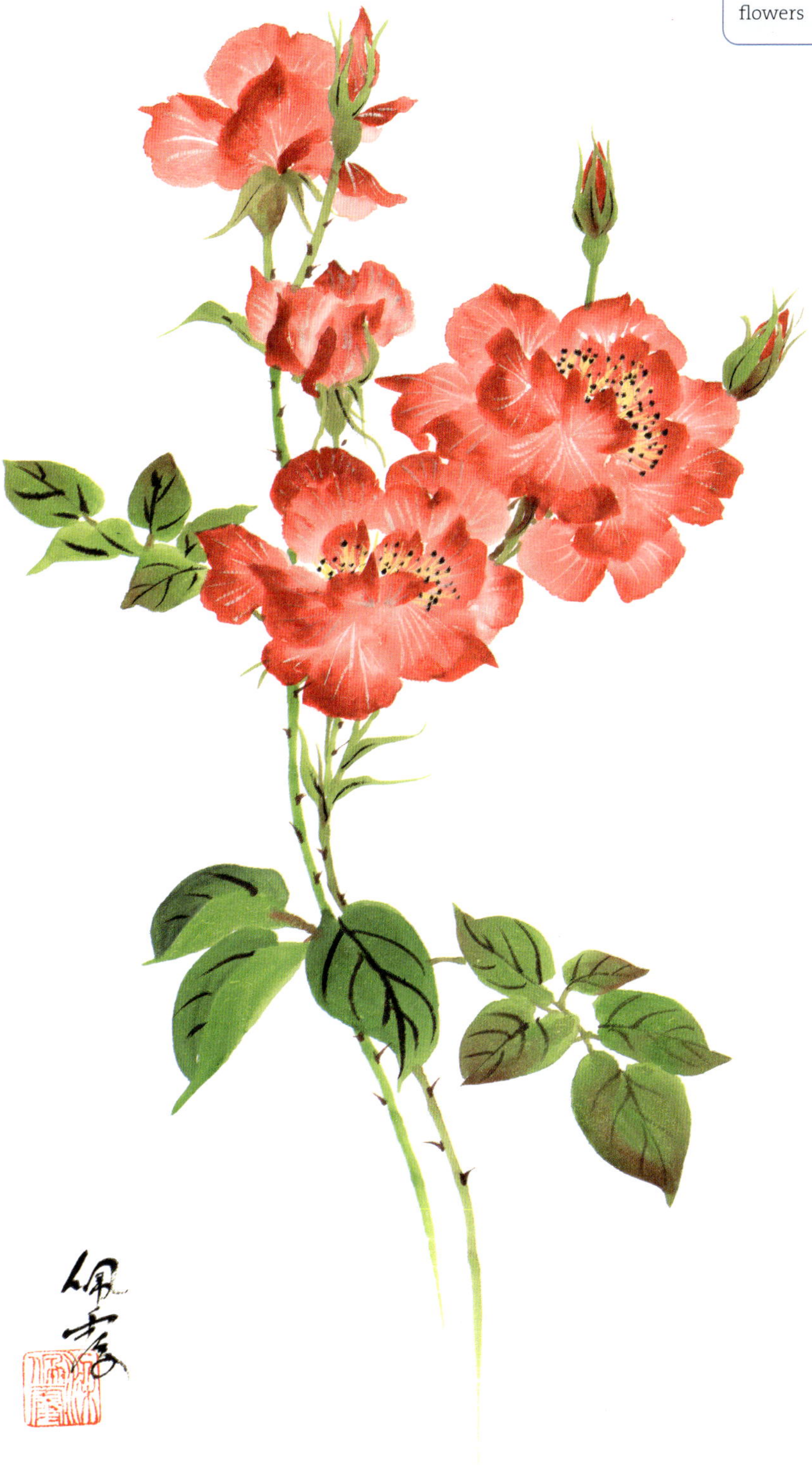

See also
leaves p83
flowers p52

BLEEDING HEART

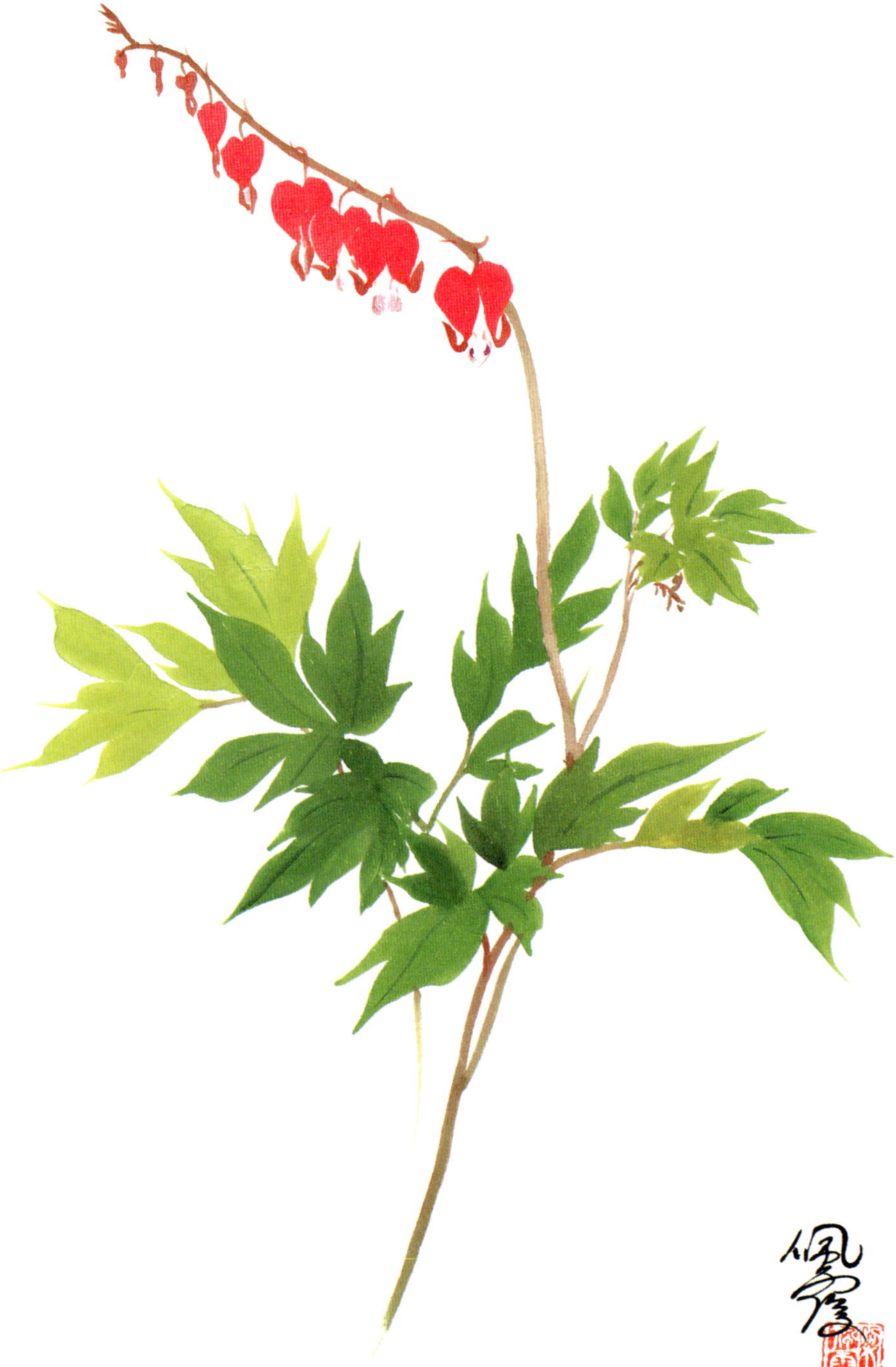

PANSY

See also

leaves	**p81**
flowers	**p126**

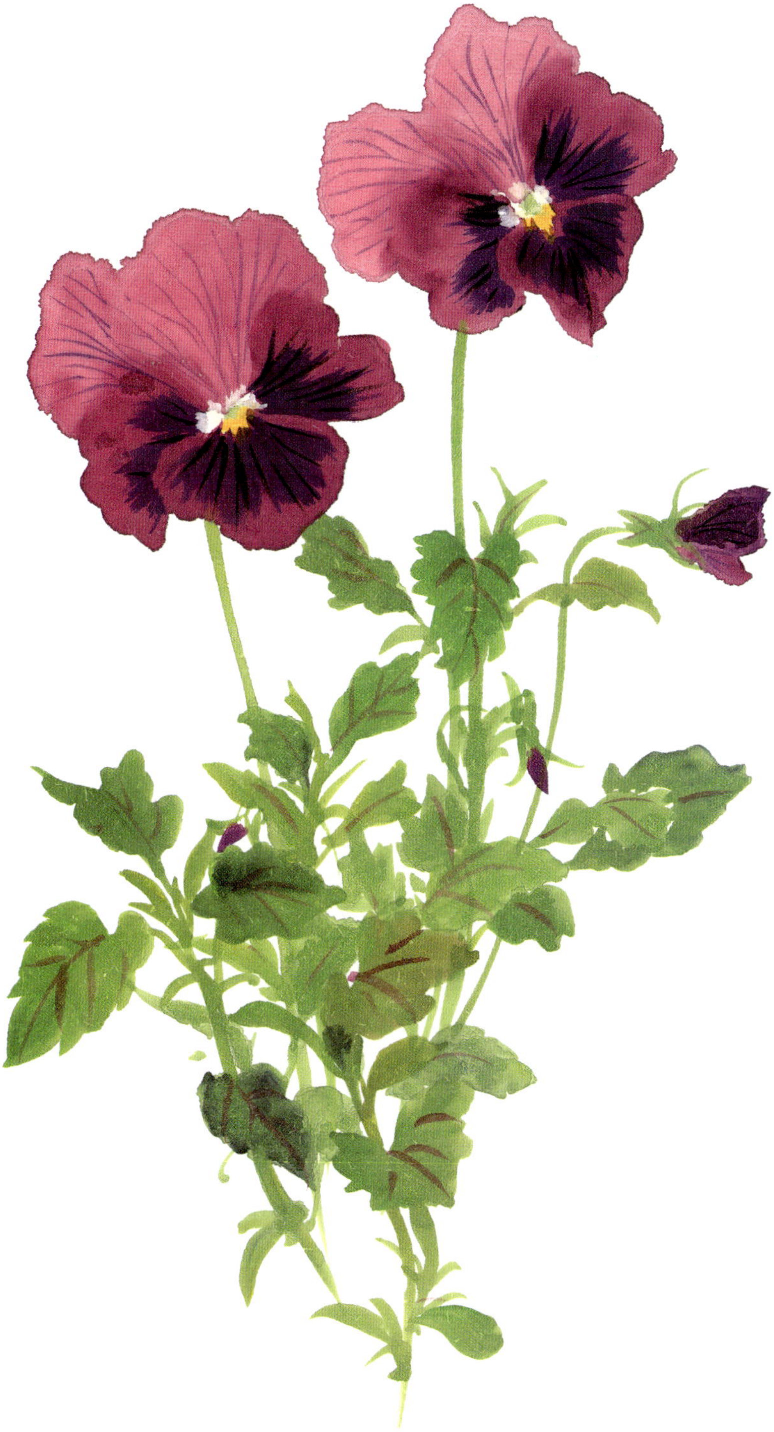

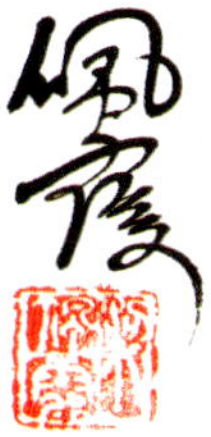

See also

leaves p82
flowers p128

POPPY

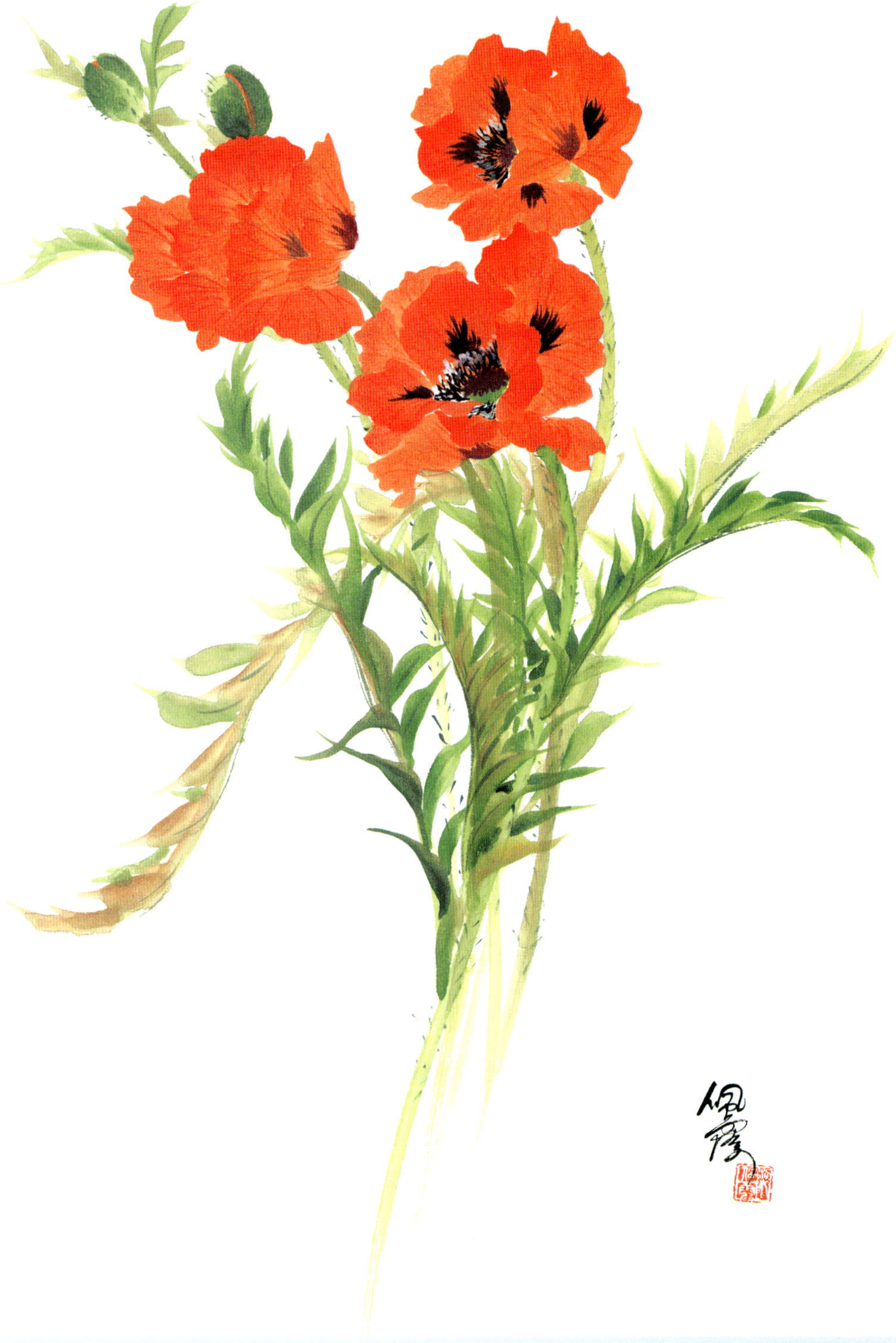

PEONY

See also
leaves p89
flowers p125

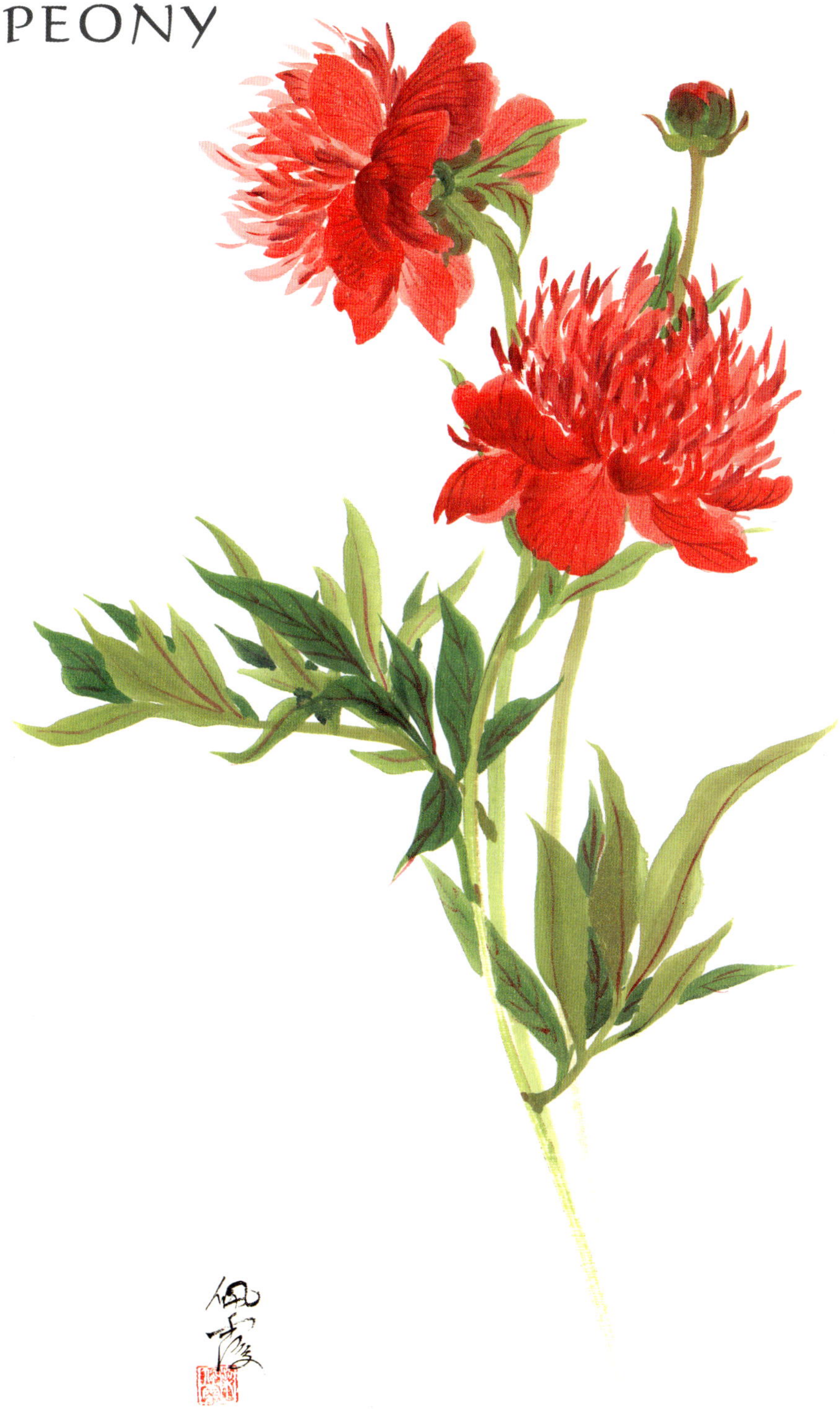

See also

leaves p67
flowers p67

AZALEA

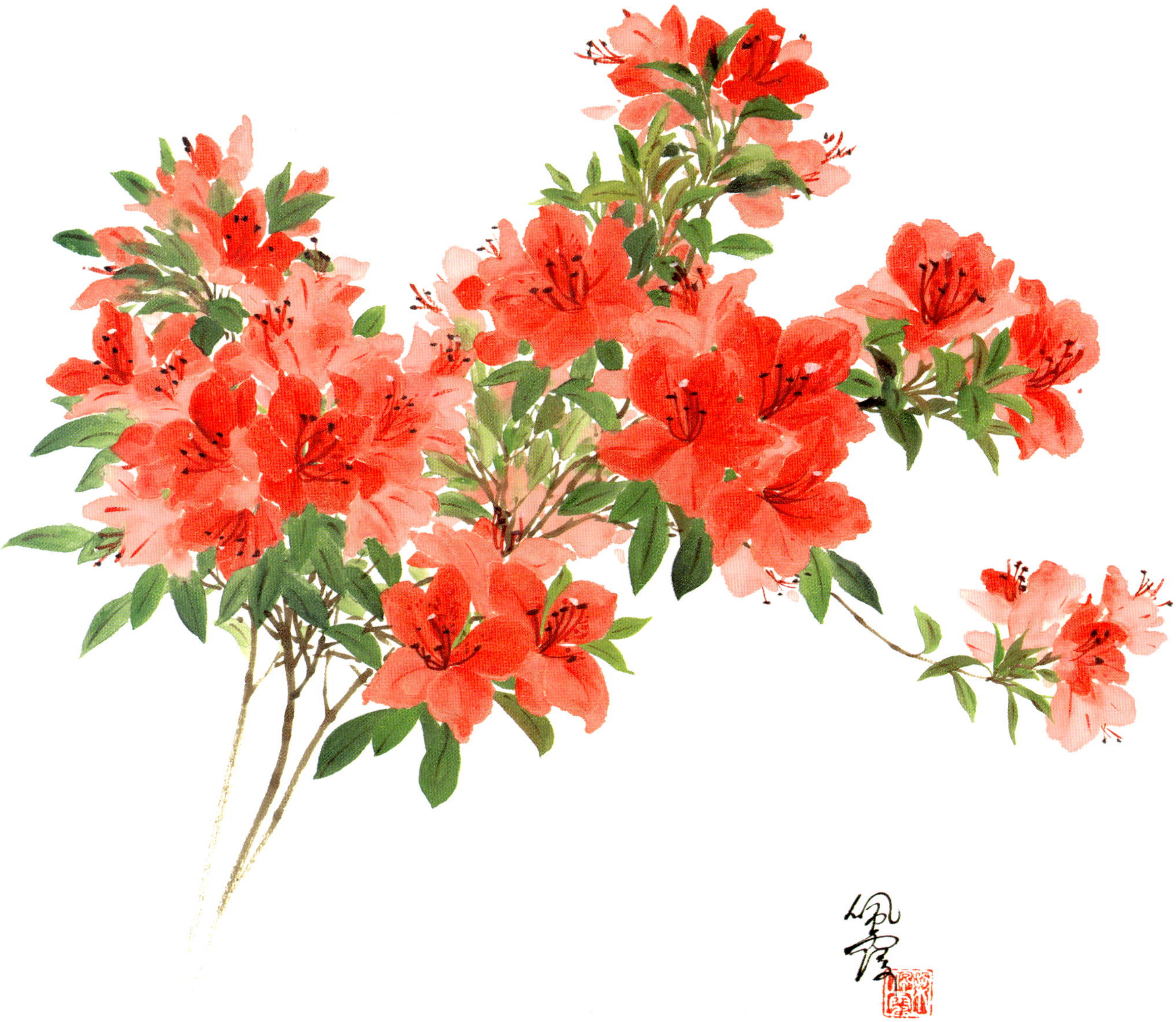

WATER LILY

See also
leaves p57
flowers p65

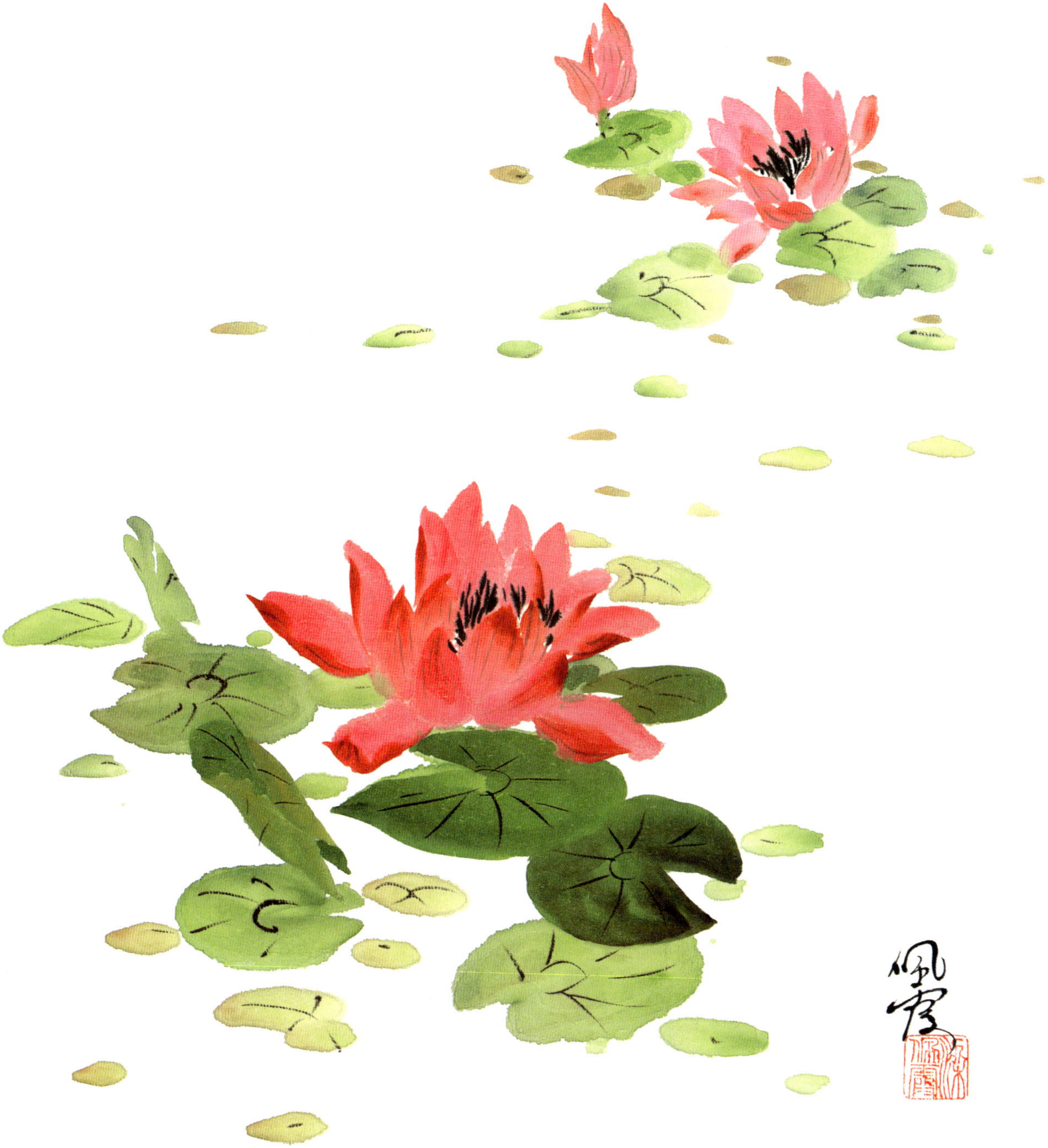

See also

leaves **p127**
flowers **p66**

LOTUS

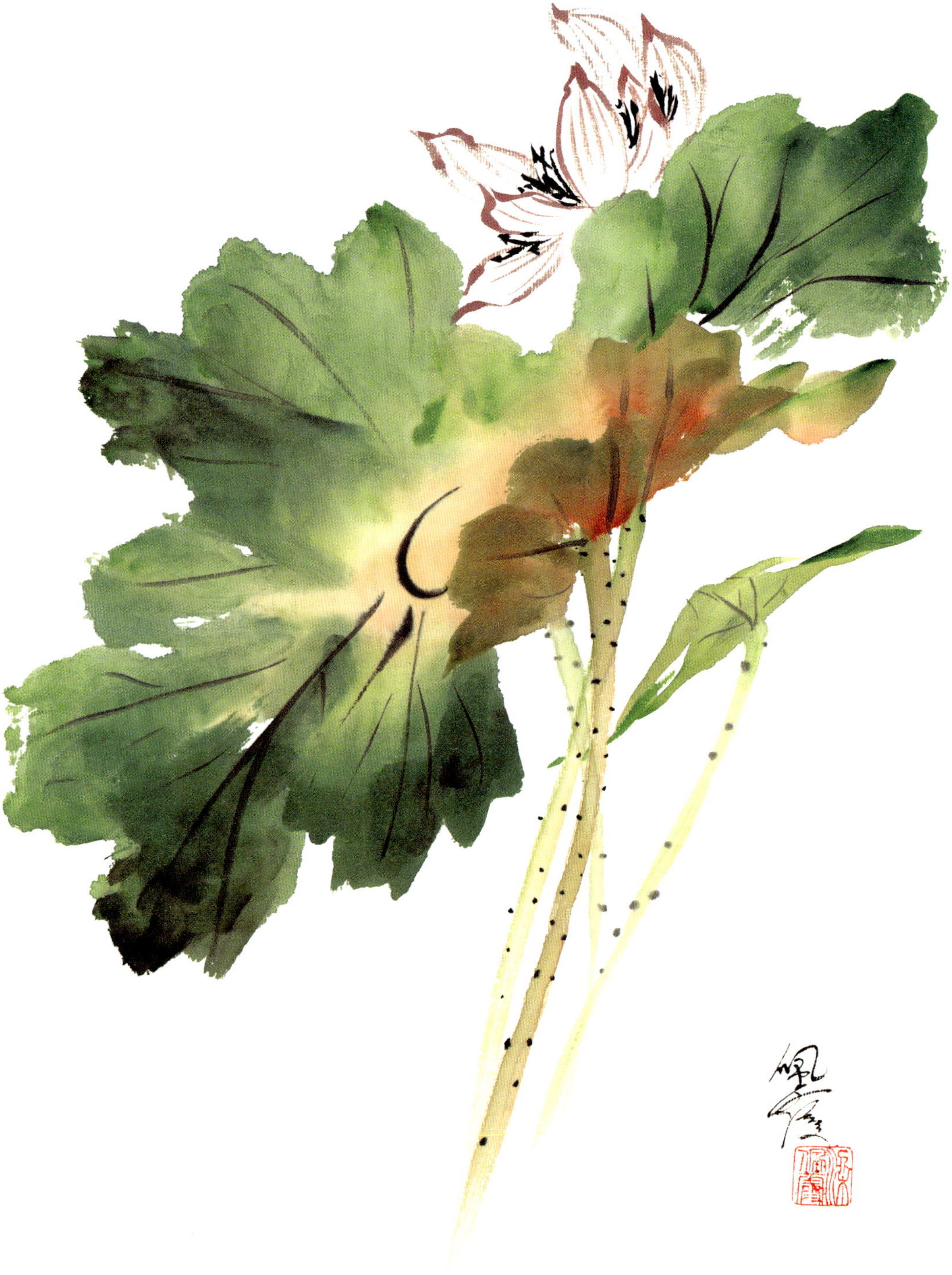

MORNING GLORY

See also

leaves p56
flowers p114

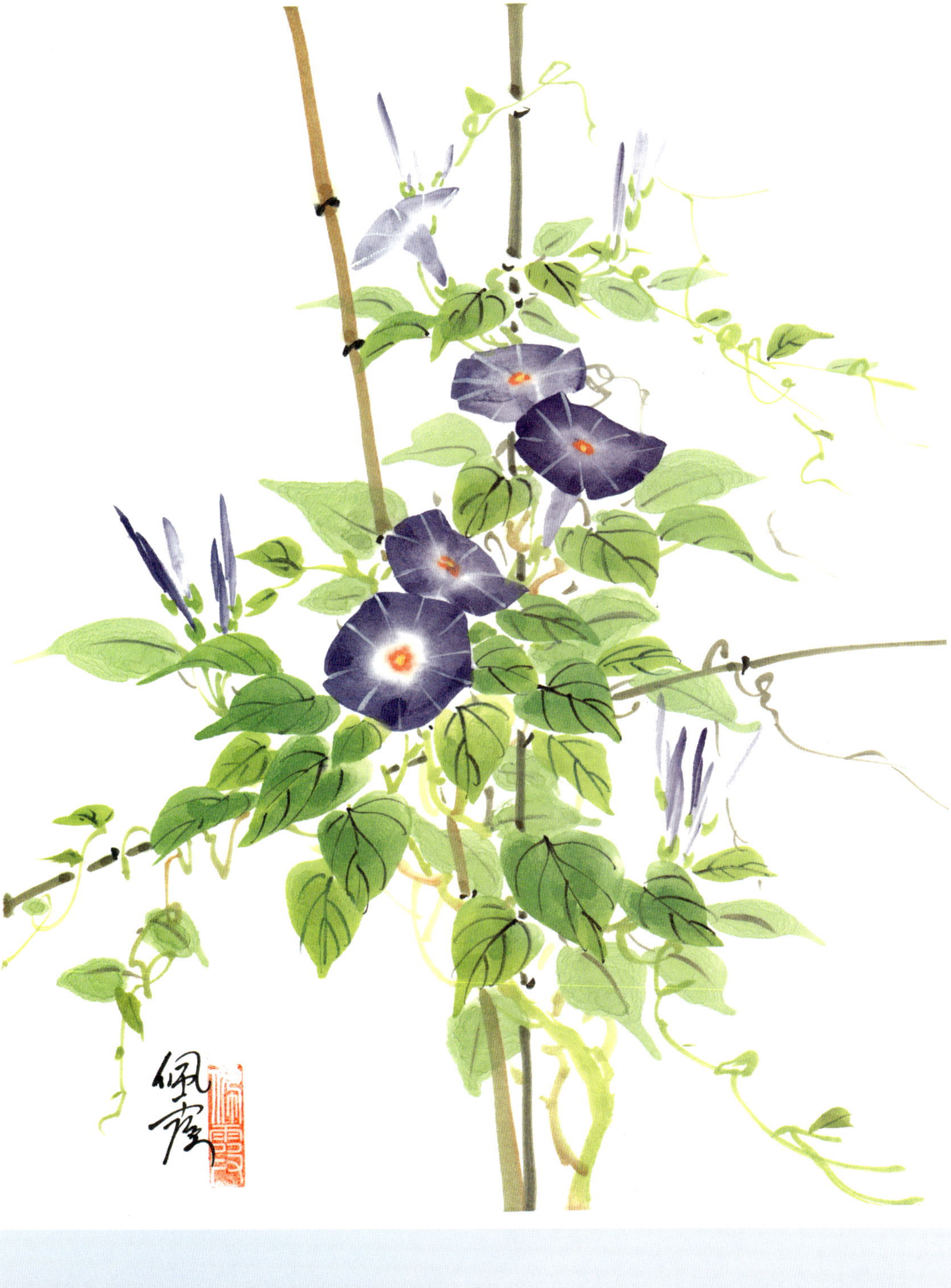

MOUNTING A XUAN PAPER ARTWORK

Xuan paper is usually very thin. It needs to be backed with a thicker paper before framing. Painting on Xuan paper creates wrinkles which will turn into creases when it is being pressed onto the thicker paper. The whole mounting process is designed to smooth the Xuan paper to get rid of the wrinkles and bind it onto a heavier paper.

The traditional method of mounting is an art in itself. Good mounting requires experience and skill. Although improvements have been made and new tools have been invented to make the method easier to master, it is still a complicated technique which will put many people off. The process involves wetting the artwork and using rice starch to bind the artwork to the heavier backing paper. Handling a wet Xuan paper requires great care. Though the gum in Chinese ink and colours should make them permanent on paper, they can still run when wet. Most mounting masters would have learned the art of touching up Chinese artworks but most of us are not equipped with such skill.

I have developed an alternative method of mounting and many of my pupils find it very successful.

MATERIALS AND EQUIPMENT FOR MOUNTING

A Xuan paper artwork

Metal rule

Pencil

Sharp craft knife or scissors

A piece of thick cardboard at least 3/4 in (2 cm) bigger than the artwork all round. Thickness of cardboard preferable is 550 microns with matt finish. I use acid free cardboard for quality.

A1 size newsprint allowing ten pieces for each artwork, fewer if the artwork is small.

Plasticine

Spray mount

Two heavy boards (a heavy weight or two big books will serve the purpose).

A fine spray (a good quality garden spray will work very well).

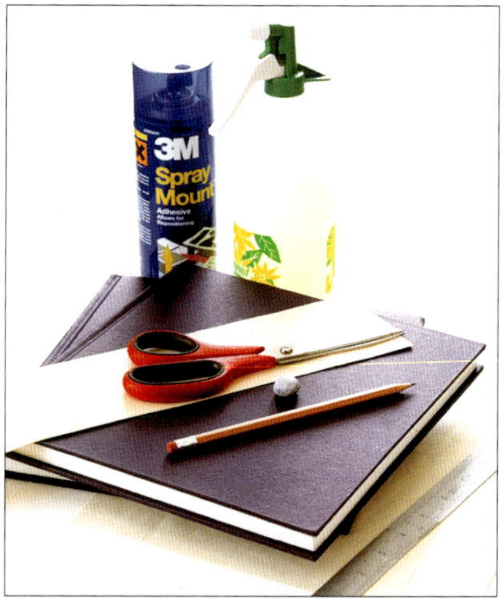

Step 1. Decide how big you want your artwork to be. It is easier to start with a rectangular artwork. When you are more experienced, you will be able to mount artwork of any shape. Add at least 1 in (2 to 3 cm) all round to the measurements of your artwork and draw straight lines with a pencil on your artwork to confirm the size and shape. Cut off excess paper with a sharp knife or a pair of scissors.

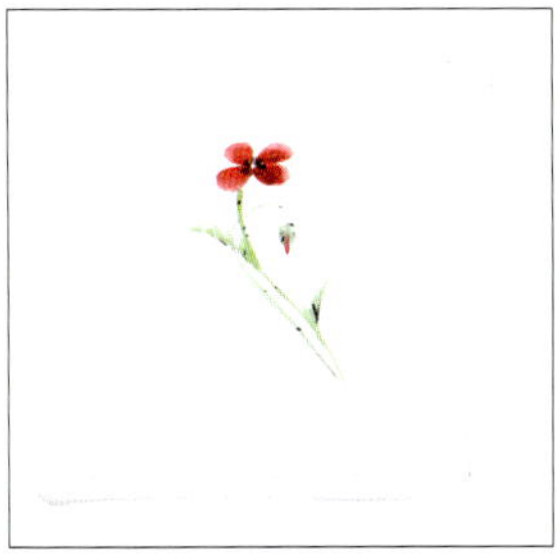

Step 2. Lay the artwork on the cardboard. Mark the outline of the artwork on the cardboard. Mark another rectangle with dimensions at least 1 in (2 to 3 cm) bigger than the artwork all round. Cut out the cardboard along this new rectangle with a sharp knife or a pair of scissors. Label the top or bottom edge so that you will know where to place the artwork later on. If you are mounting more than one artwork at a time, it would be better to label each piece of cardboard with the title of that artwork so there is no confusion. I have used ink marker to make things clear in this particular project. If you want to remove the markings after mounting, it is better to use pencil.

Step 3. Cut or tear a piece of newsprint into long strips of about 4 in (10 cm) wide. Fold one side of each strip lengthwise so that you will have a straight edge to every paper strip. Make sufficient strips to cover the four edges of the cardboard.

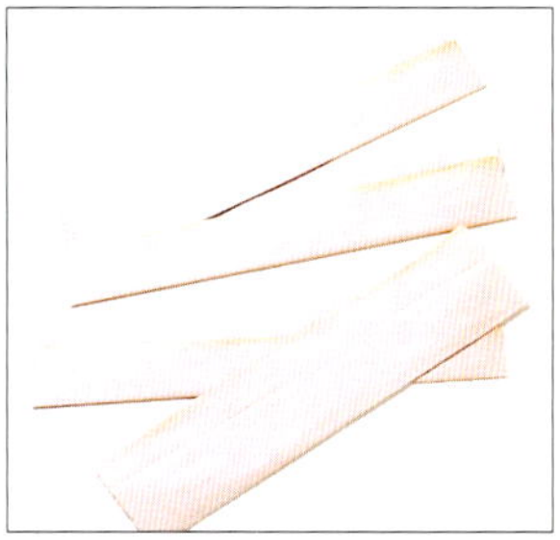

Step 4. Stick small bits of plasticine along the outer edge of the pencil line on the cardboard at about 2 in (5 to 6 cm) intervals.

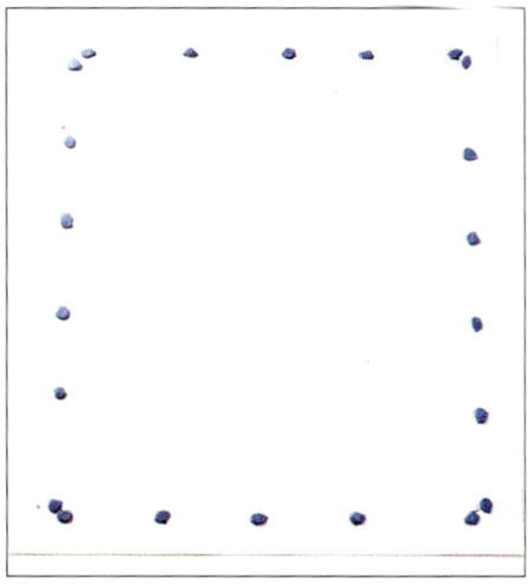

Step 5. Place the strips of newsprint with the folded side matching the markings of the artwork on the cardboard. Stick the strips with the plasticine covering the space around the cardboard so that only the space for the artwork is exposed.

Step 6. Clean the two heavy boards. Lay one on a flat surface with two layers of clean newsprint on top.

Step 7. Lay another layer of clean newsprint on a flat surface. Place the artwork upside down on the newsprint. Spray clean water lightly on the back of the artwork with the garden spray. Do not wet the artwork too much. At places on the Xuan paper where there are heavy creases, sprinkle a little more water. Spraying water sparingly on the artwork will relax the paper so that it can be stretched when it is mounted on the cardboard.

Wrinkles are removed in this way.

Step 8. Place the damp artwork onto the newsprint on the heavy board. Cover it with two more layers of newsprint and place the other heavy board on top. Put a heavy weight on top of the board. This will allow the newsprint to absorb some of the moisture in the Xuan paper. The board and the weight will keep the Xuan paper flat.

Step 9. Spray evenly all over the exposed area of the cardboard with spray mount. Then remove all the news-print strips and the plasticine covering the edges. Lay the cardboard on a flat surface.

Step 10. Remove the weight and the heavy board on top of the artwork. Transfer the artwork to the cardboard on the exact space you marked previously for the artwork. Make sure to match the pencil marks. Do not press at this stage until you are sure that the artwork is perfectly lined up.

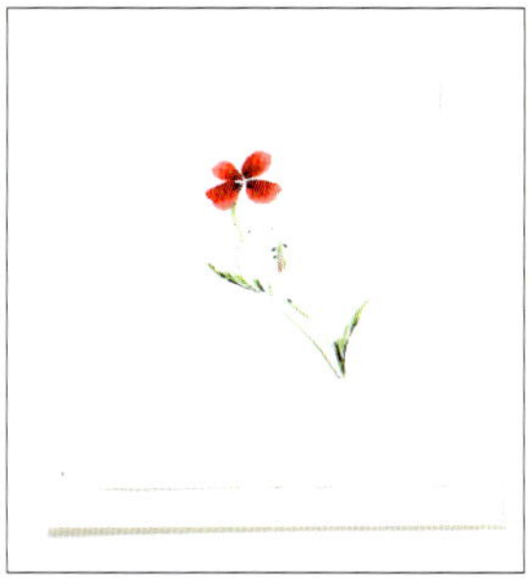

Step 11. Place a a piece of clean newsprint on top of the artwork and press lightly from the centre outwards. Lift the newsprint to see if there are any creases. If so, the artwork can be lifted and relayed at this stage. Any bubbles can be removed by pressing. Once you have lifted the newsprint it is best to change to a clean piece because the one used before may carry a bit of loose ink or some colours from the artwork. If you use it again, you may transfer the smudge onto the artwork.
When there are no creases and the artwork is in the right place, place a clean newsprint on top of the artwork and press hard with your palm. Start from the centre and work your way outwards. Make sure you press on every bit of space of the artwork. The artwork is now properly mounted.

Step 12. If the artwork is still damp, sandwich it between clean newsprint and heavy boards until it is completely dry.

ADDING A COLOUR WASH

You can add a colour wash to a piece of Xuan paper before or after completing a painting. If you add a colour wash after finishing a painting, it will be safer to apply the wash to the back of the painting. If you want to add a colour wash to a clean piece of paper, you can apply it to either side of the paper. Follow the instructions below to apply a colour wash to a piece of Xuan paper.

MATERIALS AND EQUIPMENT

A piece of Xuan paper, with or without a painting

A Hake brush at least 2 in (5 cm) wide

Two big pieces of clean newsprint

A wide container such as a bowl for mixing colour. This container has to be wide enough for the brush to dip in to

Watercolour of your choice

Plenty of newspaper to protect from splashes of coloured water

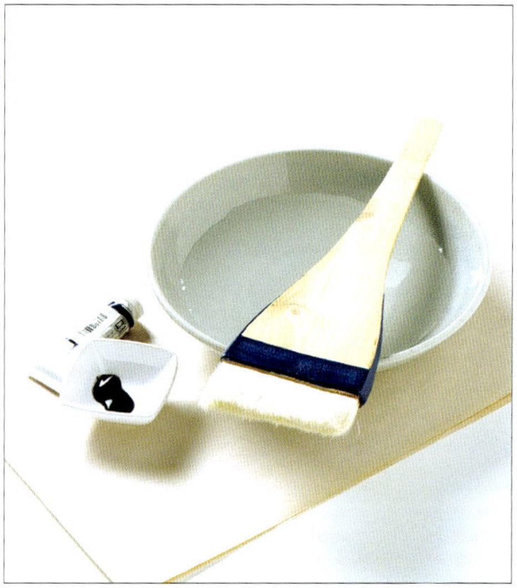

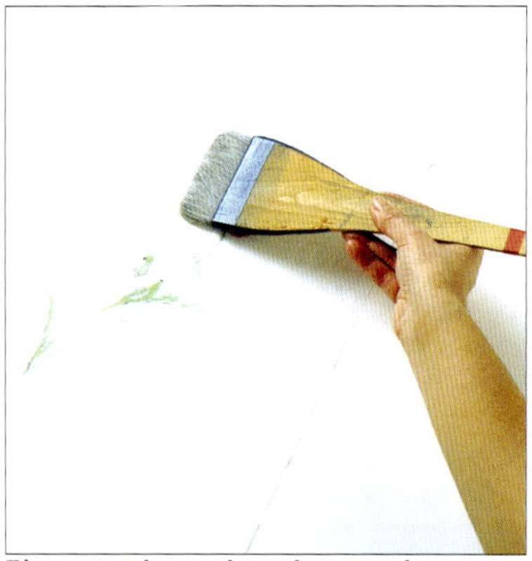

Fig. 1. Applying the colour wash.

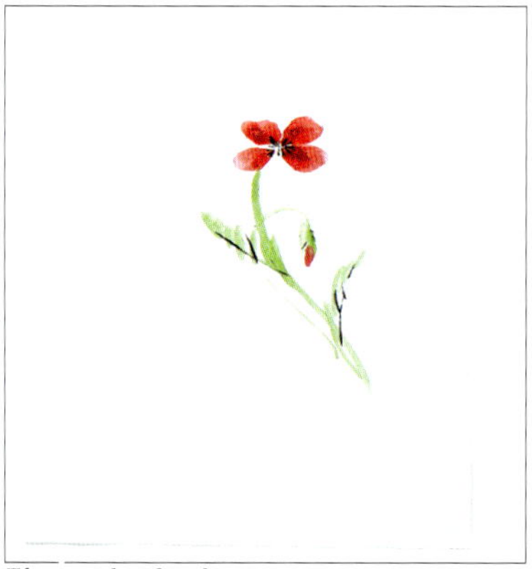

Fig. 2. The final painting.

Step 1. Lay plenty of newspaper on the surface you are going to work on.

Step 2. Mix a colour wash in a wide container by diluting the watercolour of your choice to the tone you would like.

Step 3. Place a piece of clean newsprint on the newspaper and lay the piece of Xuan paper on top of the newsprint. If the Xuan paper is an artwork, lay it upside down.

Step 4. Fully load the Hake brush with the colour wash. Apply the wash, beginning from the top of the Xuan paper and going from one side to the other.

Step 5. Reload the brush with the wash and apply a second strip of wash close to the first one, overlapping the first one slightly. Make every application in the same direction. Going in the opposite direction will cause creasing (see Fig. 1).

Step 6. Continue to add more wash strip by strip until the whole Xuan paper is covered with the colour wash.

Step 7. Cover the wet Xuan paper with a second piece of clean newsprint and turn the pile of paper (first piece of newsprint, Xuan paper and second piece of newsprint) upside down. Peel off the first newsprint carefully and let the Xuan paper dry (see Fig. 2).

A WATER LINE

A water line is a line made by a clean damp brush to mark the position of a long flower stem or leaf stem. To prepare a clean damp brush, dip a clean brush in clean water and wipe it with a tissue to remove most of the water. A line made by such a brush is thin and quick to dry. Too wet a brush makes the line too thick and it takes too long to dry. Any brushwork on a wet line will run. A brush carrying residues of colour leaves a mark on the paper. A line made by a clean damp brush dries up quickly and leaves nothing on the paper except a slight dent to indicate the position of the line. You can use the line to indicate a stalk and paint flowers or leaves along it. When you have finished painting all the flowers and leaves in position, you can then add sections of stalk on the water line wherever it is visible. Plants with long flower stems and long leaf stems such as honeysuckle, sweet pea, bleeding heart, phlox and fuchsia are painted using this technique.

GREENS

Green is the main ingredient for painting leaves, but there are many tones of green. The following are those used in this book:

Sap green
This is the basic green for general painting.

Dark green
Mix two parts of sap green with one part of indigo. This green is used for painting mature leaves.

Light green
Mix one part of sap green with one part of gamboge. This green is used for painting young leaves.

Lemon green
Mix one part of sap green with one pàrt of lemon yellow. Use this green to paint young leaves in early spring. The light green made by using gamboge is too warm for this time of the year.

Olive green
Mix two parts of sap green with one part of burnt sienna. This green is used for painting older leaves. Some plants such as wisteria have this green in their early sprouting leaves.

SUPPLIERS

US

Dick Blick Art Materials
P.O. Box 1267
Galesburg,
IL 61402-1267
USA
FIND NUMBER FROM OUTSIDE US
Tel: (800) 828-4548
Fax (800) 621-8293
www.dickblick.com

Rochester Art Supply
150 West Main St.
Rochester, NY
14614
USA
Tel: 001 (585) 546-6509
Fax: 001(585) 546-5028
www.fineartstore.com

OAS (Oriental Arts Supplies)
21522 Surveyor cir
Huntington Beach,
CA 92646
USA
Tel: 001-714-969-4470
Tel: 1-800-969-4471

China Art Material and Art Books
China Cultural Centre
970 North Broadway
Suite 210
Los Angeles
CA 90012
USA
Tel: 213-626-7295
Fax: 213-617-7656
www.ocac.gov.tw

Oriental Culture Enterpises
Co. Inc.
13 - 17 Elizabeth St
2nd Fl
NY 10013
USA
Tel: 001 (212) 226-8461
Fax: 001 (212) 431-6695
www.oceweb.com/en/

UK

Jacksons Art Suppliers
1 Farleigh Place
London
N16 7SX
Tel: 020 7 254 0077
Fax: 0207 254 0088
www.jacksonart.com

Guanghwa Co. ltd
7 Newport Place
London WC2H 7JR
Tel: 0207 437 373 CHECK NUMBER
Fax: 0207 831 0137
GET WEBSITE

Paper People
Slade Farm
Morchard Bishop
Crediton
Devon
EX17 6ST
Tel: 01363 85050
Fax: 01363 84660
GET WEBSITE

SAA (Society for All Artists)
PO Box 50
Newark
Notts
NG23 5GY
UK
Tel: 01949 844050
Fax: 01949 844051
www.saa.co.uk/Shop

London Graphic Centre
16-18 Shelton Street
London
WC2H 9JJ
Tel: 0207 759 4500

Australia

Wills Quills
Shop 1,
166 Victroia Avenue
Chatswood
NSW
Auatralia 2069
Tel: (61) 02 9411 2627
Fax: (61) 02 9419 6031
www.willsquills.com.au

AD Art Supplies
44 Buckley Street
Footscray
Vic 3011
Tel: (61) 03 9687 5845
Fax: (61) 03 9689 4200
GET WEBSITE

INDEX

A

accessories 25
alum-sized Xuan paper 23
angle of brush 29, 92, 96
  for fan brushstroke 100, 101, 105
  for long dot 50
  for reverse fan brushstroke 111
  and wrist movement 28, 29, 30
  see also direction of brush handle
arm movements *see* elbow movement; wrist movement
astilbe 48
azalea 67, 148

B

bamboo 8, 98-99
  leaves 73
  side brushstroke used for 92, 94
basic techniques 10, 26-42
  constructing a flower painting 59, 130
  traditional methods for orchid 40
  see also dry brush techniques; water line; wet brush techniques
black hair brushes 14, 15, 28
bleeding heart 144
  flower stalks 52
  leaves 83
branches 95, 109
brown hair brushes 14, 16
brushes *see* Chinese brushes
brushstrokes 8, 10-11
  combining 118-129
  direction of brush handle 30, 85, 92
  dot 44-45
  fan 100-101
  long dot 50-51
  short 60-61
  sliding the brush 50, 51, 124
  width and size 92-93, 100, 111
  see also angle of brush
buddleia 47
buds 63, 104, 114, 126
  short brushstroke 63, 104, 114, 126

C

camellia 140
  flowers 121
  leaves 74
Chinese brushes:
care of 19
  holding 28-30
  loading *see* loading the brush
  'opening' 17-18
  for rough and dry brushwork 14-15, 19
  sizes of 16
  types of 14-17
Chinese national flower 108
Chinese orchid 8, 40-41
chrysanthemum 8, 116-117
  flowers 62
  leaves 107, 115
clematis 133
  flowers 120
  leaves 78
climbers 49, 77
  elbow movement used for 35
  side brushstroke used for 97
coloured paper 23, 48
colours 25
  greens 155
  multi-colour effects 39
  for three-dimensional effects 45, 46, 53, 58
  washes of 48, 154
  see also loading the brush
composition:
  basic techniques 59, 130
  lilac 59
cotton paper 23
curves, and wrist movement 32-33
'cutting' paper 23

D

daffodils 90-91
  flower heads 54
direction of brush handle 30, 85, 92
  and wrist movement 28, 29, 30
  see also angle of brush
dot 10, 44-45
  for flower heads 46-48, 102, 104
  for trees and climbers 49
dry brush techniques 14-15, 95, 97
  brushes for 19
  painting dots 44, 45

E

elbow movement 10, 34-35
for press and lift 37, 84
for side brushstroke 92, 96
equipment *see* materials

F

fan brushstroke 100-101
angle of brush 100, 101, 105
for flower heads and blossom 102-105, 121, 122, 125, 126
for leaves 106-107, 127
flower stalks *see* stalks
flowers:
four Chinese flowers 8-9
symbolism of 108
four Chinese flowers 8-9
framing *see* mounting artwork

G

geraniums 132
flower heads 103
leaves 106
greens 155
gypsophila 48

H

Hake brushes 14, 17, 18, 154
hibiscus 138
flower heads 33, 105
leaves 80
honeysuckle 134
flower heads 63
leaves 77
hydrangea 141
flower heads 53
leaves 79

I

ink 12, 24
bamboo painting 98-99
loading the brush 31, 38
ink stick 24
iris 135
flowers 122
leaves 88

L

lavender 47
leaves:
elbow movements for 35
long brushstroke 86-89
long dot brushstroke 55-59
reverse fan brushstroke 115
short brushstroke 60, 67-83
wrist movements for 33
see also stalks
Leopard and Wolf brush 16
lilac:
flower heads 46, 58
leaves 55, 58-59
lily 136
flowers 64
leaves 76
lines:
and elbow movement 34-35
and wrist movement 32-33
loading the brush 10, 30, 31, 38, 39
see also three colour loadings; two colour loadings
long brushstroke 84-85
for leaves 86-89
long dot 50-51
for flower heads 52-54, 65, 104
for leaves 55-59
long slender leaves 86
lotus 150
flowers 66
leaves 127

M

materials 12-25
for colour washes 154
for mounting 152
mixing dish 25
'Moon Palace' paper 20
morning glory 151
flowers 114
leaves 56
Mountain and Horse brush 15, 17, 18, 95
mounting artwork 25, 152-153
mulberry paper 23
multi-colour effects 39

N

national flower of China 108
newsprint 25
non-outline style 8, 116
paper for 20, 23
non-stopped brushwork 96

O

orchid 8, 40-41
Orchid and Bamboo brush 16
outline style 8
paper for 23
wrist movement for 33

P

paints *see* colours; ink
pansy 145
leaves 81
paper 20-23, 152
coloured 23, 48
peony 147
flowers 125
leaves 89
as national flower 108
plum blossom 8, 102, 108-109

poppy 146
- flowers 112, 128
- leaves and stalks 82

press and lift 10, 36-37, 41
- for long brushstroke 84
- for short brushstroke 60

projects:
- bamboo 98-99
- chrysanthemum 116-117
- daffodils 90-91
- lilac 58-59
- orchid 40-41

plum blossom 108-109

R

Red Bean brush 16, 17

reverse fan brushstroke 110-111
- for flowers 112-114, 120, 122, 124, 125, 128
- for leaves 115

rose 143
- flowers 113
- leaves 75

rough and dry effects *see* dry brush techniques

rounds, wrist movement for 32-33

S

Shirley poppy 112, 139

short brushstroke 60-61
- for buds 63, 104, 114, 126
- for flower heads 62-67, 90, 120, 125
- for leaves 60, 67-83

side brushstroke 92-93
- for climbers 97
- for stalks 96
- for trunks 94-95, 97

size:
- of brush 16
- of brushstroke 92-93, 100, 111

sizing, of Xuan paper 23

sliding the brush 50, 51, 124

soft-hair brushes 14

stalks:
- bleeding heart 52
- chrysanthemum 116
- leaf stalks 71
- marked by water line 71, 76, 77, 155
- poppy 82
- side brushstroke used for 96

stopped brushwork 95, 96
- non-stopped 96

symbolism:
- of bamboo 98
- the four Chinese flowers 8
- of plum blossom 108, 109

T

techniques *see* basic techniques; dry brush techniques; water line; wet brush techniques

three colour loadings 31, 39, 54

three-dimensional effects 45, 46, 53, 58

tone:
- and three-dimensional effects 45, 46, 53, 58
- two-tone effects 31, 38

tough-hair brushes 14

traditional:
- painting methods 40
- symbolism 8, 98, 108, 109

trees 49, 95

trunks:
- painted before flowers 109
- side brushstroke used for 94-95, 97

tulip 142
- flowers 124
- leaves 87

two colour loadings 10, 31, 39
- for dots 45, 57
- for fan brushstrokes 110
- for short brushstrokes 61

two-tone effects 31, 38

W

washes, of colour 48, 154

water lily 149
- flowers 65
- leaves 57

water line 71, 155
- flowers painted on 52
- positioning the stem 76, 77

watercolours 25

weights 25

wet brush techniques 44, 45, 50, 51
- dot brushstroke 44, 45
- long dot brushstroke 50, 51
- *see also* water line

white hair brushes 14

width of brushstroke 92-93, 100, 111

wisteria 137
- flower heads 104
- leaves 72

wolf-hair brush 15, 16, 17

wrist movement 10, 32-33
- brush direction and angle 28, 29, 30
- for fan brushwork 110
- for press and lift 36, 41, 60

X

Xuan paper 20-23, 48, 152

From the author

I deeply appreciate the tremendous support my family have given me. During the time I wrote this book, my family was scattered all over the world. My husband was working in Asia, my daughter was studying in Australia, and my sisters were in Hong Kong and Canada. Each of them frequently emailed and phoned to encourage me.

It was my son in England who gave me the most support. He made sure that my computer was in excellent working condition every day so that I could carry out my writing smoothly. Without him, there would not be a book.

The eagerness of my friends and pupils for this book to be published so that each of them will own a copy indeed means a lot to me. Now they will have their wishes fulfilled.

I was not an easy pupil to teach. My three masters who taught me painting and the two teachers who taught me calligraphy would certainly agree. I constantly questioned the styles, the methods, the artistic approaches . . . My thanks for the patience of my masters and teachers. I am on my own now. I am very sure that they would be very proud of me. They all can smile now that they do not have to answer any more of my questions.

Thanks, folks. Thanks for being there along my long journey of being an artist.